INTIMATE JESUS

The sexuality of God incarnate

ANDY ANGEL

First published in Great Britain in 2017

Society for Promoting Christian Knowledge
36 Causton Street
London SW1P 4ST
www.spck.org.uk

The author and publisher have made every effort to ensure that the external website and
email addresses included in this book are correct and up to date at the time of going to
press. The author and publisher are not responsible for the content, quality or continuing
accessibility of the sites.

British Library Cataloguing-in-Publication Data
A catalogue record for this book is available from the British Library

ISBN 978–0–281–07240–8
eBook ISBN 978–0–281–07241–5

Typeset by Lapiz Digital Services
First printed in Great Britain by Ashford Colour Press
Subsequently digitally printed in Great Britain

eBook by Lapiz Digital Services

Produced on paper from sustainable forests

For with you is the fountain of life
Psalm 36.9

To Fabi with love

Contents

Preface		vii
List of abbreviations		viii
Introduction		xi
1	Asking the question	1
2	Word become flesh	11
3	A Samaritan bride and her Jewish groom	31
4	Male intimacy	61
5	Peter, Mary and the woman caught in adultery	84
6	Intimate Jesus	98
Notes		103
Bibliography		151
Index of ancient sources		161
Index of modern authors		168
Index of subjects		173

Preface

I would like to thank the many people who have helped shape this book both by reading drafts and commenting on the ideas delivered in papers at seminars. They are too many to mention by name, but I am grateful to you all for your insights. I am also grateful to those friends whose response to this project was something along the lines of 'Are you sure?' Your concerns have reminded me throughout the writing of the book that I am treading on holy ground. I hope I have followed the straight and narrow path.

Particular thanks must go to my mother, the late Evelyn Angel. She was a woman of remarkable faith: brought up in the Plymouth Brethren, married into the Church of England and ministered in the Holy Spirit. I thought I had better warn her about my latest book project so as to avoid shock later on. When I told her I was writing a book on Jesus' sexuality in the hope that it might allow us to identify with him more closely in our own frail sexuality, she responded: 'At last. About time somebody did!'

So this book is at least in part dedicated to all those who wonder where their sexuality fits into their spirituality, and I hope that what I have written will at least encourage you to pray to a God who understands.

I would also like to thank my father, Gervais Angel, who has once again spent many hours on the manuscript, both proofreading and preparing the indexes. Thank you for being so willing to be 'heavy-laden' and for giving me 'the rest'!

My greatest thanks go as ever to my wife, Fabiola, who changed continent, culture and language to come and live with me. She is also the reason that I think there is a fountain of life from which we can drink. It is to her, my best friend, my beautiful lover and my fellow parent of our two wonderful sons, that I dedicate this book.

Abbreviations

AB	Anchor Bible
ABD	*Anchor Bible Dictionary*
'Abot R. Nat.	*'Abot de Rabbi Nathan*
ABRL	Anchor Bible Reference Library
AnBib	Analecta Biblica
Apoc. Mos.	Apocalypse of Moses
ApOTC	Apollos Old Testament Commentary
BAR	*Biblical Archaeology Review*
BCOTWP	Baker Commentary on the Old Testament Wisdom and Psalms
BDAG	Bauer et al., *Greek-English Lexicon of the New Testament and Other Early Christian Literature*
BECNT	Baker Exegetical Commentary on the New Testament
b. 'Erub.	*Babylonian Talmud, tractate 'Erubin*
Bib	*Biblica*
BibInt	*Biblical Interpretation*
BJS	Brown Judaic Studies
b. Ketub.	*Babylonian Talmud, tractate Ketubbot*
BNTC	Black's New Testament Commentaries
b. Qidd.	*Babylonian Talmud, tractate Qiddušin*
BST	Bible Speaks Today
BTB	*Biblical Theology Bulletin*
CAP	A. E. Cowley, *Aramaic Papyri of the Fifth Century B.C.*
CBQ	*Catholic Biblical Quarterly*
CEJL	Commentaries on Early Jewish Literature
ConBNT	Coniectanea Neotestamentica or Coniectanea Biblica: New Testament Series
DJD	Discoveries in the Judaean Desert
ECC	Eerdmans Critical Commentary
FF	Foundations and Facets

HALOT	Koehler et al., *The Hebrew and Aramaic Lexicon of the Old Testament*
HeyJ	*Heythrop Journal*
HThKNT	Herders Theologischer Kommentar zum Neuen Testament
HTR	*Harvard Theological Review*
HUCA	*Hebrew Union College Annual*
IB	*Interpreter's Bible*
ICC	International Critical Commentary
JBL	*Journal of Biblical Literature*
JJS	*Journal of Jewish Studies*
JSJ	*Journal of the Study of Judaism in the Persian, Hellenistic, and Roman Periods*
JSNT	*Journal for the Study of the New Testament*
LSJ	Liddell, Scott, Jones, *A Greek-English Lexicon*
LXX	the Septuagint
m. 'Abot	*Mishnah, tractate 'Abot*
m. Ketub.	*Mishnah, tractate Ketubbot*
m. Pesaḥ.	*Mishnah, tractate Pesaḥim*
m. Soṭah	*Mishnah, tractate Soṭah*
NCB	New Century Bible
NCBC	New Cambridge Bible Commentary
NHC	Nag Hammadi Codex
NIB	*The New Interpreter's Bible*
NICNT	New International Commentary on the New Testament
NICOT	New International Commentary on the Old Testament
NovTSup	Novum Testamentum Supplement Series
NRSV	New Revised Standard Version
NT	New Testament
NTL	New Testament Library
NTS	*New Testament Studies*
OCD	*Oxford Classical Dictionary*
OT	Old Testament
PNTC	Pelican New Testament Commentaries
SBL	Society of Biblical Literature
SBLDS	Society of Biblical Literature Dissertation Series

SJT	*Scottish Journal of Theology*
SNTSMS	Society for New Testament Studies Monograph Series
SP	Sacra Pagina
SVTP	Studia in Veteris Testamenti Pseudepigraphica
T. Benj.	Testament of Benjamin
t. Ber.	*Tosefta Berakot*
TDNT	Kittel and Friedrich, *Theological Dictionary of the New Testament*
T. Levi	Testament of Levi
TLG	*Thesaurus Linguae Graecae*
t. Qidd.	*Tosefta Qiddušin*
T. Sol.	Testament of Solomon
WBC	Word Biblical Commentary
WUNT	Wissenschaftliche Untersuchungen zum Neuen Testament
ZAW	*Zeitschrift für die alttestamentliche Wissenschaft*

Introduction

I want in this book to ask the question: how did God experience human sexuality? Churches are as divided over issues of human sexuality today as they have been at any other time. The resulting debates are significant and help to inform Christian understanding and teaching. However, they can seem to lack humanity. Many of us who have experienced difficulties over the relationship between our sexuality and traditional Christian teaching (with regard to issues such as marriage, divorce, singleness, homosexuality, bisexuality, transsexuality, freedom of sexual expression or lack of it – the list could be endless) have sometimes wondered where the teachings of the faith coincide with our basic humanity. The justifications of Christian viewpoints (and they can be many, varied and conflicting) can lose credibility as sometimes they apparently fail to take into account what it feels like to be human. Many of the moral questions we ask are important. However, most of us find it much easier to listen to someone who understands what we are going through than we do a moral argument. Hence my question: how did *God* find living out *his* human sexuality?

I do not ask this question with the intention of being irreverent, churlish or defiant. I ask it as a devout man of faith. The Christian faith teaches me that God became human in the person of Jesus of Nazareth. Given the struggles most of us have over sex, I am intrigued as to how he managed (or even flourished!) in this area of his humanity. I also find the comment I hear too often with regard to Jesus and sexuality – that he was tested in every respect as we are, yet was without sin (using Heb. 4.15) – somewhat disheartening. It suggests that Jesus' experience of human sexuality was all temptation and no goodness. I cannot accept that this is the whole story of Jesus and his sexuality as it seems so at odds with his own views on sex. He taught that it was created by the one true good God (Matt. 19.4–7; Mark 10.6–9).[1] If sex and sexuality are part of God's good creation, then he could not have thought that it was all temptation and sin. Given this viewpoint, how did he experience his own sexuality? Just because he seems to have been single does not mean he did not experience human sexuality;[2] he would simply have woken up every morning without a wife next to him,[3] which only raises more questions of how he lived out (or coped with) his sexuality. Given, moreover, that God was incarnate as a man, and I am also a man, I find the whole question particularly intriguing, as his experience of his sexuality cannot have been totally removed from my own. And as my faith encourages me to imitate Christ, it might be helpful to know how he did it.

I realize that I am not the first to ask this question. The churches and the Christian creeds have asserted for roughly two millennia that God became man in the person of Jesus. This implies that he experienced human sexuality, and male sexuality in particular. This is obvious really, and has not escaped the notice of some down the centuries. Artists, novelists and dramatists have explored the subject of Jesus' sexuality in various ways over the years – primarily by exercising their imaginations well beyond anything written in the Gospels or other ancient texts that purports to tell us of Jesus' life or person.[4]

Theologians seem to have been more reticent. Very few professional theologians discuss the sexuality of Jesus at all, and even fewer ask how God experienced human sexuality. In the twentieth century, William E. Phipps raised the question in *Was Jesus Married?* but his ideas have not met with widespread acceptance.[5] Scholarly studies of Jesus tend to focus on his teaching and mission.[6] Much of what has been written on the subject of his sexuality has centred on the *Secret Gospel of Mark* and the *Gospel of Jesus' Wife* (both of which were discovered in the last hundred years and have been hailed by their discoverers as very early Christian texts). The *Secret Gospel of Mark* suggests a possible homoerotic liaison between Jesus and a young man,[7] while the *Gospel of Jesus' Wife* is a fragment written in Coptic containing a line in which Jesus says 'my wife'.[8] However, many scholars view both texts as modern creations rather than as genuinely ancient.[9] The majority do not view them as giving us any reliable information about Jesus' sexuality or marital status.[10]

Someone who does ask questions of Jesus' sexuality cautions us against thinking that we can come to any firm conclusions. Dale Martin notes that we all approach biblical texts with certain questions that interest us in mind, and with particular ways of reading those texts. Not only does he observe that our perspectives shape the way we read biblical texts, but he suggests that none of us have the right way to read the text – there are simply different ways of doing it.[11] I take his point but only partially agree. People read biblical texts from very different viewpoints and see quite different things in them, but this does not necessarily make every reading equally valid. At a very basic level I remember a sermon in which the preacher apparently failed to notice that, in the command he was discussing, his text included the word 'not'.[12] A reading which takes account of the whole text is surely better than one which omits to do so. Biblical understanding often moves forward by means of people noticing elements of texts which others have missed; sometimes, however, the readings offered read into texts things which are not there. These readings are surely not as good as those which carefully assess what a text does and does not say. Biblical texts can stand as witnesses against some of the ways that we try to read them.[13] So I will now outline my approach to reading the biblical texts I study here. Then at least readers will know where (I think) I am coming from.

In this book, I wish to explore what the Gospel of John might tell us about the sexuality of God incarnate. Given that John portrays Jesus as the 'Word made flesh', this seems to be an appropriate place to begin my enquiry. Others have already begun the exploration of sexual themes in the Gospel, particularly in relation to the story of the woman at the well and the presentation of the figure of the beloved disciple.[14] I will draw on their work. However, I shall start with John as narrator of the Gospel. He is a very able storyteller who uses numerous narrative techniques to great effect in his portrayal of Jesus.[15] One such technique is his use of signals (which Alan Culpepper playfully calls 'nods, winks, and gestures') to show that there is more going on in certain parts of the text than you might notice on first reading. Through these nods and winks John invites us to stop, read again, think and see what else is going on beneath the surface.[16] I shall start with one of these nods.

John notes that the disciples do not dare to ask Jesus why he is talking to the Samaritan woman, or what his intentions are in talking to her (John 4.27). (Along with the early Church fathers, but probably unlike most modern scholars, I take the author of the Gospel to be Jesus' disciple John, the son of Zebedee, who was writing in Ephesus around AD 80–85 and who is the beloved disciple of the narrative.)[17] They are afraid to ask him what he is doing because they suspect him of something sexually untoward. John was embarrassed to ask Jesus these questions at the time. However, the fact that he could eventually write his account suggests that much later in life he was no longer embarrassed. In dropping this remark into his narrative, John tips us the wink that he is no longer shy about Jesus' sexuality. In doing so, he invites us to lose any reticence we might have about the subject and to re-read his Gospel for further insights into Jesus' sexuality. He drops a trail of breadcrumbs.

Going back to the prologue to his Gospel (John 1.1–18), John inserts two hints into his narrative. He says Jesus became 'flesh' after using exactly this word to refer to sexual desires. He does this in a text where he describes Jesus as the 'Word' or 'Wisdom' of God – a figure who had been sexualized (and desexualized) in contemporary and ancient Jewish religious writings. He also uses an image of Jesus 'the only begotten god' lying in the breast (or lap) of the Father, picking it up later in the Gospel as he introduces the character of the beloved disciple in words and images which would most likely evoke homo-erotic ideas in contemporary Greek and Roman minds. Moving back to the story where John nudges us to ask about Jesus' sexuality, we notice that it takes the form of a betrothal narrative. Having been tipped the wink, we notice the breadcrumbs and are encouraged to follow where they lead.

But as we follow we need to remember that this is a trail of breadcrumbs and not a street paved with gold. We are studying a minor sub-theme in the Gospel. John makes his purpose clear (John 20.30–31) and his main purpose is not to explore the sexuality of Jesus. Nonetheless, as he introduces Jesus to the audience he does play with the idea of God experiencing both the frailty and beauty of human sexuality, and our somehow seeing something of his glory in this experience. John puts Jesus on the spot in a potentially flirta-tious conversation with a tough but touchy woman who misreads the signs and is having none of it. Possibly courting controversy within his own Christian community and the Greco-Roman world outside, he uses motifs from homoerotic relationships (emptying them of homoerotic content) to describe the intimacy he personally shared with Jesus and which he knows Jesus longs to share with all people. Given that the churches could get embroiled in controversies over sex just as easily in the later first century AD as they can today, John was an Evangelist who enjoyed sailing close to the wind.

In order to study the texts towards which John draws us, I am going to read the Gospel as a narrative, making the assumption that John writes as a storyteller who is familiar with the narrative techniques and plot lines of the ancient Jewish, Greek and Roman worlds (as one might reasonably suspect a Palestinian Jew living in Ephesus to be). I will read the text as having been written for a Christian community which was already familiar with at least some of the life and teaching of Jesus, and in light of the fact that to understand the Gospel we need to presume some knowledge which the Gospel itself does not provide. A case in point would be the commands of Jesus. John assumes that his audience knows what they are (John 14.15; 15.10) but never tells us what they are.[18] I am also going to read the text in its final form (i.e. including chapter 21, although I recognize that some scholars do not think it belonged to the first version of the Gospel).[19]

Reading the Gospel primarily as a narrative has its pitfalls, especially when you are following up a nod and a wink. The risks of over-reading a text or allowing your perspective or interests to colour your reading are ever-present.[20] I am aware of this, but how far that awareness extends to not doing it I leave up to each reader to decide. I shall provide reasons and where necessary arguments for my interpretations of texts, particularly where I suggest that other authors may not quite have grasped what John is saying. However, where these arguments are potentially long-winded and interrupt the flow of the reading, I shall endeavour to confine them to the notes in the interests of making my reading of the text and my overall argument about John's presentation of Jesus' sexuality easier to follow.

I am aware that my reading of the Gospel may be controversial – not least because I follow ancient commentators in thinking it was written by an eyewitness to Jesus' ministry, namely his disciple John. So I wish to make two things clear at the outset. First, although I think John drew on his memories and probably those of other eyewitnesses, I also think that he exercised considerable freedom in framing his story using contemporary narrative techniques and literary artistry. I do not believe the overall argument of this book stands or falls with Johannine authorship. If this Gospel was written by an unknown author then the argument simply needs reframing in terms of authorship. I would ask readers with a different view of authorship to do so. Second, discussing the cultural context of the Gospel entails looking at some ancient texts which are sexually explicit. I have tried to give a clear picture without being salacious. I apologize in advance to any who might find this material offensive.

1

Asking the question

Just at that moment his disciples came and they were aston-
ished that he was talking with a woman but nobody dared ask
him 'what are you after?' or 'why are you talking with her?'

(John 4.27)

This scene from the Gospel of John may well be very familiar, but I
suspect that the implications of John's words may be less so. Worn
out from his journey, Jesus has sat down by a well. A few moments
ago he sent his disciples into town to buy food, too tired to accom-
pany them himself it seems. A woman has come to the well and they
have struck up a conversation. While Jesus and the Samaritan woman
are talking, the disciples arrive back at the well.

John does not tell us whether they said anything at this moment
but he does note, in the verse quoted above, that none of them asked
the questions that were clearly on their minds. Possibly there was an
awkward silence. Possibly there was an embarrassing conversation
or exchange of greetings in which the disciples avoided putting their
thoughts into words. Whatever happened, the woman seems to have
sensed the atmosphere. Immediately after John records the disciples'
silent thoughts, he writes '*therefore* the woman left her water jar and
went back to town' (4.28). Somehow she sensed that this was a scene
she would rather exit, as this group of men was making assumptions
about the conversation she found uncomfortable.

The key words are the ones I have translated 'but nobody dared
ask him'. In the Greek in which the Gospel of John was originally
written, the words 'but' and 'him' are missing. (I supply them simply
to make the translation flow better.) The three Greek words I render
'nobody dared ask' literally translate as 'of course nobody said' or
'absolutely nobody said'. John reassures his readers that the disciples
would not dream of asking aloud the questions they were asking in
their heads, conveying a sense that they felt the inappropriateness
of those questions. They could see exactly how embarrassing their

1

questions would be if they did ask them aloud, and so they kept them to themselves.

The disciples were silent in order to keep their thoughts from Jesus, but in doing so they did not tell each other what they were thinking either. John tells the story brilliantly. He notes the disciples' astonishment that Jesus was talking with a woman and comments that nobody dared ask him what he was after, or why he was talking with her.[1] John does not tell us explicitly whether each of the disciples knew at the time what the others were thinking, but as he describes the scene later in life he clearly believes that they had all been drawing the same kind of conclusion. They all thought that Jesus was after something. They assumed that he had some kind of sexual motive, but none of them was brave enough to tackle him.[2]

What are you after?

In explaining the disciples' reluctance to ask Jesus either of the questions that were going around their heads, biblical commentators tend to point to Jewish wisdom literature and the sayings of rabbis which discourage men from talking to women.[3] Rabbi Yose ben Yohanan of Jerusalem taught that men should not talk much with women, particularly the wives of other men, as doing so brought trouble and landed one in hell – as well as wasting time better spent on studying the law (*m. 'Abot* 1.5). This advice was well known if not always heeded, as illustrated by a story of Beruriah, the wife of Rabbi Meir. Beruriah was a woman famed for her wisdom, learning and character. When one day she met Rabbi Yose the Galilean on the road, he asked her directions to the city of Lydda, but in too many words for her liking. She told him how he should have phrased his question and then rebuked him, 'Foolish Galilean, did not the Sages say this, "do not engage in much talk with women"' (*b. 'Erub.* 53b).

The majority of contemporary commentators prove deafeningly silent when it comes to explaining *why* the rabbis or Jesus or any other man might wish to avoid talking to women, or what kind of trouble they thought this might bring upon them.[4] Those that do tend to give incomplete or unconvincing answers.[5] Perhaps the disciples were keen that Jesus avoid scandal.[6] Perhaps they were shocked that Jesus was speaking to the woman because they thought he was too tired to speak.[7] Perhaps, as Rabbi Yose ben Yohanan taught, they were concerned that Jesus was wasting time that could have been more profitably spent, for example studying Torah.[8] But none of these explanations accounts for the disciples' failure to ask Jesus 'what are *you* after?' This question implies that at least part of the problem lies in Jesus' intentions towards the woman. Besides, John is hardly likely to suggest that Jesus ought to have spent more time studying Torah (see e.g. John 1.17).

Perhaps the first question, 'What are you after?' was addressed (albeit silently) to the woman rather than Jesus. The Greek text can be interpreted in this way.[9] But this interrupts the flow of the text. The disciples are amazed that Jesus is talking with a woman, not that she is talking with him. So why would they want to ask her anything? They want to know what *he* is up to, and so both questions are most naturally addressed to him.[10] Possibly then, the disciples fail to ask these questions because they admire Jesus' moral character and know he cannot be up to anything untoward.[11] However, this fails to answer the obvious counter of why such questions entered their heads in the first place.

A minority of commentators are less coy, commenting to the effect that 'sexual innuendo is not far from the surface of the disciples' unspoken questions'.[12] This would seem very likely. Rabbi Yose ben Yohanan probably had it in mind when he warned that conversing with women can lead a man into trouble and land him in Gehenna (*m. 'Abot* 1.5). This is very much the message of Proverbs 7.1–27. The same message was alive and well in Jewish wisdom literature around the turn of the eras, as illustrated by these words of the Jewish teacher Ben Sira (Sir. 9.3–9 NRSV):

> Do not go near a loose woman, or you will fall into her snares.
> Do not dally with a singing-girl, or you will be caught by her
> tricks. Do not look intently at a virgin, or you may stumble
> and incur penalties for her. Do not give yourself to prosti-
> tutes, or you may lose your inheritance. Do not look around
> in the streets of a city, or wander about in its deserted sections.
> Turn away your eyes from a shapely woman, and do not gaze
> at beauty belonging to another; many have been seduced by a
> woman's beauty, and by it passion is kindled like a fire. Never
> dine with another man's wife, or revel with her at wine; or your
> heart may turn aside to her, and in blood you may be plunged
> into destruction.

Rabbi Yose ben Yohanan, Proverbs and Ben Sira all agree that carelessly associating with women can bring trouble on a man and plunge him into death or destruction by leading him astray into sexual misdemeanours (Prov. 7.21–27).[13] So, as George Foot Moore put it, 'the rabbis, in their endeavour to "keep a man a long way from sin," took manifold precautions against the excitement of lustful thoughts through the senses, and administered their warnings with liberal threats of damnation'.[14] Among his precautions for avoiding adultery, Ben Sira recommends that men should avoid walking around the deserted parts of any town and communicating with any woman who may be off limits.

Jesus does not seem to act according to this code. He is alone in a deserted place outside town at a time when few if any people might be expected to turn up. The heat at noon would probably have made this an uncomfortable and hence unpopular time of day to carry the heavy burden of a full water jar back from the well. Yet rather than avoid communicating with the Samaritan woman, Jesus initiates conversation. By the time the disciples get back from town, he is doing things they would expect him as a righteous man to avoid. It is little wonder that they are amazed. They suspect him of being up to no good.

This has been an uncomfortable thought for many Christians over the centuries. Commenting on the story, Augustine, Bishop of Hippo (AD 354–430) suggests that the disciples are amazed in a positive way. Seeing Jesus at work saving this lost woman, they wonder with joy at his ministry to her. Concerning the questions that they do not dare to ask, Augustine asserts (*Tractates on the Gospel of John* 15.29) that the disciples were marvelling at a good thing and not suspecting an evil thing. However, Augustine's very denial that they suspect something untoward indicates that he was aware of this possibility. Either he thought the disciples suspected something was wrong or he knew that others thought as much. But, like the disciples at the scene, he did not dare admit it.

Nobody dared ask

We will look in more detail at the story of the woman at the well in Chapter 3. For now, though, I will focus on the words I have translated 'nobody dared ask'. They are wonderfully ironic. In telling the story of the disciples' embarrassment and timidity, John has written these questions down for his audience and all the world to read and hear. In doing so he demonstrates that he no longer believes or feels that the questions are off limits, because one of the disciples who did not dare ask them at the time is now doing precisely that.

John Chrysostom, Archbishop of Constantinople (AD *c.* 347–407) suggests that, towards the end of his life, 'when he enjoyed greater confidence and was bold in the love of Christ' (John Chrysostom, *Homilies on John* 33.3), John the Apostle does ask the two questions that had been on his mind by the well. Chrysostom does not explain why the disciples believed Jesus was speaking to the Samaritan woman, although he thinks they marvelled at his humility in talking to her. Despite his own silence on their reasons for failing to say what was on their minds, however, Chrysostom offers the intriguing idea that John's experience of the intimate love of Christ as the beloved disciple gave him the courage later in life to ask what had felt unaskable on that day.

The apostle's boldness is an invitation to the Gospel audience to come alongside him and ask what may be awkward, difficult or embarrassing questions of Jesus' sexuality.[15] By telling us what the disciples did not dare ask on the day, John introduces the subject of Jesus' sexuality and invites us to go back over the Gospel to see what he has written about it.[16] According to the prologue, Jesus was God incarnate, the Word made flesh, God become fully human (John 1.14). This entails Jesus experiencing human sexuality physically, mentally, emotionally and spiritually. Living in a culture which celebrated human physicality and sexuality, the apostle John, once he had claimed that Jesus was the Word incarnate, could hardly avoid questions about Jesus' experience of human sexuality.

Entering the baths with the beloved disciple

Irenaeus, Bishop of Lyons (AD *c.* 130–*c.* 200) tells a story about the beloved disciple which he heard from Polycarp, Bishop of Smyrna (AD *c.* 69–*c.* 155). John had moved from Palestine to Ephesus where he was engaged in leading and teaching the Church. When, one day, he was going to the baths he noticed that the heretic Cerinthus was there too. John rushed from the baths without bathing, shouting to all and sundry to leave quickly just in case the buildings collapsed – presumably in divine judgment on Cerinthus (Irenaeus, *Against Heresies* 3.3.4).

Although Irenaeus tells the story as part of his narrative about the preservation of the truths of the Gospel, it offers an interesting piece of incidental information. The apostle John seems to have been a regular at the baths, like many people in cities where there were Roman baths. Irenaeus tells the story as if his presence at the baths were perfectly normal. He mentions the fact that John left without bathing in order to highlight how quickly he got out (thanks to the evil that lay within and the divine wrath that it might incur), giving the impression that he did not normally leave so quickly or without bathing. Irenaeus and Polycarp imply that John enjoyed the baths on a regular basis, and so would have been familiar with their culture.

People who could afford the leisure time, or who could cultivate lucrative relationships there, would visit the baths regularly. The baths were as much a health club and social centre as a hygiene facility. Typically, the bath house would comprise an *apodyterium* or changing room, a *tepidarium* or warm room, a *caldarium* or hot room and a *frigidarium* or cold room. There might also be a *palaestra* or courtyard where exercise could be taken. While people exercised and bathed they would relax, engage in conversation, sort out their social calendars and maybe do a little business.

On paying the entrance fee, people headed for the changing rooms where they would strip naked and leave their clothes with an attendant or slave. They might then take exercise. This could involve running, weight lifting, throwing the javelin or discus, wrestling or some other sport, or a variety of other physical activities. Unlike in modern gyms, exercise was undertaken naked. Once people had worked up a sweat and their physical exertions were completed, they would enter the baths.

People would use the baths in a certain order based on the cleansing of the skin, although it was also a physically pleasurable experience. Normally, they would enter the warm room first. Particularly if they had not worked up a sweat through exercise, the *tepidarium* warmed their bodies and so gently prepared them for the hot room. In the *caldarium* they would sweat much as in a modern sauna or steam room, and maybe take a quick dip in a hot plunge pool. The idea was to sweat the impurities out of the skin. In the hot room an attendant or slave would rub their bodies down with oil and then scrape the oil off with a blunt metal scraper called a *strigil.* While the rubbing of the oil into the skin formed a pleasurable massage, this bathing ritual also performed an important hygienic function. The impurities sweated out of the pores would be caught up in the oil and scraped away with it, so cleansing the skin. After this, people would enter the cold room. In the *frigidarium* they would plunge into the cold waters and their pores would quickly close up, thus preventing further impurities from entering. Their bathing now complete, people might socialize further or leave for their late afternoon or evening engagements.

Some baths in the Roman empire were more ornate than others; some were large complexes with additional bathing rooms. Some had swimming pools attached, and elegant exercise grounds. Some even had libraries and were not simply social and health clubs but centres of education. In the first century AD, the baths at Ephesus (known as the Scholastica baths after the wealthy Christian woman who restored them in the fourth century) were a three-storey complex. On the ground floor, two entrances led to the changing room. There was one suite of baths with a *tepidarium,* a *caldarium* and a *frigidarium.* The upper storeys may have been used for further health therapies. Doubtless the behaviour of the clientele of the many Roman baths throughout the empire differed according to time and place, but they did share a common culture. Most probably, the sexual prowess and encounter which we know from contemporary literature was common to bathing culture across the empire. John would have encountered this when he went to the baths.

The naked wrestling that took place between men seems to have been a source of homoerotic feeling and attraction for some. In Xenophon of Ephesus' romantic novel *Anthia and Habrocomes* (first century AD), Hippothous talks of falling in love with the handsome Hyperanthes because of the way he grappled with his opponents' bodies in wrestling matches (Xenophon of Ephesus, *Anthia and Habrocomes* 3.2.2), while in Achilles Tatius' romantic novel *Leucippe and Clitophon* (late first or early second century AD), Menelaus tells Clitophon that loving other men is superior to loving women, not least because you can enjoy struggling naked with the object of your affections in wrestling matches in the gym even before entering any romantic relationship together (Achilles Tatius, *Leucippe and Clitophon* 2.38.4). The Roman satirist Martial (AD 40–c. 104) plays on this aspect of sporting culture when he writes of liking a particular wrestler not just because of the wrestling but also the sex (Martial, *Epigrams* 14.201). The link between wrestling and sex was strong enough to be a familiar motif in novels and satirical poetry.

The baths and gymnasium were places where people would admire others, fall for their physical beauty and find sexual partners. Martial teases an acquaintance for constantly looking at the penises of athletic young men (Martial, *Epigrams* 1.96.12–13). Not all these admiring looks were homoerotic; some men simply engaged in the age-old custom of comparing size. The Roman novelist Petronius (d. AD 66) tells the tale of Ascyltos leaving the baths for the changing rooms to find his clothes had been stolen. As he wandered around naked, trying to find his clothes and his slave, quite a crowd gathered gazing at his loins in humble admiration (Petronius, *Satyricon* 92).

Checking out the bodies of others was not an activity limited to men looking at each other in the baths: men and women would also size each other up. Knowing that she wants to sleep with him, Martial asks Saufeia why she will not bathe with him. He wonders whether she worries that seeing her in the nude may put him off (Martial, *Epigrams* 3.72). On another occasion he asks Galla (another woman who wants to have sex with him) why she will not bathe with him. This time he is slightly less arrogant – perhaps she is afraid that seeing *him* in the nude will put *her* off (*Epigrams* 3.51). Naked athletic contests and admiring looks at the baths seem to have encouraged social encounters of various kinds. Martial notes that Cotta never invites anyone to dinner unless he has bathed with them. Having bathed with Cotta many times, Martial asks himself why he has never been invited to dinner. He decides Cotta does not like him nude (*Epigrams* 1.23).

Sexual attraction, flirtation and admiring one another's bodies, then, were part of the culture of the Roman baths. Given that both exercise and bathing were undertaken in the nude this may not be very surprising. Both Greek and Roman cultures had a more fluid understanding of sexual attraction than many modern ones; hence, sexual attractions and liaisons might be with members of the opposite sex or the same sex, particularly for men. Some relationships might be quite mercenary, so that both partners knew what they were getting: sex for money and money for sex. Others might be classically romantic, one partner falling head over heels in love with the body and soul of another.[17]

Since the baths were a major social hub and a centre of community, where relationships were formed and broken, where people met and doubtless gossiped, it would be hard sometimes to miss what was going on. If the apostle John was a regular at the baths, as both Irenaeus and Polycarp seem to suggest, he would have been more than familiar with the romantic and sometimes sordid sexual entanglements that began there. Reading the prologue to the Gospel of John (John 1.1–18) with this in mind, it becomes very difficult to believe that John could possibly have described Jesus as the Word become flesh without realizing that others would naturally hear this in terms of Jesus' physicality and sexuality.[18]

Who dares sins?

Given the culture within which John ministered and wrote his Gospel, he could not then have avoided the implication of his statement that Jesus was the Word of God made flesh. The Greek and Roman myths prevalent across the Roman empire told many stories of gods becoming human and having sexual encounters, or more generally simply having sex with human beings to whom they were attracted, whether that involved them coming to earth or taking the object of their affections into the heavens. Those hearing the words of John's opening statement would automatically make the assumption that this Word of God experienced human sexuality as part of the experience of becoming human.

The sexuality of Jesus is hardly the major plot line of the Gospel. From its opening statement to its closing chapters, the Gospel of John presents Jesus as divine, the Son of God who is one with God the Father, and the one whom God the Father has sent to bring light and life to a broken and sinful world. It climaxes with an invitation to the reader to accept these truths: 'but these things are written so that you should believe that Jesus is the messiah and the Son of God, and that believing you should have life in his name' (John 20.31).[19]

But John does not ignore the sexuality of Jesus either. His comment on his silence so many years ago by the well shows that he has come a long way since then. Between that day and the time when he wrote the Gospel, John grew in his knowledge and understanding of the love of Christ – a love which he elsewhere describes as casting out all fear (1 John 4.18).[20] When he came to tell the story, he was no longer afraid to open up and ask his questions. Whatever the reasons for the disciples' reluctance to ask Jesus about his possible sexual motivations that day by the well, they had disappeared from John's heart and mind by the time he wrote his Gospel. Possibly his experience of Christ's love made him more comfortable with the idea of God in Jesus experiencing human sexuality. At any rate, it was nothing about which he needed to be embarrassed any longer.

2

Word become flesh

A very few words can sometimes carry the profoundest of truths. Such is the case with the words from the prologue to the Gospel of John: 'and the Word became flesh' (John 1.14). But these words are the first in which John says anything about the sexuality of Jesus, and so they need close examination. Doing so involves studying in some detail what John writes about the nature of Jesus, which in turn entails investigating what John says about Jesus' divinity and his relationship with the Father, as well as thinking about the ways in which John pictures Jesus' humanity. Exploring such matters may seem to take us away from the primary focus of our discussion. However, if we are to understand how John pictures Jesus' sexuality, we need to see it as part of his wider portrait of Jesus: God made human, Word made flesh.

And the Word was God

John opens his Gospel with the magisterial lines: 'in the beginning was the Word and the Word was beside God and the Word was God' (John 1.1). He goes on to describe the Word as being alongside God in the beginning and creating all things which exist (1.2–3). As this opening statement of the Gospel proceeds, we discover that the Word becomes flesh and is full of grace and truth (1.14). This gives the clue to the identity of the Word, as just before the prologue closes, John mentions that grace and truth come through Jesus Christ (1.17). John identifies the Word as Jesus.

In identifying Jesus as the Word in his opening lines, John signals to his readers that he expects us to see Jesus through this lens, inviting us to see Jesus first and foremost as the Word. This is the perspective through which we are to understand all his other images of Jesus and within which we are to draw them together to form a coherent overall picture. It is therefore important that we gain a reasonable understanding of what John was trying to communicate through calling Jesus the Word.

Jesus, Word and Wisdom of God

Exactly what it means to describe Jesus as the Word has been the subject of considerable debate down the centuries. Even within the last hundred years, many ideas have been put forward to explain what John may have had in mind as he chose those words. The difficulty lies in there being so many different more or less plausible options for interpreting them in the Jewish, Greek and Roman cultures of the first century AD. The Greek word for 'Word' (*logos*) would be heard differently by members of different philosophical schools and religious groups.[1] So the wisest course of action is to read the term in its current context in John and proceed from there.

The Word is identified as existing in the beginning alongside God (John 1.1). The fact that John repeats this assertion (1.2) in the opening statement of the Gospel makes clear that he wants his readers to hear it clearly. The Word has existed throughout all time with God. John describes the Word as an 'only son of a father' (1.14) and then as an 'only begotten god' who is in the bosom of 'the Father' (1.18). In this way, he invites us to read the relationship of God and the Word as being like that of a father and a son. However, as he makes clear at the end of v. 1, John does not want to picture two gods existing alongside each other in heaven.[2] God and the Word have distinct identities but the Word is God.

John develops the contemporary Jewish doctrine of God further in his prologue. Jews in the first century AD believed that the God of Israel was the creator of the whole world. The classic statement of this teaching is found in the opening chapter of the book of Genesis. God transforms the watery chaos into the beautiful and good creation over six days and rests on the seventh (Gen. 1.1—2.4a). John alludes to this story. His opening words, 'in the beginning', Greek *en archē*, are identical to those opening the Genesis story of creation (Gen. 1.1 LXX).[3] Just as God creates by speaking in the Genesis account, so John has the Word of God create all things (John 1.3). However, whereas the Genesis creation account clearly refers to one God who creates the world, John has one God but two distinct divine identities in the Word and the Father, and the Word of God has become the creator.

The picture John paints of the Word as creator is very like that in Proverbs 8.22–31.[4] There the figure of Wisdom claims that God created her at the beginning of all his works, before the world or anything in it was created. Wisdom was acting like an artisan alongside God as he created. (In the LXX Wisdom fits and joins for God as God creates the world.) The author or compiler of the book of Proverbs pictures God creating the world with another spiritual being. Beyond naming it Wisdom, Proverbs leaves the nature of this being (divine, poetical, metaphorical or something else) largely undefined. Nevertheless, John seems to draw on this image in picturing the Word of God as creating the world and existing alongside God the Father before all things.

Wisdom, Word and Second God

This image raised questions in Second Temple Judaism about what kind of angelic or divine figure Wisdom was.[5] Another spiritual being which is not identified as an angel, and has existed from eternity alongside God in heaven, could very easily be mistaken for a god even if she were the first of all God's creations. This point was not lost on Second Temple Jews, and a number wrote of Wisdom in ways which attempt to explain her nature, and to reconcile her existence with their belief in only one God.

The Wisdom of Solomon (written between 30 BC and AD 50) identifies Wisdom with God and assumes they have two identities that are distinct (Wisd. 7.24—8.1).[6] It describes Wisdom as 'a vapour or mist of the power of God' and 'an emanation of the glory of the Almighty' (7.24). Neither description clarifies exactly what Wisdom is; the language of vapours and emanations seems more poetic than plainly descriptive. However, both these descriptions preserve the idea that Wisdom comes from God and so has no identity apart from God. Both maintain the exalted status of Wisdom and suggest that there is a difference between Wisdom and all other creations. Wisdom comes directly out of God (as a 'vapour' or 'emanation'), whereas God speaks everything else into being. Like Proverbs, the Wisdom of Solomon pictures Wisdom present at creation (9.7), ordering all created things (8.1) and sitting alongside the throne of God in heaven (9.4, 10). Wisdom is a Spirit which enters human lives, makes them wise, and enables them to listen to God and his prophets (7.27). As Wisdom comes from God's very being, Wisdom also reflects the true nature of God (7.26). So the Wisdom of Solomon builds on the picture in Proverbs, suggesting that Wisdom comes from the heart of God and is not entirely separate from God, although she has a distinct identity.

The Wisdom of Ben Sira or Sirach (written around 190–175 BC and translated by the author's grandson around 130–100 BC) also develops the traditions in Proverbs describing Wisdom.[7] Wisdom dwells in the assembly of the Most High (Sir. 24.2); Wisdom is enthroned in the highest heaven (24.4); Wisdom is subservient to and obedient to the one true creator God who created her (24.8); God created Wisdom before all things (24.9); Wisdom was present with God at the time of creation (24.5–6);[8] Wisdom serves God and comes from the mouth of God (24.3), seeking holy souls in which to abide (24.7). The unity of God and Wisdom may be less clear in Sirach than in the Wisdom of Solomon, but the pre-eminence of Wisdom is unmistakable, as is her presence with God at creation.

The Jewish philosopher Philo (*c.* 20 BC–*c.* AD 50) also writes of a figure like Wisdom. Philo calls this figure by many names, including '[God's] firstborn Word' (Philo, *On the Confusion of Tongues* 146) and God's 'firstborn son' (*On the Confusion of Tongues* 146; *On Dreams* 1.215). In Proverbs 8 Wisdom is the firstborn of all God's creations and in these two texts Philo identifies the firstborn, or Wisdom, with the 'Word' (Greek *logos*). He identifies the divine Word with Wisdom at various points in his writings (e.g. Philo, *Allegorical Interpretation* 1.65; *On Dreams* 2.242–245). Like Proverbs and the Wisdom of Solomon, he believes that the Word was the instrument through which God made the world (Philo, *On the Cherubim* 127; *On the Special Laws* 1.81); like Proverbs, the Wisdom of Solomon and Sirach, he sees the Word as revealing the nature of God. He describes the Word as the image of God (Philo, *On Flight and Finding* 101) and as the angel of the Lord whom Philo takes to be God appearing as an angel, reflecting the nature of God (Philo, *On Dreams* 1.238–239). Like the Wisdom of Solomon and Sirach, Philo identifies Wisdom with God and preserves the idea that Wisdom and God have distinct identities. Like the apostle John, he prefers the use of the term Word (*logos*), rather than Wisdom, to refer to this figure.

While there may be differences in the way in which Proverbs, the Wisdom of Solomon, Sirach, Philo and John conceive of the nature and work of the Word or Wisdom, there are clear similarities. They all see Wisdom as closely identified with God and yet having an identity distinct from God. They all understand Wisdom to have been involved in or present at creation. John is not entirely original in his portrayal of the Word – although he is in identifying the Word as Jesus Christ. Given that he opens his Gospel with this statement about Jesus being the Word, at one and the same time God and yet in identity distinct from God, John pictures Jesus not simply as divine but as God himself, alongside the Father.

Father and Son

John describes the Word as an only child of a father (John 1.14) and as God the only son who lies in the breast of the Father (1.18), thus identifying the Word as the Son of God the Father right at the start of the Gospel. By identifying the Word with the Son, John indicates that the Son is both God and beside God whom he names the Father (1.18). The relationship of God and the Word is the model for the relationship of the Father and the Son.

From the start John portrays this relationship as one of intimacy and love. This is evident from the description of God the only Son in the breast of the Father (1.18).[9] There is a parallel with the beloved disciple lying in Jesus' breast at dinner (13.23), which we shall consider in more detail in Chapter 4, and which suggests a dining image here.[10] God the only son reclines (as on an ancient dining couch) close to the Father who lies behind him, their bodies one against the other. Ancient dining rituals placed the most important guests next to the host. The Son reclines in the place of highest honour, one of physical intimacy. We know from elsewhere in the Gospel that John believes God is Spirit (4.24) and so does not intend this bodily image to be taken literally. Both the Father and the Son are spirit in heaven, the Word taking on physical human form only at the incarnation. However, this serves to reinforce the fact that, by using an image of physical closeness, John intends his audience to hear from the outset that the relationship of the Father and the Son is marked by intimacy.

Love lies at the heart of the relationship between the Father and the Son and of their actions. The Father sends the only Son into the world in order to save it (John 3.16–18; cf. also John 6.40) because the Father loves the world (3.16). The Son does not believe he is compelled to lay down his life but chooses to do so for others (John 10.17–18); his voluntary gift of his life demonstrates how great is his love for humanity (cf. John 15.13). By way of response to the Son's loving offering of himself, the Father loves the Son (10.17). The Father and Son, then, have a relationship of mutual love which results in the self-giving of God the Son, through which he shares with the world the love he shares with the Father. On account of his love for the Son, the Father has placed all things in the Son's hands (John 3.35).

The distinct identities of the Son and the Father are reinforced by the many sayings in which Jesus notes his dependence on the Father. He does the will of the Father just as a boy in the ancient world would learn his trade from observing his father (John 5.19, 30);[11] he speaks only as the Father instructs and tells only what he has seen in the presence of the Father (John 8.28, 38); he does only the works the Father tells him to do (John 10.22–39). At the same time Jesus claims that he is the Son of God and that he and God the Father are one (John 10.30, 36), and elaborates on this assertion of unity by claiming that the Father is in him and he is in the Father (John 10.38). Here Jesus develops ideas introduced in the prologue that the Word was both God and had identity distinct from God the Father.

Jesus invites those who believe in him to enter the relationship of the Father and the Son. Talking to his disciples at the Last Supper he says that he will send the Spirit upon his disciples. When they receive the Spirit, they will know that they live in him, and that he lives in them and in the Father. In keeping his commandments, the disciples will demonstrate their love for Jesus and experience the love of the Father and the Son. Just as the Father and the Son love each other and live in each other, and as the Son obeys the Father, so the disciples will experience the love of the Father and the Son as they live in the Son, and he lives in them (John 14.8–24).

These themes are gathered together in Jesus' prayer to the Father before he goes to the garden and the cross (John 17.1–26). Acknowledging that the Father has given him authority to offer eternal life, he commits himself to the way of the cross, asking that the Father will glorify him in his presence just as the Father did before the world was created. Knowing that he faces crucifixion, Jesus as Son commits those who have believed in him to his heavenly Father for divine protection. Just as he taught his disciples that they would experience the loving relationship of the Father and the Son, Jesus now prays that they might experience the unity of the Father and the Son and the love the Father and the Son share.

The relationship of the Father and the Son introduced in the prologue is developed throughout the Gospel. Jesus explains that the Father and Son are one, that they live in each other and love each other. The Father has loved the Son from before all time and the Son responds by doing as the Father shows and instructs him. However, the Son responds freely to the Father not out of compulsion but out of love. The Son invites all people into this relationship and draws those who believe into it by the work of the Spirit. Those who believe in the Son experience the unity and the love which is shared by the Father and the Son. Both the Father and the Son are God, and John models their relationship on the relationship of God and the Word with which he begins his Gospel.

Jesus the great 'I AM'

John reinforces his presentation of the divinity of Jesus through a number of sayings that use the words *egō eimi* (Greek for 'I am' or 'I AM'). In the story of the burning bush, God famously identifies himself to Moses as 'I AM' or 'I AM WHO I AM' (Exod. 3.14). In the LXX this is translated into the Greek phrase *egō eimi ho ōn*, which literally means 'I am the being', although 'I AM WHO I AM' are the words that normally appear in English translations.[12] In other places in the LXX, the words *egō eimi* are used to identify the one true God of Israel (e.g. Deut. 32.39; Isa. 41.4; 43.10, 25; 45.18–19; 46.4; 51.12; 52.6). Jesus uses the phrase *egō eimi* many times in the Gospel of John, recalling the 'I AM' of Exodus 3.14 LXX and these other LXX texts. Tracing the way John employs these sayings throughout the Gospel also helps us to understand how he sees the divinity of Jesus.[13]

The first time Jesus uses the phrase, he is talking to the Samaritan woman. She has just told him that she knows the messiah is coming (John 4.25). Jesus replies *egō eimi ho lalōn soi*, which means literally 'I am the one speaking to you' (4.26) or, paraphrasing to capture the whole meaning, 'I am the messiah of whom you speak, the person talking to you'. Not only are the first three words of his reply, Greek *egō eimi ho*, the same as the first three words of the divine name in Exodus 3.14 LXX, they recall even more closely words of the Lord God in Isaiah 52.6 LXX: *egō eimi autos ho lalōn*, 'I AM he the one speaking'. By making these allusions, John has Jesus recall the divine name in order to identify him not simply as the messiah but also as God.[14] John has already informed his audience that Jesus is God by virtue of being the Word and the Son of God. Now he has Jesus reveal his nature as messiah and Son of God to the Samaritan woman, who then believes in him. Her journey to belief in Jesus as messiah and Son of God prefigures those of the hearers of the Gospel, whom John hopes will in turn believe (John 20.31).

John develops the identity of Jesus as the Lord God Almighty more strongly in the next 'I AM' saying. The disciples are in a boat on the Sea of Galilee. The sea is rough because of a strong wind. Jesus walks on the sea and comes near the boat. The disciples are terrified but Jesus says to them, *egō eimi*, and tells them not to fear (John 6.16–20). The *egō eimi* here almost certainly recalls that of Exodus 3.14 LXX because of the way in which Jesus is portrayed as walking on the sea. The Greek words used for walking on the sea (*peripateō* + *epi* + *thalassa*) are found together in the Bible only in four places: in this story and its equivalents in Matthew and Mark (Matt. 14.22–33; Mark 6.45–52), and at Job 9.8. The image of God walking on the sea in Job 9.8 recalls ancient myths in which God conquers the sea (which represents God's mythical enemy, evil and chaos). In recalling this image, Matthew, Mark and John picture Jesus as the Lord God who defeats all evil. Here again John identifies Jesus as the one true God.[15]

John follows this with a series of 'I AM' sayings where Jesus uses imagery to describe his ministry among humankind: 'I AM the bread of life' (John 6.35; cf. 6.41, 48, 51); 'I AM the light of the world' (8.12); 'I AM the gate' (10.7, 9); 'I AM the good shepherd' (10.11, 14); 'I AM the resurrection and the life' (11.25); 'I AM the way, the truth and the life' (14.6); and finally, 'I AM the vine' (15.1, 5). There are other 'I AM' sayings that identify Jesus as God. In debate with the Jews over whether Jesus' father is God, he declares 'before Abraham was I AM' (8.58).[16] The reaction of his dialogue partners is to pick up stones to throw at him – presumably for blasphemy.[17] They hear this as Jesus claiming to be divine.[18] John uses many 'I AM' sayings to identify Jesus as the one true God of Israel ('I AM WHO I AM').

Other 'I AM' sayings explore the relationship of the Father and the Son. As bread of life Jesus comes from heaven and does the will of the Father (John 6.38–40). Jesus has seen the Father as he has come from being with God (6.46), for as the Word he was with God. Referring to his crucifixion, Jesus says that when the Jews have lifted up the Son of Man, then they will know that *egō eimi* and that the Father validates

Jesus' ministry (8.28) – implying that God is Father to Jesus the divine Son. Jesus' claim that 'I AM the good shepherd' means that as such he knows his sheep as he and the Father know one another. He lays down his life for the sheep and so the Father loves him (10.14–18). Jesus will look after all those whom the Father has given him (10.27–29) because he and the Father are one (10.30). In his claim 'I AM the vine', Jesus abides in the love of the Father and keeps his commandments (15.10). All these speeches identify Jesus as the great 'I AM', the divine Son of his heavenly Father – just as the Word was God and was with God.

My Lord and my God

Down the centuries Thomas has been famous for doubting the resurrection of Jesus. Having missed the first resurrection appearance to the disciples gathered in the house where they are staying, he declares that he will only believe if he sees the nail marks in Jesus' wrists, and can put his finger in these marks and his hand in Jesus' side (John 20.25). A week later Jesus appears, bearing the marks, and invites Thomas to do just that (20.27). Thomas declares, 'my Lord and my God' (20.28). John's picture of the divinity of Jesus reaches a climax in this declaration.

Although others, like John the Baptist, Nathanael and Martha, have declared him to be the Son of God (John 1.34, 46; 11.27), this is the first time in the narrative of the Gospel that any character has declared Jesus to be God. The Greek words that Thomas uses are *ho kurios mou kai ho theos mou*. In the LXX, the word *kurios* translates the Hebrew term YHWH (or 'I AM WHO I AM'), the name by which God reveals himself to Moses (Exod. 3.14). Therefore, Thomas' declaration implies that he identifies Jesus fully with the Lord God Almighty. By using the pronoun 'my' Thomas also makes clear that he owns and worships Jesus as such.

Assuming the Gospel was written in the late first century AD, John cannot have missed another resonance in Thomas' words. Contemporary Roman authors record that the emperor Domitian (AD 51–96) liked to be called *domini deique nostri* (Martial, *Epigrams* 5.8.1; 7.34.8; cf. 8.2.6; 10.72.3) or *dominus et deus noster* (Suetonius, *Domitian* 13.2). Both Latin phrases translate as 'our Lord and God'.[19] So John has Thomas suggest that Jesus is not only the Lord God of Israel but also the true Lord of the whole world, over and above the

Roman emperors of the Flavian dynasty which had been ruling the world politically since AD 70.

From the start to the end of his Gospel, John reinforces the same basic point about the divinity of Jesus. Jesus is fully God, and is identified as the one true God of Israel in his walking on the water and in some of his *egō eimi* sayings. This point reaches a climax in Thomas' declaration that Jesus is his Lord and God. Throughout the Gospel, John also makes the point that Jesus, as Word of God, is both distinct from and one with God the Father.

Fully human

John not only asserts the divinity of Jesus throughout the Gospel but also his humanity. In the prologue he declares that the Word, who was God and was with God in the beginning, was made flesh (John 1.14). Whether or not John was writing in order to fight Docetism (an early heretical teaching that God was not truly human in Jesus but only appeared to be human), he certainly puts the full humanity of Jesus on the agenda of his Gospel by making it part of his opening statement.[20] Throughout the Gospel he includes details which reinforce the real and complete humanity of Jesus.

Other characters in the Gospel think Jesus is an ordinary human being. Philip describes him to Nathanael in purely human terms as the son of Joseph from Nazareth (John 1.45). The Samaritan woman leaves the well to tell her fellow citizens to come and see a man who has told her everything she has ever done (4.29). She knows that he is special – she thinks he is a prophet (4.19), and in that sense no ordinary man – but she thinks he is human all the same. Confused by his claim that God is his Father, the Jews understand Jesus in purely human terms when they identify him as the son of Joseph, noting that they know both his father and mother (6.42). Rejecting his claim to divinity, they state that Jesus is blaspheming when he claims equality with God, because he is only a human being (10.33).

Of course, the fact that characters in the Gospel thought Jesus was human is no guarantee that he was so. In the book of Tobit, none of the characters realize that Azariah (the 'kinsman' who has helped Tobit) is actually Raphael, one of the seven angels who enters the throne room of God, until he reveals his true identity at the end of the story (Tobit 12.11–15).[21] However, there are other indications that John sees Jesus as fully human, and not as an angelic or divine being who only appears human.

John presents Jesus as having a human body with normal human needs. He writes of Jesus speaking of his body, or *sōma* in Greek (John 2.21). John only uses this word elsewhere of the crucified body of Jesus (19.38, 40; 20.12) and of the bodies of those crucified with Jesus (19.31), both of whom were human beings with human bodies. As John uses the same word (*sōma*) for all three bodies, he understands Jesus to have a normal human body like those crucified with him.

John notes that the reason Jesus stayed by the well was because he was exhausted by his journey (4.6). He did not have inexhaustible angelic or divine bodily strength but was subject to the same physical limitations as all ordinary human beings.[22] Both John as narrator and the disciples within the narrative are aware of Jesus' need to eat. John notes that the disciples went to buy food (4.8) and when they came back they told Jesus to eat (4.31). In the final chapter of the Gospel, John has Jesus making breakfast by the shore of the Sea of Galilee (21.9). On getting out of the boat the disciples see a charcoal fire with fish on it. Jesus does not tell them to tuck in but to bring some of the fish they have just caught. Rather than sharing the breakfast he has already cooked he asks them to bring some more fish to barbecue. It is not as if Jesus would be incapable of sharing his few fish among only a handful of disciples, as he had done something rather more impressive in the feeding of the five thousand (John 6.1–14); there was no reason for a miracle as they had plenty of fish. The implication is that Jesus was making his own breakfast with the first batch of fish and expected the disciples to share their fish for their own breakfasts. Jesus' eating suggests his humanity, as – at least according to most contemporary Jews – angels appearing in human form did not eat earthly food.[23]

The Passion narrative also brings the audience face to face with Jesus' humanity. Jesus is flogged. The soldiers who torture him place a crown of thorns on his head and a purple robe on his body. They repeatedly punch him in the face while mocking him (John 19.1–3). They could do none of these things if Jesus was human merely in appearance. The soldiers maltreat his physical body, while Jesus cries out on the cross that he is thirsty.[24] When Jesus dies one of the soldiers pierces his side with a spear, and blood and water flow out

(19.34). While commentators since the early Church have suggested symbolic interpretations of this event, the apostle John witnesses it primarily as testimony of the physical death of Jesus (19.34–35).[25]

The resurrection appearance to Thomas underlines the point that Jesus had a physical body not simply before his death but also on his resurrection (John 20.24–29). Thomas expresses his doubts about the appearance in ways that make entirely clear his view that Jesus had a human body in his earthly life. Unless Jesus had such a body Thomas could not touch the marks in his wrists or put his hand in the hole in his side. Whether or not Thomas actually did either of these things when Jesus appeared to him – the narrative does not say (20.27–28) – he is clearly sufficiently convinced by Jesus' presence to doubt no longer that Jesus has physically risen from the dead.

But John does not simply present Jesus' humanity in terms of his physical body. He presents Jesus as experiencing human relationships and participating in normal human community. Theories abound concerning the beloved disciple but at a very basic level, hearing this aspect of John's narrative for the first time most people would simply assume that Jesus had a best friend.[26] Judging by the narratives of John 11.1–44 and 12.1–8 Jesus shared close relationships with Mary, Martha and Lazarus of Bethany. When he comes towards the tomb of Lazarus, he breaks down in tears (11.35). Jesus understood human grief in bereavement; he experienced the joy and pain of human friendship.

Jesus also participated fully in family life. There are many things John does not say about Jesus' family. What he does say, however, paints a picture of a very normal family – however many questions this raises for commentators. At the wedding of Cana Jesus retorts to his mother, 'What have you got to do with me, woman?' (John 2.4). This famously causes complications for those who would see only peace, love and harmony in the holy family. To the theologically untrained eye, however, it looks remarkably like a young man telling his mother to get off his case.[27] Although John puts it down to their lack of belief, Jesus' siblings offer him career advice, which he initially ignores (7.1–9). At the start of the Johannine narrative, Jesus draws his disciples into his family circle by taking them home with him for a few days after the wedding at Cana (2.12). Jesus was certainly concerned for his mother's needs: at his crucifixion, he asks the beloved disciple to become a son to his mother in his place

(19.26–27). Possibly he felt the responsibility of being an eldest child. Whatever the case concerning this latter speculation, John certainly portrays Jesus as involved in the life of his family.

John, then, portrays Jesus as both divine and human. He introduces Jesus as the Word who was God and was with God from the beginning, and has the Word made a human being. Throughout the narrative of the Gospel he develops both points in various ways, and in his closing chapters he continues to portray Jesus as both fully human and fully divine.[28] The Thomas narrative sums it all up rather well. Thomas' doubts about the physical resurrection of Jesus are entirely removed through encountering him. He recognizes the physical Jesus he knew before his death. In his words of recognition, he also ascribes full divinity to Jesus, using of him terms normally reserved for the Lord of heaven and earth.

And the Word became flesh

The first words that John uses to state that in Jesus God became a human being, 'and the Word became flesh' (John 1.14), set the tone for understanding the humanity of Jesus within the text of the Gospel. While they clearly convey a broader meaning, they also hint at Jesus' sexuality, and not simply because sexuality is part of humanity. John chooses a term for flesh which in context specifically highlights the sexuality of Jesus. In choosing words which allude to the sexuality of the Word or Wisdom of God, John enters into dialogue with some of his Jewish contemporaries who also developed earlier ideas of the sexuality of Wisdom.

Words are best understood in context. John utters the line 'and the Word was made flesh' immediately after his comment about the rejection and acceptance of the Word by those to whom he came (John 1.11–13). His own did not receive him and to those who did he gave the right to become children of God. John underlines this by contrasting those who are born of God by believing in the name of the Word with those who were born physically into Second Temple Judaism. He uses three phrases to deny that people are born into the people of God through natural descent or procreation: 'not by bloods', 'not of the will of flesh' and 'not of the will of a man' (1.13).

There have been disagreements down the centuries over the finer nuances of meaning of these phrases. Whether or not John implies the mixing of the blood of the father and the blood of the mother in using the plural 'bloods' in 1.13a does not change the substantial meaning that he seeks to convey – that people are not made children of God through procreation and being born Second Temple Jews.[29] Rather they are made children of God, whether they are ethnically Jewish or something else, by believing that Jesus is the messiah and Son of God (John 20.31).

Augustine contended that 'will of flesh' refers to the sexual desire of a woman, as both Genesis and Paul use the Greek term *sarx* to refer to a woman in the context of sexual relationships (Gen. 2.23 LXX; Eph. 5.29; Augustine, *Tractates on the Gospel of John* 2.14). So he thought that 'will of flesh' referring to female sexual desire and 'will of a man' referring to male sexual desire complemented one another, whereas Calvin claimed that 'will of flesh' and 'will of a man' meant the same thing, as throughout Scripture 'flesh' simply refers to mortal human nature (body and soul).[30] Modern commentators give various nuances to the words. For example, Brant reads them as expressing 'blind desire with no intent to procreate'.[31] Few if any today agree with Augustine, but whatever the exact connotation, there is consensus that 'will of flesh' refers to sexual desire.[32]

Importantly the term *sarx* bears no connotations of sin in the Gospel of John (as it does in the writings of Paul, e.g. Rom. 7.5, 14, 18, 25).[33] John contrasts *sarx* with Spirit in order to emphasize the limitations of humanity, its inability to save itself and to see the truth of God without divine revelation (John 3.6; 6.63; 8.12). Although *sarx* therefore connotes the frailty of humanity and its inability to escape sin and evil of its own efforts, it does not necessarily denote only people who are destined to die in their sin. Jesus uses *sarx* of all people, including those whom the Father gave to him to save (John 17.2). John also uses the term of Jesus' physical body (6.51), particularly his body broken on the cross to give eternal life to humanity (6.53–56). As both Augustine and Calvin suggested, John seems to use *sarx* with connotations of the weakness of humanity (Augustine, *Tractates on the Gospel of John* 15.6–7).[34] So when John uses the term to describe the Word becoming human, he intends the reader to understand that Jesus took on the weakness of human flesh. The picture of Jesus exhausted by the well makes the point nicely (John 4.6).

But this is not the dominant note in the use of the word in John 1.14. The immediate context uses it to refer to human sexuality and specifically to sexual desire (John 1.13). These two verses are the only places in the prologue which use the term *sarx*, which makes it rather difficult not to read the usage in v. 14 in the light of that in v. 13.[35] So, when John describes the physical humanity of Jesus, he does so by using a word which he also uses in the immediate context to refer to sexual desire. Through his choice of words, John suggests that sexual desire was part of God's human experience.

John could have expressed himself otherwise.[36] He could have had Jesus become a man using the Greek word *anthrōpos*; he has the Samaritan woman, the Temple police, the man born blind, the Pharisees, the Jews, the chief priests, Caiaphas, the woman in the courtyard and Pilate call Jesus *anthrōpos* (4.29; 7.46; 9.11, 16; 10.33; 11.47, 50; 18.14, 17, 29; 19.5; cf. 5.12).[37] He could have used the Greek term *anēr* ('man' or 'male'); he uses this term of men elsewhere in the Gospel (e.g. 4.16–18). But he does not do so here. Similarly, he could have used the term *sōma*, body, to suggest that Jesus took on human physical form. He uses *sōma* of Jesus' body elsewhere (2.21; 19.31, 38, 40; 20.12). But he prefers to use *sarx* when he speaks of the Word becoming human.

Accidents do happen, but John seems to have chosen this word quite specifically. He uses the word *sarx* elsewhere to mean frail flesh, and he has used it quite clearly of sexual desire in the previous verse. If John did not draw attention to the disciples' belief that sex lay behind Jesus' conversation with the woman at the well (4.27), I might be more inclined to read the sexual connotation of 'flesh' in 1.14 as accidental or coincidental. However, given that John does precisely this, it seems more likely that he intends his audience to hear that as the Word made flesh Jesus experienced sexual desire, and that he did so in the frailty of human nature. Jesus did not use divine powers to avoid the challenges of human sexuality or to overcome the temptations of sex. Instead, John suggests, Jesus experienced the joys and difficulties of sexuality with all the weaknesses and needs of any other human being.

Desire and glory

On the one hand this statement has Jesus experience human sexuality (and specifically sexual desire) as part and parcel of being human, with all the frailty that entails. On the other John intends his audience to hear that this is precisely where they may see the glory of the one true God. Before claiming that he and his contemporaries saw the glory of God in Jesus as the Word made flesh (1.14), he describes Jesus as living, or more specifically becoming a tent (or tabernacle) among us. The tent and glory recall the exodus from Egypt when the glory of God came and settled in the tabernacle (Exod. 40.34–35). As the Word made flesh Jesus becomes the new place where God lives on earth and from which his glory is made known.[38] Given the connotations of *sarx* in this context, making Jesus the place where people see God's glory suggests that the glory of God is visible in the way Jesus lives out his sexuality – as part of his life and works more generally.[39]

This statement seems all the more remarkable when you consider that sexuality was normally excluded from the tabernacle or Temple. When Israel settled in the land, the functions of the tabernacle were in time taken over by the Temple, which became the place where God dwelt. Ritual purity laws delineated who could enter the Temple and when. Men who had had an emission of semen, men and women who had had sexual intercourse and women who were menstruating were not able to enter the Temple until the required time had elapsed and the required rituals had been performed (Lev. 15). The Temple was to be kept free from any ritual defilement associated with human sexuality.

Among some of John's Jewish contemporaries, this ritual separation of human sexuality from the presence and glory of God had been strengthened. The Roman historian Josephus (AD 37–*c*. 97) extends the purity provisions of the Torah concerning menstruation and impurity after childbirth in order to maintain the purity of the Temple (e.g. Josephus, *Jewish Antiquities* 3.11.3§261; 3.11.5§269).[40] The book of Jubilees (second century BC) identifies the Garden of Eden with the Temple and so places sexual intercourse between Adam and Eve outside the garden (Jub. 3.4–14).[41] The Torah declared men ritually unclean after any emission of semen until the evening and after bathing (Lev. 15.16). The Essenes extended this command so that, after an emission of semen, men could not enter the Temple until three days had passed and they had washed themselves and their clothes (11QTemple XLV, 7–12).[42] For these Second Temple Jews, sex and the ritual purity of the Temple were incompatible.[43]

John offers a radically different perspective. By making the Word *sarx*, and specifically the tabernacle from which people saw the glory of God, he places human sexuality and sexual desire within the heart of the Temple in the humanity of Jesus Christ. God is no longer separated from human sexuality; instead human sexual experience lies right at the heart of God in the person of the Word made flesh. John goes so far as to suggest that he and his contemporaries saw the glory of God in Jesus' humanity, including his sexuality and experience of sexual desire.

Wisdom and desire

If John was deliberately engaging in dialogue with Philo and Sirach in the prologue to the Gospel, then his use of the Word (or Wisdom) further develops this theme of Jesus revealing the glory of God at least in part through his sexuality and sexual desire. John uses the figure of Wisdom as the model for his depiction of Jesus as the Word of God, drawing on the ways in which these Jewish contemporaries of his interpreted the figure of Lady Wisdom in Proverbs 1—9.

Following Proverbs 1—9, Philo depicts both Wisdom and Folly as women (Philo, *On the Sacrifices of Cain and Abel* 21–28). Taking his cue from Proverbs 7, he depicts Lady Folly as an adulteress. She wears only the most fashionable and expensive clothes and jewellery, indulges incessantly in spa treatments and reeks of perfume. She lures unsuspecting young men into her trap with promises of a life of unbridled pleasure, relaxation and freedom from responsibility (Philo, *On the Sacrifices of Cain and Abel* 21–25). By contrast Lady Wisdom is austere, plain and prudent (Philo, *On the Sacrifices of Cain and Abel* 26–28).[44] In Proverbs Lady Wisdom nevertheless encourages young men to become her lovers, using mildly erotic language to depict the acquisition of Wisdom (Prov. 4.5–9; 7.4).[45] Philo strips her of the few sexual allures she possesses in Proverbs. This seems very much in line with his general view that although sex is necessary for procreation, both sexual passion and indulgence in physical pleasures are evils to be avoided. Although sex forms part of marriage, Philo condemns acts of unbridled sexual passion not only with the wives of others but also between husbands and their own wives (Philo, *On the Special Laws* 3.9).[46] He depicts Wisdom without sexuality and so avoids affirming sexual passion.[47]

Sirach 51.13–21 offers a very different depiction of Wisdom. Although this is a hymn in praise of Wisdom, it appears to develop the mildly erotic language of acquiring Wisdom found in Proverbs

1—9. Double meanings abound in the text, particularly the Hebrew text. Sirach claims to have found much 'instruction' or 'seductive speech' in Wisdom (Sir. 51.16; 11Q5 XXI 14). He is determined to 'enjoy' Wisdom (Sir. 51.18a; 11Q5 XXI 15),[48] zealous for 'good' or 'pleasure' (Sir. 51.18b; 11Q5 XXI 15). He has 'set his soul ablaze for her', or his 'soul grappled with her' (Sir. 51.19; 11Q5 XXI 15–16). He promises not to let up in her moments of exultation (11Q5 XXI 15–16). Sirach finds Wisdom in a state of purity and so ready to have sexual intercourse (Sir. 51.20). He says that his loins have been stirred up to seek her (Sir. 51.21). The depiction of Wisdom here could not contrast more strongly with that of Philo. Sirach offers a highly erotic undertone to his praise of Wisdom.[49] He talks of 'sexual intercourse, female nakedness, and orgasm' alongside 'lines . . . praising God', so bringing Eros into the sacred sphere and breaking down the boundary between the two set up within ritual practice.[50] Ironically, however, the poem assumes the continuation of such rituals relating to sexuality (Sir. 51.20 LXX), and so ruptures the boundary between sex and the sacred more in poetic imagination than in practice.[51]

These two very different depictions of Wisdom both develop the sexualized figure of Wisdom in Proverbs 1—9. John offers his own view of the sexuality of Wisdom or the Word. Whereas Philo sees sin in sexual desire and puts a gulf between it and the Wisdom of God, and Sirach breaks down the barrier between sex and the sacred only in poetry rather than practice, John incarnates the Word in flesh, *sarx*, a word he has invested with connotations not simply of human sexuality but sexual desire, and so has the one true God experience sexual desire as a human being. John further claims that he and his fellow disciples saw the glory of God in this. The boundary between sex and the sacred is well and truly broken as God takes on human sexuality.

John has also done another remarkable thing in making the Word flesh. Read in twenty-first-century terms, this is an extremely inclusive piece of theology. Little can really be made of the grammatical gender of Wisdom and Word. Wisdom (Greek *sophia*) is feminine and Word (Greek *logos*) is masculine. Even if one were to try to make something out of the grammatical gender of Wisdom in Proverbs, Wisdom of Solomon and Sirach, the fact remains that the term John uses is grammatically masculine. Besides which, the grammatical genders of *sophia* and *logos* do not necessarily imply anything about the human gender of Jesus. However, the same cannot be said of the *figure* of Wisdom, on which John clearly draws in his portrayal of the Word. This Wisdom is not only grammatically feminine but is always portrayed as a female figure in Proverbs and the Second Temple Jewish literature. Jewish wisdom literature plays on the femininity and female sexuality of this figure.[52] The Greek and Roman deities of Wisdom, Athena and Minerva respectively, are goddesses. When John the Apostle recalls the figure of Wisdom in his presentation of the Word, his audience would naturally think of a female figure and likely recall her sexuality. Nothing John says in the prologue indicates the gender of the Word before v. 15, where John the Baptist talks of 'the one coming after me' in words which indicate that this person is male.[53] So when John the Apostle claims that the Word was made flesh, the female figure of Wisdom is still in mind. The original audience probably knew that Jesus was the Word made flesh, and John certainly tells them this in v. 17. However, the fact remains that at the point he writes of the incarnation of the Word, the audience has both the female figure of Wisdom and (at least soon afterwards) the male person of Jesus in mind. This militates against any reading of the text which suggests that John has only one gender or its sexuality in mind when he introduces the incarnation. Given the sexualization of Wisdom in Proverbs and Second Temple Judaism, the sexual connotation of *sarx* in v. 13 and the identification of the Word as Jesus in v. 17, John most likely has both male and female sexuality in view. Jesus' gender was physically male and John writes of him as such throughout the Gospel. However, as he introduces him in the prologue, Jesus is gendered theologically as both male and female. The sexuality of both genders is taken into his incarnation.

John seems to underline this point in choosing to make the Word flesh. The Greek word *sarx* could be used to refer to both male flesh (e.g. Gen. 2.21 LXX) and female flesh (e.g. Gen. 2.23 LXX). Occasionally, the LXX uses the term as a euphemism for penis (Ezek. 23.20 LXX) or in reference to circumcision (e.g. Gen. 17.21);[54] however, the context or combination of words in which *sarx* appears makes it clear when the word refers to male or female flesh or body parts. The LXX uses *sarx* to refer to many sorts of flesh, human and animal – but when it refers to human flesh, it normally refers to both male and female flesh.[55] When writing of the incarnation of the Word, John chooses not to use the word *anēr* (man, male) but the gender non-specific *sarx*.[56] Given that he does not signal the gender of Jesus until v. 15, the audience may reasonably hear a more general reference to humanity in the word *sarx* – although the vast majority will know that John refers to the man Jesus.

Right at the start of his Gospel, then, John makes a statement about Jesus' sexuality in the phrase 'and the Word was made flesh'. These few words carry depths and layers of meaning which unfold as the Gospel proceeds. Primarily they bear witness to the revelation that in the person of Jesus the one true God has become human: as the Word of God, Jesus is both God and has a distinct identity from God. Jesus the Word made flesh is God. However, in the same few words John also hints at the sexuality of Jesus. Having used the term *sarx* (or 'flesh') to refer to sexual desire in the verse immediately preceding the statement 'the Word was made flesh', he intends his audience to hear in that statement that God experienced human sexuality including sexual desire in Jesus. Moreover, in identifying Jesus with the female figure of Wisdom, John manages to include both male and female sexuality theologically in the incarnation.

John also suggests that he and his contemporaries saw the glory of God in Jesus' experience of human sexuality, and specifically of sexual desire. He guards against the notion that Jesus used his divine power to control either his sexuality or any of the challenges or temptations it presented. Rather he introduces Jesus' sexuality in terms that suggest Jesus experienced sexual desire in all the frailty and weakness of normal people. He had to face his sexuality as any other human being, with all the difficulties that entails. John and his contemporaries beheld the glory of God in the way Jesus lived his life (and supremely in his death on the cross). They also saw his glory in the way Jesus experienced and lived out his sexual desire. And in order to explain how they saw his glory in this, John tells stories and explores friendships.

3

A Samaritan bride and her Jewish groom

The first of the stories in which John explores Jesus' sexual desire more fully is the aforementioned narrative of the woman at the well. The story is about the revelation of Jesus as the saviour of the whole world, including the much-despised Samaritans (John 4.42).[1] Here John uses a standard plot which was familiar to ancient Jewish audiences, namely 'guy meets girl at well and they get married',[2] to tell the story of the God who woos humanity back into relationship with him. But there is a twist in the tale. In telling this story of Jesus the saviour whom he wants his audience to believe in so that they may have life, John also develops his picture of Jesus the man in whose sexual desires and behaviour he and others have seen the glory of God.

This story of God wooing humanity as a bride develops one of the themes introduced in the prologue: that of the Word being in the world which refused to know him, coming to his own but being rejected by them, and giving to those who believed in him the right to become the children of God (John 1.13). It forms a contrasting pair with the story of Jesus meeting Nicodemus by night (3.1–21). Nicodemus is a leader of the Jews. He meets Jesus in the dark, has more questions than faith and has not expressed belief by the end of the story. The Samaritan woman, who belongs to a people despised by their Jewish neighbours, meets Jesus in the light, talks with him and not only believes but brings others to believe in him.[3]

Around these two stories John portrays Jesus as a bridegroom. He introduces Jesus to the role of the groom at the wedding at Cana (John 2.1–11), while via John the Baptist he develops the idea of Jesus as the groom in his teaching of his own disciples (3.22–36). Through the story of Jesus talking with the Samaritan woman at Jacob's well, John completes the portrayal. He does not imagine that Jesus was actually married – or at the very least he leaves no clear clues if he did.[4] Rather, as John the Baptist indicates, for Jesus being bridegroom means being the messiah (3.28–29). His marriage is metaphorical and refers to the salvation of humanity.[5]

This metaphor of marriage finds deep roots in the Old Testament. The prophets picture God as both suitor wooing his beloved and as husband, the object of his affection being the nation of Israel or Judah, the covenant people (Jer. 2.2–3). Sometimes the suitor has been rebuffed or the husband has been betrayed by his adulterous wife (e.g. Jer. 3.1–11, 20). Sometimes the jilted husband pronounces a curse on or divorces or widows his unfaithful wife (e.g. Ezek. 16). At other times, he longs to woo her back or restore their relationship (e.g. Isa. 54.4–8; 62.4–5; Hos. 2.1–15). The metaphor of courtship and marriage describes the sometimes difficult relationship between God and the covenant people. By depicting Jesus as a bridegroom, John continues this story of the marriage of God and his people – but with a twist.[6]

Becoming the groom

John first depicts Jesus as bridegroom while narrating the story of the wedding at Cana in Galilee (John 2.1–11). Jesus' mother is there, while Jesus and his disciples are also invited. (This detail counts against any reading of the story as one of Jesus' marriage, as he would hardly have been invited to his own wedding.)[7] The wine runs out, and Jesus' mother tells him of the scandal and instructs the servants to follow Jesus' directions. They do so, and the water with which they fill the jars changes into wine. The master of ceremonies tastes the wine and compliments the groom on saving the best wine until last. The story is full of humour.

We are unaware of any relationship between the happy couple and Jesus' mother, the fact that she is invited (2.1–2) suggesting she is a guest rather than family. Providing food and drink of sufficient quality and quantity was a matter of family honour, so for the wine to run out is a social disaster.[8] Family reputation is at stake. None of this prevents Jesus' mother from stepping feet first into someone else's delicate family situation.[9] Without any authority or role, she tries to organize Jesus and tells the slaves what to do.

Jesus' response, 'What have you got to do with me, woman?', Greek *ti emoi kai soi*, uses words also found in other biblical stories. They only ever appear, either in the LXX or elsewhere in the NT, as words spoken between enemies (Judg. 11.12; 4 Kgdms 3.13;

2 Chron. 35.21; 1 Esd. 1.24; Mark 5.7; Luke 8.28), or in the case of the widow talking to Elijah someone who thought the person she was addressing had become an enemy (3 Kgdms 17.10).[10] Jesus wants to put clear blue water between his interfering mother and himself. (And to be fair, he has a point.) The situation is embarrassing for all concerned. The lack of wine has nothing to do with his mother and he wants to steer well clear of it, and of her.[11]

The groom appears to have been responsible for the provision of wine at the wedding (John 2.10). He may have been made aware of the problem. However, he has had nothing to do with solving it. He has probably spent a great deal of money on wine already and has likely served the best he could afford – just as the master of ceremonies says grooms usually do (2.10). However, after the miracle the master of ceremonies congratulates the groom for reserving the best wine until last. This comment, although kindly meant, would hardly have complimented the groom. Instead it implied that the wine he had provided was pretty rough stuff. To add injury to insult, the groom very likely had no idea where the decent wine came from, and he could not tell anybody without losing family honour – hardly something he would want to do on his wedding day.[12]

Behind the humour lies an important truth that John signals to the attentive reader. The groom was responsible for the provision of wine. Jesus was responsible for this miracle and so for the provision of wine. Through performing the miracle Jesus takes on the role of a bridegroom.[13] John has already presented Jesus as the Word and so as God. In making Jesus adopt the role of a bridegroom, John hints that Jesus is God, seeking to restore his relationship with the covenant people.

The Baptist and the bridegroom

John the Apostle links this narrative to another, about John the Baptist (John 3.22–36).[14] Offering his disciples a reflection on a situation that has arisen (3.27–30), the Baptist reminds them he is not the messiah (cf. John 1.20) but has been sent ahead of the messiah (cf. John 1.15). He has already proclaimed Jesus as the messiah (John 1.29–30, 35–36). John compares his relationship to Jesus the messiah with that of a bridegroom and his best friend (John 3.28–29). This offers an interesting take on the traditional image of the courtship and marriage between God and the covenant people. In the prophetic tradition, the groom is always God and never the king of Israel. The Second Temple Jewish texts imagine the messiah or messiahs as priests, kings and warriors, but not as the bridegroom of the covenant people. The marriage of the messiah to the covenant people seems to be a Christian innovation (e.g. 2 Cor. 11.2; Eph. 5.25–33). Within the narrative, then, John the Baptist is saying something quite novel.[15]

Knowing who Jesus is, John the Baptist rejoices at the marriage of the messiah and his bride, the people of God. He expresses his joy in the picture of the best man rejoicing at the 'voice' or 'shout' or 'noise' (Greek *phōnē*) of the groom (John 3.29).[16] Many interpretations have been suggested as to what the voice of the groom refers to. It might refer to a marriage attendant hearing the groom's voice as his procession approaches the house of the bride.[17] It could refer to sweet nothings the groom whispers to his bride as they enter the wedding ceremonies.[18] Possibly it refers to the joy of the groom on the birth of children.[19] Many think it refers to 'the triumphal shout by which the bridegroom announced to his friends outside [the bridal chamber] that he had been united to a virginal bride'.[20] Others believe it refers to the groom calling the best man (who has been waiting for this moment outside the bridal chamber) to collect the proof of the bride's virginity after sexual intercourse.[21]

Our evidence for what happened at Jewish weddings in the first century is fairly meagre, which makes it hard to reconstruct the scene.[22] However, some doubt has been cast on the reliability of the traditions cited by scholars about the role of friends or best men and whether they ever waited outside the bridal canopy to check either that the marriage was consummated or that the bride was a virgin (*b. Ketub.* 12a).[23] Given that the couple would have entered the bridal canopy after the wedding procession to consummate the marriage while others were still feasting, a simpler suggestion presents itself.[24] The final prayer of the groom's blessing pronounced at the betrothal of the wedding reads:

> Praised are you, Lord our God, king of the universe, who created gladness and joy, groom and bride, rejoicing, song, mirth, delight, love, friendship, peace, and companionship. Lord our God, may there soon be heard in the cities of Judah and in the streets of Jerusalem the voice of gladness and the voice of joy;

the voice of the groom and the voice of the bride; the joyous shouts of grooms from their bridal chambers, and of youths from their [marriage] celebrations. Praised are you Lord, who causes the groom to rejoice with the bride.[25]

The language is clearly sexual and alludes to grooms shouting with joy from the wedding chambers where they are consummating their marriages.[26] In light of this, the suggestion that the *phōnē* or 'noise' of the groom is his ecstatic moaning or shouting during sex seems the most plausible.[27]

John the Apostle thus develops the theme of Jesus the bridegroom through John the Baptist's use of the sexual image of Jesus as a groom after he has made love to his bride on their wedding night. Admittedly we are in the world of metaphor here. Neither the Baptist nor the Apostle is suggesting that Jesus had sex or that he was married. John the Baptist simply develops the traditional language of the marriage of God to the covenant people, placing Jesus as messiah in the role of God and the covenant people in the role of the bride. (Having already identified Jesus as the Word of God in the prologue, John the Apostle also expects his audience to hear that in Jesus God has come to wed his bride, the covenant people.)[28]

John the Apostle admits to being selective with his material and to cutting quite a lot of material he could have used when writing his Gospel (John 20.30). It is therefore interesting that he chooses to include the metaphor of sex on the wedding night to describe the Baptist's delight at Jesus' ministry. None of the other Evangelists record this particular saying.[29] By picturing Jesus the Word as making love to his bride, John pictures God consummating his marriage to the covenant people. In these words of the Baptist the Gospel makes the sexuality of God incarnate explicit in a metaphor. What the disciples thought but hardly dared admit to thinking of Jesus that day by the well, John the Apostle now depicts quite openly in the words of the Baptist.

Jesus and the woman at the well

The scene is now set for the bridegroom messiah to meet his bride. Jesus has been identified as the groom (John 2.1–11; 3.29). John the Baptist has anticipated his wedding to his bride, the covenant people, in a relatively sexually explicit image. Now John the Apostle turns from sexual imagery about the bridegroom messiah to a narrative in which the real flesh-and-blood Jesus meets a woman alone in a secluded place, at a time of day when few locals are likely to turn up and the disciples will not be back for a while. In developing the traditional 'boy meets girl' plot to tell the story of the Word meeting the Samaritans and giving them the right to become children of God (cf. John 1.12), John replaces the human betrothal narrative with the story of the divine marriage of God and the people he calls into relationship with himself. Throughout the narrative John's main purpose remains to show that Jesus is the messiah and Son of God and to encourage his audience to believe in him, but by placing him in the ancient equivalent of a singles bar he also sheds some light on Jesus' sexuality.[30]

The well

Jesus is travelling back to Galilee by way of Samaria. Near the city of Sychar he stops at Jacob's well. Exhausted, he sits down beside the well. It is about noon, so it is probably hot.[31] He has sent his disciples into town to buy something to eat (John 4.8). The Samaritan woman meets him by the well.

The location is significant. In the typical betrothal narrative, the groom or his surrogate travels to a foreign land. There he meets a girl by a well. Often at this point one or other of them draws water from the well. The girl rushes home to announce the arrival of the stranger. The stranger is normally invited to eat and then becomes betrothed to the girl.[32] The well makes good sense as a meeting place for these soon-to-be-betrothed couples, since in biblical poetry it can symbolize fertility and sexuality (e.g. Prov. 5.15). Examples of this betrothal narrative form are found in the stories of how Isaac and Rebekah (Gen. 24.1–27), Jacob and Rachel (Gen. 29.1–12) and Moses and Zipporah (Exod. 2.15–21) got engaged.

Storytellers followed these typical patterns creatively. While by and large retaining the form of the particular kind of story they were telling, they would add twists or change the plot where it helped them to make particular points. So, whereas the story of Isaac and Rebekah follows quite typical plot lines, the groom's surrogate meeting a girl of impeccable credentials – beautiful, hospitable, hard-working and a virgin (Gen. 24.15–20) – after which the marriage is swiftly arranged (Gen. 24.28–51), Jacob has to work hard to marry Rachel, the woman he really loves, despite the fact that his seven years' labour seems for him but a few days (Gen. 29.20). Tellingly, when he meets her at the well he rolls the stone away from its mouth to water Laban's flocks. This detail suggests that opening his well (marriage with Rachel) will involve working for Laban (Gen. 29.10).[33]

When John has Jesus arrive in the foreign country of Samaria where he meets a woman by a well, the three details – foreign country, woman and well – suggest that John is using the betrothal narrative form. The way he has set up the narrative confirms this impression. He has made Jesus the true bridegroom at the wedding of Cana, after which John the Baptist has proclaimed Jesus the bridegroom messiah of the covenant people. By placing his narrative of Jesus meeting a woman at a well in a foreign country, John the Apostle signals that his story of the bridegroom messiah is about to reach a significant moment: the one where the groom meets his girl.[34] Because John uses the opening motifs of a familiar narrative form, he sets up certain narrative expectations. We expect that the woman will be not only marriageable but of impeccable credentials. We expect the man and woman to get betrothed. We expect the woman will come from the wider family, while not being close kin. John plays with these expectations, as we shall see.

Indeed, although he has placed the story within his larger narrative of God's marriage to the covenant people, John subverts this narrative too. Jesus does not meet a Jewish woman but a Samaritan woman. The Samaritans laid claim to the same God, but the bride is well aware that Jews do not mix with Samaritans (John 4.9). The insult thrown at Jesus later in the Gospel – 'are we not right that you are a Samaritan and have a demon?' (John 8.48) – sums up rather well the attitude that, she fears, contemporary Jews have towards her and her kind. The woman Jesus meets seems unsuitable because she comes not only from outside the family but also from a people despised by the family.[35]

By the end of the narrative, John tells us that the marriage was not with covenant people after all but with Samaritans.[36] Many Samaritans from Sychar have come to believe in Jesus on account of what the woman tells them about her encounter (John 4.39–42). The bridegroom messiah does not marry the girl but the people. He does not marry his own people (like Nicodemus) here, but people from another 'fold' (cf. John 10.16). The story puts flesh on the bones of

John's statement in the prologue that his own did not receive him and that he gave the right to become the children of God to all who believed in his name (John 1.11–13).

However, all this is jumping ahead. Another detail at the beginning of the story suggests that this tale might move in a different direction from the perfect betrothal narrative. When John talks of Jesus he uses the term spring, *pēgē*: Jesus comes to and sits down by the spring of Jacob (John 4.6). The only other place in the narrative where 'spring' or *pēgē* occurs is on the lips of Jesus himself (4.14); the woman identifies the watering hole merely as a well or *phrear* (4.11–12). John associates Jesus with the 'spring' and the Samaritan woman with the 'well'.[37] Jesus uses the term spring of the 'water' which he gives, bubbling up to eternal life (4.14). The woman knows the well is deep – she has to use a bucket to get any water from it – and she gives the impression that she would gladly never have to come to it again (4.11, 15). Jesus seems quite excited about his spring of living water, whereas the woman appears pretty fed up with her well. The pair seem to be starting their conversation from very different places, and John plays on this to great effect.

John also exploits the ambiguity of the language of springs and wells in the story. Both terms are found in the erotic love poetry of the Bible. Proverbs uses the metaphors of spring (*pēgē*) and well (*phrear*) to steer young men towards enjoying sex exclusively with their wives, advising them to drink water from their own 'spring of wells', Greek *pēgē phreatōn*, and to keep their 'fountain of water', *pēgē tou hudatos*, to themselves alone. By making love only to his own wife, a young man might preserve both himself and his wife from adultery and its consequences (Prov. 5.15–18 LXX).[38]

The Song of Solomon uses these terms similarly. The virgin bride is a sealed 'fountain', *pēgē* (Song of Sol. 4.12), her 'channel' a garden 'fountain', *pēgē* and a 'well' of running water, *phrear* (Song of Sol. 4.15).[39] The terms 'well' and 'spring' could bear connotations of lovemaking and sexual attractiveness.[40] However, the metaphorical use of 'well' does not always bear a positive sexual connotation. Proverbs refers to the adulteress as a narrow 'well', *phrear* (Prov. 23.27 LXX), and a deep pit.[41] John plays on all these connotations of the terms 'spring' and 'well'.

He also subverts the traditional plot line in other respects. The women who arrive at the well in betrothal narratives are generally eligible for marriage.[42] John, on the other hand, introduces his female protagonist as 'a woman from Samaria' (4.7). Not only does the term 'woman', Greek *gunē*, give no hint as to whether she is single, married or divorced, but the fact that she is a Samaritan makes her distinctly ineligible for marriage to the Jew Jesus.[43] There are normally many people around the well;[44] there is, after all, safety in numbers. But when Jesus arrives, his disciples soon disappear to buy food. He seems to be all alone when he meets the Samaritan woman (4.7–8). John takes the perfectly respectable betrothal narrative form and opens up the story in ways which suggest that something less than desirable might happen.

Living water

Jesus asks the woman for a drink, which within the betrothal narrative is classically the first step of courtship. Jesus is tired and thirsty because of his journey, and John leaves any further motive behind Jesus' question ambiguous for the moment.[45] She is suspicious of his intentions and brushes him off, drawing attention to the fact that he is a Jew and she is a Samaritan and the two do not mix. However, this is not all she wants to communicate. If she had done she would simply have asked, 'How come you, a Jew, ask me, a Samaritan, for a drink?' Instead she asks 'How come you, a Jew, ask me, a Samaritan *woman*, for a drink?' (4.9a). She draws attention to the fact that she is a woman.[46]

John gives us reason to believe that she makes this comment to ward off any untoward attentions she might otherwise receive from this Jewish man. She follows up her question with the observation 'Jews do not associate [Greek *sugchrōntai*] with Samaritans'.[47] The Greek verb can mean various things. It might mean 'share things in common', so Jesus cannot drink from the same vessel that she does for fear of contracting ritual uncleanness.[48] Ordinarily it means 'make use of', 'be friendly with' or 'take advantage of'.[49] Given the context of a betrothal narrative, 'be friendly with' or 'take advantage of' seems to lurk in the subtext.[50] Knowing what the men one meets by wells can be like, she brushes him off with the comment 'Jewish men do not get friendly with Samaritan women' (John 4.9b).[51] The audience can almost hear her thinking that she has met his type by wells before.

A comparison of her response with those of the typical marriage-able maidens of biblical betrothal narratives makes it most unlikely that she is flirting with Jesus. Rebekah responds 'drink, my lord' to Abraham's servant before drawing water for all his camels (Gen. 24.18–20). Admittedly Rachel has no time to draw water for Jacob as he leaps up and opens the well himself, but at least she runs home and tells her father so that he is invited home (Gen. 29.9–14). Jethro's daughters are somewhat slow on the uptake and may have forgotten to invite Moses home (Exod. 2.20), but at least they are surprised at his help in drawing water, suggesting they expected to do this them-selves (Exod. 2.19). The ideal bride seems to have been willing to show hospitality, even if she requires some prompting. The response of the Samaritan woman (more or less 'Where's your bucket?') con-trasts greatly with the ideal response and shows a complete lack of hospitality. She gives the impression that she intends to nip this romance in the bud (as do all her comments until v. 15).[52]

Jesus' reply says exactly what he wants to say: 'if you knew God's gift and exactly who is the one saying to you "give me a drink", *you* would ask *him* and he would give you living water'. His words offer a hint that he is the God of salvation. The only other place the phrase 'the one saying to you', Greek *ho legōn soi*, occurs in the Bible is Isaiah 41.13 LXX where God speaks words of salvation to his people.[53] However, his hint is entirely lost on her and does not allay her suspicions. The term for gift, Greek *dōrea*, was used quite commonly of wedding presents,[54] and the ambiguity may be deliberate: this may be the wedding gift of the bridegroom messiah to his bride, the Samaritan people. However, the woman has reason to be wary. First he asks for a drink by a well. Now he drops hints about lover's gifts.[55]

Jesus' offer of living water gives room for further confusion. Living water, Greek *hudōr zōn*, had various connotations. It could simply mean 'running water' or 'spring water'. Hagar finds a well of spring water, Greek *phrear hudatos zōntos* (Gen. 21.19 LXX).[56] Spring water was used in various cultic rituals: for example, the ritual cleansing of a leper (Lev. 14.5–6 LXX).[57] So 'living water' might bear cultic connotations. 'Living waters' might connote salvation, as in the prophecy of rivers of living water flowing from Jerusalem (Zech. 14.8 LXX) and God identifying himself as the fountain of living water, Greek *pēgē hudatos zōēs* (Jer. 2.13 LXX).[58] However, like 'spring' and 'well', the phrase 'living water' could also carry sexual connotations.

The Song of Solomon refers to the woman's 'channel' as a well of 'living water', Greek *phrear hudatos zōntos* (Song of Sol. 4.15 LXX).[59] Jesus offers the Samaritan woman salvation, but given the many connotations of 'living waters' she could be forgiven for mishearing his offer as some kind of sexual advance.[60]

The Gospel audience may be fully aware of Jesus' meaning. However, John the Apostle has not yet made it clear in the narrative. We discover this only later in the Gospel at the feast of Tabernacles when Jesus cries out, 'if anyone is thirsty let them come to me and let the one who believes in me drink – as the Scriptures said "rivers of living water flow out of his belly"' (John 7.37–38). The living water here is the Spirit of God which gives life (7.39).[61] Although the exact words of Jesus' quotation cannot be found in any Scriptures we possess today, the thought is remarkably close to that in Jeremiah 2.13 LXX where God identifies himself as the 'spring of living water', Greek *pēgē hudatos zōēs*.[62] Since John has not yet made Jesus' meaning clear to his audience, they like the woman might suspect Jesus of flirting with her.

So, assuming that he is after something other than water, she offers an immediate rebuff: 'you do not have a bucket and the well is deep' (John 4.11a). She answers him at the literal level of his request for water and his offer of spring water.[63] Her approach to what she assumes are unwanted sexual overtures is to kill off the conversation at this literal level.[64] In pointing out his lack of a bucket, there may also be a hint of a put-down. Assuming he is playing on the sexual connotations of 'living water', her words carry a subtext along the lines of 'you are not getting anything out of me, sonny, so move on by'.[65]

This does not discourage Jesus, who answers her riposte that he can hardly think himself greater than Jacob with the observation that anyone who drinks water from this well will soon be thirsty again. His water, however, will become a 'a spring of water welling up to eternal life' (John 4.14). The superiority of his water is clear enough as it not only quenches but dispels thirst. Equally clear is that Jesus is using 'living water' as a metaphor, for there is no such thing as water which once drunk quenches thirst for ever. The Greek words quoted recall Jeremiah 2.13 LXX which identify God as the source of living water, meaning salvation.[66] Jesus (who is God and so greater than Jacob) offers something better than water: salvation.

John develops his understanding of Jesus the Word of God here. Sirach presents Wisdom calling out to people that they eat of her fruits. She claims that those who have eaten of her will hunger for more and those who have drunk of her will thirst for more (Sir. 24.19–21). Jesus' words seem to allude to this saying of Wisdom.[67] However, they contrast the works of Wisdom as Sirach knew her with the life-giving Word as John knew him. The Wisdom of Sirach leaves the righteous person hungering and thirsting for more. The Word of God in Jesus gives wisdom which satisfies completely, so that the one who believes in him will never thirst again. (This contrast echoes that in the prologue: 'the law came through Moses, grace and truth through Jesus Christ', where both 'the law' and 'grace and truth' are identified as grace – in John's words, 'grace instead of grace', John 1.16b–17.)[68]

Jesus may be talking about the life-giving Wisdom of God but the woman is not hearing him that way. At this point in the dialogue, however, she begins to soften, or perhaps weaken. Rather than rebuffing him again, something seems to strike a chord as this time she responds: 'give me this water so that I stop getting thirsty and coming here day after day to draw water' (John 14.15). At one level, she gives a literal answer to a literal offer. If he really can produce this magic water that prevents thirst recurring, then she is happy to drink it. However, they both know that this is not what Jesus is talking about. What she does not know is that they are talking at cross purposes. He is talking about wisdom, life and salvation. She assumes that he is offering her some kind of sexual relationship. Her response suggests that she has become more open to the idea of finding 'living water' with him.[69]

(Let us take a moment to ponder briefly and in parentheses on how this decision reflects on the woman's character. In a few words' time, the history of her relationships will be revealed and it does not appear, at least on first sight, to be either a happy or a successful one. She has known and lived with quite a few men. Whatever the reasons, these relationships have not lasted, and nor is she married to the man she currently lives with. She appears to arrive at the well alone rather than with the other girls from the town. Later in the story she gets away as quickly as she can from the judgemental silence of the disciples. Her personal history gives the impression that she would like a relationship with a man but has not had much success in relationships to date, while her responses to Jesus suggest that she is wary of men, particularly the sort that hang around wells at times of day when no one else is about. I suspect that she is a woman who has seen the worse side of men but has not yet lost hope. She appears understandably self-protective and wary, and yet open to at last finding a man who might be able to give her what she wants. She comes across as confident yet vulnerable. Perhaps when she finally responds to what she thinks Jesus is saying, she is putting her personal history and fears tentatively to one side and asking herself whether things might actually work out with this man.)[70]

At this point Jesus acts to stop their talking at cross purposes any further. (If they have not been hearing different subtexts, then the abrupt change in conversation from 'living water' to marital and other sexual relationships becomes hard to explain.)[71] Jesus asks the woman to fetch her husband (John 4.16). Both Jesus and the woman know that her request for his 'living water' has indicated a willingness to get involved with him. The fact that she does not ask Jesus why he changes the subject gives the impression that she knows exactly why he has done so.[72] The conversation now becomes awkward, and she replies that she has no husband (4.17a). Technically she is telling the truth. Possibly she is trying to cover up embarrassment at the fact that she was softening at what she thought were Jesus' advances when she already had a partner;[73] possibly she thinks he is trying to work out whether she is single.[74] Jesus then makes a comment that reveals he knows her relationship history: 'you have got that about right when you say "I don't have a husband" because you have had five husbands and now the bloke you have is not your husband' (4.17b–18a). Perhaps he is being ironic, or maybe he is giving her the benefit of the doubt; or maybe he wants to affirm her but he follows up with the words 'you have told the truth' (4.18b).[75] Although tones of voice are difficult to reconstruct from any text, I imagine that Jesus does not speak harshly to her. Since she later disappears as soon as she thinks the disciples are making assumptions about her (4.27–28), we might wonder why she would stay talking to Jesus if she found him judgemental. For the narrative to work, we have to assume that she finds Jesus approachable enough to stay, however embarrassing she finds anything he says.[76]

The fact that the woman has had five husbands has left commentators feeling free to speculate about her past and offer varied assessments of her moral character, both in their own eyes and those of ancient audiences.[77] Many assume fault on her part, speaking in terms of 'matrimonial maladjustment', 'dubious reputation' and the like.[78] The Greek may suggest that she is living with a married man.[79] Given that the rabbis did not generally approve of a woman marrying more than three times, some read her serial monogamy and current adultery as evidence of her moral laxity.[80] (Though the woman was Samaritan and we simply do not know whether Jewish and Samaritan divorce law, customs and attitudes were the same.)[81] One interpretation suggests that she was not married to any of the six men with whom she had lived.[82]

Others have urged caution in making such assessments, suggesting that her husbands might have divorced her, more than one may have died, and some legal impediment might prevent her marrying legally now.[83] Possibly she has been caught in the custom of levirate marriage and the sixth brother refuses to marry her.[84] Maybe her husbands divorced her on account of infertility or loss of beauty, or 'an overready wit and tongue'.[85] On the other hand, particularly in the case of infertility, multiple remarriages are hard to explain, as she would gain a reputation as barren.[86] So perhaps, having been widowed or rejected five times, she is living with a male relative rather than someone else's husband.[87] *She* might even have asked her husbands for divorces because they were tanners or coppersmiths, or because they had boils and she could not take it any more (see *m. Ketub.* 7.9–10). Like Sarah in the book of Tobit, she may have lived the tragedy of losing each of her husbands as a result of their death – and the current man may be unwilling to chance becoming the next one to die.[88]

There is much that John leaves ambiguous about her personal history.[89] However, this we can know. Jesus tells her to 'go fetch your man [Greek *anēr*]' (John 4.16), the word 'your' suggesting he means her husband. She responds, 'I do not have a man [Greek *andra*]' (4.17a). She does not qualify what sort of man she does not have. We would expect her to do so if she were not talking of a husband. Jesus' comment, 'you have had five men [Greek *andras*] (4.18) refers to her marital history because they are still talking about her husbands. So, when he goes on to say 'the [bloke] you have now is not your man', Greek *nun hon echeis ouk estin sou anēr* (4.18), he uses the same Greek word for 'husband' (*anēr*) that both he and she have used in the immediately preceding verses. Given the use of the same vocabulary, it seems unlikely that we have moved from sexual relationships (including marriage) to kinship relationships.[90] That she has a man indicates she is in a sexual relationship with this man. However, Jesus says nothing about what has led to her current marital status and relationship situation.[91] She might be largely a victim or entirely to blame. Should we be tempted to fill in this gap, we should only do so from clues in the text.[92] The fact that neither Jesus nor John enquires further into the reasons for her situation is instructive.[93] The nearest John gets to suggesting anything about her beyond the bare facts of her personal history is that she seems cautious of men who hang about wells but would love to find a decent bloke.

I see you are a prophet

Exposure of any shaming event, action or relationship in life is never easy. However gentle the revelation, embarrassment is certain to follow. This is awkward for the Samaritan woman. Her response indicates some of the discomfort she feels: 'sir, I see that you are a prophet' (John 4.19). In other words, she realizes that he has special insight, which means he knows things about people that others simply cannot know. Standing before someone with such knowledge is unlikely to leave anybody feeling particularly comfortable. If Jesus knows this about her, what else does he know?

So she changes the subject. She talks about where Jews and Samaritans worship: Samaritans worship on Mount Gerizim, whereas Jews worship in Jerusalem (John 4.20). She has not chosen this new subject at random. Racing through her head has been the conversation to date. A single man at a well in the middle of the day when nobody else is around has asked for a drink and then offered her 'living water'. Of course she was going to assume that he wanted sex. But then he seemed like such a nice guy. How was she to know he was religious? If only she had stopped to think. Religious guys mean something else by 'living water'. They will be thinking of purification rituals. Awkward. She chose the wrong 'living water'. What to do? Pick up on what he was really talking about. So she begins the conversation about places of worship.[94]

John has not written down any of this internal dialogue. However, if we accept that the dialogue turns on the various meanings of 'living water', we will find that it flows more naturally. Unless the woman has misunderstood Jesus and assumed sexual innuendo, then his comment about her going to find her husband makes for a frankly odd next statement in the conversation. (I am assuming Jesus was not in the habit of hanging around wells in order to unmask adulteresses through creepy irony in disjointed conversations.)[95] If she now thinks she has got the wrong end of the 'living water' stick, then this next change in conversation makes complete sense because she now thinks he was talking about religion rather than sex.[96] If this is not the case, the change in subject is inexplicably random. There is no good reason to assume abrupt changes of subject when the various meanings of 'living water' provide a golden thread which makes coherent sense of the conversation.[97]

Jesus cuts across this new topic of conversation, closing down consideration of the relative merits of the different cultic centres of Judaism and Samaritanism (John 4.21–24). He informs the woman that the time is coming when people will worship God in spirit and truth rather than in temples.[98] In introducing the Spirit (the living water of John 7.38–39), he tries to bring the conversation back to the salvation he longs to offer her and her people.

From her perspective, the conversation is going from bad to worse. First he was not talking about sex. Now he thinks she has religion all wrong too. In an attempt to restore her dignity, she responds: '[at least] I know the messiah is coming who is called "the Christ"; when he comes, he will explain everything to us' (John 4.25).[99] In adding 'to us' the woman tries to put herself back on an equal footing with Jesus. Neither of them (not even he) knows the truth, she is saying. Only the messiah does. They both need to accept their limited knowledge graciously. Like other characters in the Gospel, the Samaritan woman does not know Jesus' identity. This line gives John exactly the narrative cue he needs.

John the Apostle now plays on words the Baptist has spoken: 'I am not the messiah', Greek *ouk egō eimi ho christos* (John 1.20; 3.28). When the Samaritan woman says she knows the messiah called the Christ, Greek *christos*, is coming, Jesus replies 'I am he', Greek *egō eimi* (4.25). John uses the same string of words, Greek *egō* + *eimi* + *christos*, that the Baptist used to deny he was the messiah for Jesus' declaration that he is the messiah. When the Baptist most recently denied being the messiah, in the same breath he described Jesus as the bridegroom (3.28–29). Jesus now confesses that he is the messiah to the Samaritan woman at a well in a betrothal narrative. The bridegroom messiah the covenant people expected has been offering his gift of 'living water' (that is, salvation) to the rejected Samaritan.[100]

John develops the theme further. Jesus' words of response, 'I am he, the one talking to you', Greek *egō eimi ho lalōn soi* (John 4.25), echo words of the Lord God Almighty through the prophet: 'I AM, I AM the LORD speaking', Greek *egō eimi egō eimi kurios lalōn* (Isa. 45.19 LXX) and especially 'I AM he who speaks', Greek *egō eimi autos ho lalōn* (Isa. 52.6 LXX). As with all the other 'I AM' sayings, the *egō eimi* recalls the name of God, 'I AM WHO I AM', Greek *egō eimi ho ōn* (Exod. 3.14 LXX). John wants the audience to hear that Jesus is the Lord God Almighty.[101] The Word was with God and the Word was God. It is not only the bridegroom messiah who has courted the Samaritan woman at the well, but the Word who is one with the Father. John develops the prophetic motif of the Lord God courting Israel here as God invites the rejected Samaritans back into his covenant marriage.[102] Now Jesus and the woman need no longer talk at cross purposes. Jesus has made his claim to being messiah clearly (and has intimated that he is God). All she has to do now is respond.[103]

Nobody dared

Just as the real conversation is beginning, the disciples arrive. John has led his audience to read the disciples' silent questions ('what are you after?' and 'why are you talking to her?') to indicate that they suspect Jesus of making advances towards the woman.[104] Having set up the story as a betrothal narrative, he has played on the phrase 'living water' in such a way that the woman herself has suspected Jesus of trying it on with her, while Jesus has brought up the question of her husband, leading to the disclosure of her relationship history. There is too much sexual material in the narrative to avoid the conclusion that John expected his audience to hear the disciples' questions as revealing their suspicions that Jesus was up to no good.

What John the Apostle does here is remarkable. He seems to work into the betrothal narrative a spiritual twist which he has been setting up from the beginning of the Gospel. In the prologue, he spoke of the true light coming to those outside his people and making them children of God. He developed this theme using the OT image of God as the bridegroom and husband of Israel, identifying Jesus as the bridegroom in the wedding at Cana and the words of the Baptist. He used classic betrothal narrative motifs to signal that the betrothal of Christ to those not his own was about to take place. He has Christ meet by a well not simply a Samaritan, but in all likelihood one rejected by at least some of her own people. God meets the one who is not part of the covenant family. They talk and finally he reveals himself as the bridegroom messiah and covenant God. At this climactic moment, we are expecting the woman to turn and believe in him – this is the expectation John has been setting up all along. Instead, however, we see the shocked disciples casting sexual aspersions in an awkward silence.

But John has not wrecked his narrative. He upsets his audience's expectations quite deliberately. (Given the time and space devoted to setting up this narrative anti-climax, it is hard to believe that he did it accidentally.) At the moment the Gospel audience expects a classic spiritual message ('Christ has come to save all people in all nations no matter what anyone else thinks of them'), John holds up to them the sexuality of Christ.[105] Within and through this narrative John communicates to his audience that the people who met Jesus, including those who spent the most time with him, experienced him as being like any other man. He was a man with all the sexual desires, drives and motivations that are part and parcel of masculinity. Without this assumption, the narrative would make no sense. Unless she read Jesus this way, the woman would have no reason to brush Jesus off. If the disciples had thought otherwise, their silent questions would never have entered their heads.

John builds up an expectation in the audience that he is going to spiritualize the betrothal narrative. He puts everything in place for the audience to assume that he will move away from sexuality as a theme – right down to the connotations of 'living water' progressing from sex to worship and then finally to salvation. At the critical moment, when we fully expect the spiritualizing of the betrothal narrative to be complete, John trips us up. He returns to the sexuality which underlies every betrothal narrative and focuses our attention on Jesus' sexuality.

John not only shows no embarrassment about drawing attention to Jesus' sexuality but he deliberately brings it into his Christology (his theological understanding of Jesus). Immediately before this embarrassing moment the Samaritan woman speaks of the messiah and Jesus claims to be the messiah (John 4.25–26). Immediately afterwards the Samaritan woman departs for town where she tells everybody what Jesus said and asks if he really could be the messiah (4.28–29). The seemingly incidental comment about the disciples' reactions draws attention to the genuine sexuality of the bridegroom messiah. But John has not simply identified Jesus here as the bridegroom messiah. He has Jesus' words recall texts in Exodus and Isaiah to identify him as the Lord God Almighty. In doing so, he makes it clear that in this scene at the well (much as they did not recognize it at the time) he and the other disciples saw something of the sexuality of God incarnate – and in that, his glory.

Pause for thought

The woman finds the return of the disciples uncomfortable. Her departure is premature. Not only does she not finish her conversation but she leaves before completing what she came to do. She has come to the well to draw water (John 4.7), but she leaves her jar behind her. Why does she rush away in the middle of her conversation and forget the water she came to draw? Many suggestions have been made.[106] John gives only one indication of her motive: '*therefore* the woman left her water jar and went away to town' (4.28).

John demonstrates himself to be a subtle narrator here. His 'therefore' relates back to the disciples' amazement that Jesus was talking with a woman and the questions that they were asking in their heads but dared not voice out loud.[107] They clearly interpret the situation as sexually motivated or charged. The woman escapes the situation as soon as she can, and John gives the impression that she assumes that the disapprobation of the disciples is directed towards her.[108] Possibly some of it was, but John does not specify this. The disciples do not ask 'what does she want?', but they are wondering silently of Jesus, 'what do you want?' John makes it clear that they are questioning Jesus' motivations and behaviour.[109] The woman appears to feel judged, when the disciples are actually judging Jesus.

But the disciples have no right to judge Jesus in this negative light. They have not witnessed anything that happened before their return from Sychar. The disjunctions of their unfairly negative judgement of Jesus, the awkwardness for them of what they think they see, and the scene the audience has actually witnessed invite a re-reading of the narrative so far. How exactly has Jesus behaved towards this woman? Given that the characters in the story read Jesus as a man with normal sexual drives, what does John's audience make of him as readers? Given that John has paused to say that no one dared voice their thoughts, and in doing so has signalled to his audience that he is now voicing his thoughts and is no longer embarrassed to do so, he seems to invite them to consider what they are to make of the sexuality of Jesus in this narrative.

In setting the scene, John has used vocabulary which recalls not simply betrothals but erotic love poetry (Song of Sol. 4.12–15) and counsels against adultery (e.g. Prov. 5.15–20). He has built moral ambiguity into his story. From the outset, the audience has been invited to check out the characters' sexual behaviour. Nothing in the narrative suggests that Jesus is anything other than very tired, after a drink of cold water, and offering the Samaritan woman the life that God now longs to give to all. Given her misunderstanding, Jesus could have taken advantage of her. Most men find sex comforting (and as John has led us to believe, Jesus has all the sex drive of the next guy). They are at the proverbial watering hole, she may well now be willing, and it is noon so nobody else is likely to turn up. But he chooses not to, and acts in a way that avoids either of them doing anything they could (or should) regret. He puts her long-term spiritual need before any short-term physical desire he might have. They both know enough of her story to realize that she has not had the happiest of relationships. Even if all her marriages have been excellent and her husbands have died, she has suffered the tragedy of loss and for some reason cannot tie the knot with her current man. So she lives a life of shame. Jesus offers her salvation and life in abundance (cf. John 10.10). The immediate context in which the offer is made is the brokenness of her relationships and her sex life. It was the hint that things might not all be well in that regard that led Jesus to make this offer in the first place.

The disciples are far from understanding the reality of the situation. To be fair, they show Jesus the respect they believe he deserves by not asking their questions aloud. Given their culture, the audience can easily understand how they come to the conclusions they do. However, they are wrong about Jesus' motivations. Far from taking advantage of the woman, he wants her to experience the quality of life he has come to bring to all. We now have two very important pieces of information to help answer our question of how God experienced human sexuality: that the disciples read Jesus as having the same sexual desires as the next man; and that Jesus preferred to bring healing to the sexual life of another person rather than seeking pleasure for himself in fulfilment of his own desires.

Leaving shame behind

Meanwhile the Samaritan woman has returned to Sychar. There she does something very surprising. At this stage in the typical betrothal narrative, the woman runs home and tells her father about the handsome stranger at the well, and her father invites him for a meal where they broker the betrothal. In our story, the Samaritan woman has returned to her fellow citizens, to whom she now says two things. First, she sums up Jesus' insight into her personal history with men: 'he told me everything I ever did'; then she asks 'could this man be the Christ?' (John 4.29). The exaggeration contained in that first statement (she clearly must have done many other things besides having relationships with men, e.g. eating, sleeping, drinking) offers the audience an insight into how she reads her own life.[110] Her relationships are central to her self-understanding. She hears Jesus' claim to be messiah alongside and within the context of her personal history. What is so surprising is that she talks of her past so openly.[111] Her cautious response to Jesus' request that she go and fetch her husband suggests she is quite guarded about her past relationships (John 4.17a). That she should tell the townsfolk quite so openly about that rather embarrassing scene with Jesus is therefore surprising. Even though she still wrestles with the question of whether Jesus could be the messiah, something in her encounter with him seems to have relieved her of the shame which attached itself to her personal history.

So this vignette contains one of the greatest ironies of the piece. The perfect bride ought to be a beautiful young virgin, but the woman at the well has had five husbands and is living with a man. She is anything but 'the ideal bride'.[112] Within her culture, honour and shame were powerful forces, and the shame of an improper background could act as a disincentive to marry.[113] Here the bridegroom messiah and Lord God in the person of Jesus invite the Samaritan woman into the covenant marriage. Somehow he triggers something in her which means that she no longer feels shame about her previous relationships.[114] Rather than talking about them cautiously and evasively as she did in v. 17a, she now talks about them quite openly.[115] Her encounter with Jesus has taken away the sting of shame.[116] Not only this, but the woman with the unsuitable background turns out to be the bride the messiah and Lord God long for. At one level this echoes the Lord God's wooing of Israel in Hosea and builds the theme of God in Christ calling all peoples into covenant relationship. At another, John the Apostle tells the story of Christ's interest in rebuilding the lives of people whose relationships have, for whatever reason, been broken. This narrative becomes one of Christ the sexual healer.

John underlines that last point, albeit subtly, in recalling how these Samaritans came to faith. When the woman returns home and tells them to come and see a man who told her everything she ever did (John 4.29a), questioning whether he could be the Christ (4.29b), her question in John's Greek uses the word *mēti*, which normally expects the answer 'no'.[117] This implies that she is still wrestling with the idea that Jesus might be the messiah, or that she tries to dismiss the idea altogether. It does not suggest that she has fully accepted his self-identification as messiah.[118] Although many of the Samaritans believed in him, John does not say they did so through her asking whether he was the messiah; instead it was through her words 'he told me everything I ever did' (John 4.39). Thus, he notes, they come to faith through what the woman says Jesus has revealed about her sex life[119] – through the story of Jesus uncovering a broken sex life and offering salvation.[120] The reality of her initial taste of the salvation he offers is more compelling for these Samaritans than trying to work through how their theology and his coincide.[121]

The engagement party

At this point in any decent betrothal narrative, the family settle down to a meal with the suitor who has recently become betrothed to one of the daughters.[122] Here the disciples have come back from Sychar with some food which they offer to Jesus. He refuses, saying that he has food they do not know about. When they speculate as to the likelihood of someone else having brought him a picnic (John 4.31–33), Jesus explains that his food is doing the will of the Father and completing his Father's work (4.34).

The audience already knows that Jesus believes that God sent his only Son to save the world (John 3.16–17) and that he came into the world to save all who would believe him (John 1.10–13). This is the will and the work of the one who sent Jesus (John 4.34). Therefore they are able to perceive that Jesus has been doing the will and the work of God the Father in wooing the Samaritan woman back into covenant relationship with God. The audience can see what the disciples are failing to see: that the engagement party has already begun. Jesus started the meal without them while they were away in town. He has been eating his fill in bringing this woman to an understanding of God's self-revelation in his person and messianic ministry.[123]

John reads Jesus' conversation with the Samaritan woman as both the ministry for which the Father sent him and the betrothal meal. He makes this clear by linking the Baptist's bridegroom saying with Jesus' reflection on his ministry here. Jesus uses a new metaphor to describe his ministry in Samaria: reaping the harvest (John 4.35–38). His comment that the harvest is ready refers to the Samaritans going to meet him and coming back into covenant relationship with God (4.35–36a).[124] His saying about the harvester and the sower rejoicing together (John 4.36b) recalls the Baptist's saying about the friend rejoicing at the groom's voice (3.29).[125] Despite the change of metaphor from marriage to harvest, John has Jesus recall the wedding metaphor of the Baptist at this betrothal meal.

John underlines by another means his desire that the audience read this conversation with the disciples within the context of the larger betrothal narrative. He brackets the scene within an *inclusio*. The woman's statement to the Samaritans before the scene begins that Jesus 'told her everything she ever did', Greek *eipen moi panta hosa epoiēsa* (John 4.29) is echoed after the scene ends by the statement that the Samaritans come to Jesus because of the woman's *testimony* that 'he told me everything I ever did', Greek *eipen moi panta ha epoiēsa* (John 4.39).[126] This *inclusio* suggests that the scene ought to be read in the light of the conversation Jesus has had with the woman about her personal history. So, as he talks about food and ministry, all the themes of sexuality in the text and subtext hang in the narrative air.

Jesus abstains from food at this betrothal party because following his calling is his meat and drink. His abstinence here mirrors his going without water. He asked the Samaritan woman for some but was never given any. (Since the conversation began with his request for a drink, John surely would have told us if he had received one.)[127] John has pictured Jesus choosing not to take advantage of the Samaritan woman sexually, despite having the opportunity. His abstinence from food, drink and sex coincide at this point in the narrative. John makes two points about the Word of God incarnate here: that his chief end in life is to serve the Father, and that he practises self-control over his bodily appetites (including his sex drive) in order to serve God faithfully.

Saviour of the world

Jesus' behaviour contrasts quite starkly with the stories of gods and heroes – the 'saviours' of Greek and Roman culture – which dominated the Mediterranean at this time. John's audience would be well acquainted with such stories and might well recall them at this point in the narrative. When the Samaritans arrive and encounter Jesus they believe, and come to the conclusion that he is 'the saviour of the world', Greek *ho sōtēr tou kosmou* (John 4.42). This title never occurs in the LXX and the NT only uses it twice (John 4.42; 1 John 4.14), but it had clear connotations within the wider Greco-Roman world.[128]

Within John's narrative, the 'saviour of the world' is more immediately the saviour of the Samaritans. The testimony of the townspeople of Sychar links their confession to the testimony of the Samaritan woman (John 4.42). Thus, John links their confession of Jesus 'the saviour of the world' to her confession of Jesus as 'messiah' (4.29). He has her confession result from Jesus' testimony concerning himself that he is the 'messiah' and the 'I AM who speaks' (4.26) and binds all these christological statements together to present Jesus as messiah, saviour of the world and God. Jesus' own reference to the Father within the narrative (John 4.23–24) reminds us that he is the Son of the Father, the Word who is God and is beside God. This figure of a man who was messiah, God and saviour would have carried many resonances in Greek and Roman culture. Comparisons between Jesus and their gods, emperors, kings and heroes would have been evoked.[129] Within the immediate context of this betrothal narrative the stories of their sex lives would likely have come to mind. The way they conducted themselves sexually and the way Jesus did stand in quite some contrast.

Gods

Jesus refers to himself as the 'I AM who speaks' and John uses the way this alludes to OT texts (Isa. 45.19; 52.6 LXX; cf. Exod. 3.14 LXX) to identify Jesus with God. Where the LXX uses the title 'saviour', Greek *sōtēr*, it normally uses it of God.[130] Philo writes of the 'father and saviour of the world [Greek *patera kai sōtēra tou te kosmou*] and God of things in the world' (Philo, *On the Special Laws* 2.198), identifying the one true God of Israel as the saviour of the world. Certain Greek gods were also called saviour, Greek *sōtēr*, most notably Zeus the king of the gods.[131]

According to Greek mythology Zeus was married to the goddess Hera. However, he was very well known for his infidelity. Drawing on Greek mythology but writing in Latin for a Roman audience, the poet Ovid (43 BC–AD 17) captures this in a scene from the story of Jupiter and Io.[132] Jove has fallen for Io, a beautiful young nymph. Wandering home from her father's stream one fine day she encounters the amorous Jove, who bids her follow him into the shady woods. He attempts to impress her with his pedigree – he is not some lowly minor god but the king. She knows exactly who he is and what he is after. So she flees, but to no avail. As god of the storm he covers the area with cloud, catches her and imposes himself upon her. Meanwhile Juno cannot find Jove anywhere in heaven, looks down to earth and sees some odd-looking clouds that cannot be part of a normal weather pattern. Knowing exactly what this means, she disperses the clouds to catch Jove *in flagrante*. He, however, knows his wife is on to him, so he turns Io into a white heifer to cover his tracks. Admiring his quickness but not to be outdone, Juno asks for this beautiful heifer as a gift. Jove can only comply (Ovid, *Metamorphoses* 1.588–621).

Another very well-known myth of Zeus' sex life was the story of his love for Ganymede, which occurs in various different forms. Ovid tells the story like this. The king of the gods once burned so much with love for the young Trojan lad Ganymede that he longed to become some other kind of being which could steal this beautiful young man away. So he turned himself into that most regal of birds, the eagle. He swooped down and whisked the lad away to heaven where to this day Ganymede remains his cupbearer, mixing and serving him drinks. Juno remains resolutely against the arrangement – which is Ovid's way of pointing out that her husband and the lad are lovers (Ovid, *Metamorphoses* 10.155–161).

Emperors and kings

The title 'saviour', Greek *sōtēr*, was given to those who rescued or healed other people, or in other ways saved or safeguarded their lives and livelihoods.[133] Following Ptolemy I Soter (reigned 323–383 BC), some Greek and Roman rulers were given the epithet, including Herod the Great (Josephus, *Jewish Antiquities* 14.15.8§439–444).[134] The citizens of Tiberias received the Roman general Vespasian (AD 9–79) as 'saviour' when he released the city from terrorists (Josephus, *Jewish War* 3.9.8§459), and the citizens of Rome received him as both emperor and 'saviour' (Josephus, *Jewish War* 7.4.1§63–74). Inscriptions describe various Roman emperors from the first two centuries AD as 'saviour'.[135]

Vespasian was deified on his death and so was accorded the epithet 'god' as well as 'saviour'.[136] He stayed married to his wife Flavia Domitilla all her life despite taking a mistress, Caenis, who more or less became his partner after Flavia's death (Suetonius, *Vespasianus* 3). After the death of Caenis he took various concubines and lovers (Suetonius, *Vespasianus* 21–22). Suetonius may hint at Vespasian taking a male lover but adopting the penetrative role with him (Suetonius, *Vespasianus* 13.1). Compared with other Roman emperors whose sexual exploits Suetonius recounts, however, Vespasian was remarkably self-controlled.

The same cannot be said for Julius Caesar, or for Herod the Great (roughly 74–4 BC). Herod had several wives including Malthace, Cleopatra of Jerusalem, and two called Mariamne (Josephus, *Jewish Antiquities* 15.7.5§231). He was immoderately fond, moreover, of some beautiful male eunuchs: one was his cupbearer, while another put him to bed (Josephus, *Jewish Antiquities* 16.8.1§230), probably implying some kind of sexual relationship with them.[137] Julius Caesar (100–44 BC) was deified after his death in 42 BC (Suetonius, *Divus Julius* 88), being hailed as 'god' and 'saviour'. One inscription describes him as the 'saviour of the world', Greek *sōtēr tou oikoumenēs*.[138] Suetonius reports the elder Curio calling him 'every woman's man and every man's woman' (Suetonius, *Divus Julius* 52.3). He was married to Cornelia, who died, and then Pompeia, whom he later divorced on suspicion of adultery (Suetonius, *Divus Julius* 6.1–2). Gossip suggested that he seduced many women of high standing in Roman society and had many affairs in the Roman provinces, including one with Cleopatra (Suetonius, *Divus Julius* 50–52). His excessively lengthy stay with King Nicomedes of Bithynia as a young soldier gave rise to the rumour that he had prostituted his chastity to Nicomedes. His return to Bithynia as soon as possible only fanned the flames of scandal (Suetonius, *Divus Julius* 2; 49.1–4).

Heroes

Heroes were sometimes also hailed as saviours in the ancient world, both in Greek and Jewish culture. Josephus uses the word of several people who saved others from danger in time of crisis: Joseph for providing grain in time of famine (Josephus, *Jewish Antiquities* 2.6.1§94), and Jonathan for preserving David's life (Josephus, *Jewish Antiquities* 6.11.10§240).[139] Some heroes in the ancient world were the offspring of or descended from gods or goddesses. This combination of ideas – a divine human to whom the language of saviour was attributed – may well also have recalled some of the heroes of old. Probably the most famous is Heracles or Hercules.[140] Again acclaimed as a 'saviour', Greek *sōtēr*,[141] he was the son of Zeus and received into heaven as a god on his death (Ovid, *Metamorphoses* 9.14–15, 241–272).

Heracles was married three times during his earthly life.[142] His first marriage, to Megara, ended in tragedy when he killed his wife and children (Euripides, *Heracles* 922–1015), while his marriage to Deianira ended in his own death (Ovid, *Metamorphoses* 9.98–272). On account of the trickery of King Thespius of Thespiae, who wanted all his 50 daughters to have a child by him, Heracles slept with each of the daughters (Apollodorus, *Bibliotheca* 2.4.10). When the snake-woman of Hylaia took his horses, he agreed to sleep with her to get them back (Herodotus, *Histories* 4.8–9). The ancient philosopher and biographer Plutarch (*c.* AD 50–120) claimed that Heracles' male lovers were beyond counting (Plutarch, *Erotikos* 761d). The poet Theocritus (early third century BC) tells the story of the love affair between Heracles and the golden-haired lad Hylas (Theocritus, *Idylls* 13).

Lesser heroes were also prone to sexual liaisons. Odysseus was the great-grandson of the god Hermes. Although married to Penelope, he had an affair with the nymph Calypso (Homer, *Odyssey* 5.129), breaking it off when he tired of her but not without making love for one last time (Homer, *Odyssey* 5.207–227). Aeneas was the son of the Roman goddess Venus. He was shipwrecked in Carthage where Queen Dido fell for him. Taking refuge from a storm in a cave, Aeneas and Dido made love as the skies flashed with lightning and the nymphs wailed from the mountain crags (Virgil, *Aeneid* 4.165–172). She went mad with love for him but he could not stay with her as he had a destiny to fulfil. She killed herself, and his last view of Carthage was the flames of her funeral pyre (Virgil, *Aeneid* 4.630–705).

Greek and Roman saviours and heroes were expected to be sexually active and impressive. Gods, emperors, kings and heroes would engage in sexual intercourse with various partners, both women and men, and were not subject to the bonds of marriage and chastity which others, particularly ordinary mortals, might be expected to uphold. Any 'saviour of the world' who did not take advantage of situations that enabled him both to enjoy sex and display his sexual prowess would have been a strange thing in the ancient world. Today the idea that Jesus might have been misunderstood by the Samaritan woman to have been asking for sex may be shocking for some readers. In the classical world into which John wrote, the text would have been equally surprising to many, but only because Jesus refused any liaison with the Samaritan woman. The hero has physical needs and although he must put his destiny before their fulfilment, there are occasions on which he simply has to make love to the beautiful woman (or young man) because he is a hero. He may do so reluctantly, as Odysseus does with Calypso once he has tired of her. He may do so because a beautiful woman is throwing herself at him, as Dido does with Aeneas. Making love comes with the territory – except on that day by the well outside Sychar. Jesus, God incarnate, who is hailed as the saviour of the world, redefines the sexual behaviour of the hero and god visiting earth. Exhausted by the well and longing for refreshment, he puts his physical needs aside so as to offer life and healing to another.

Reflections

We have seen how, in telling the story of the woman at the well, John uses the ancient Jewish betrothal narrative form to tell the story of Jesus as God and messiah coming to bring those outside his people into the love of God. We have also seen how, taking advantage of its major theme, John uses this narrative form to draw attention to Jesus' sexuality.

Both the disciples and the Samaritan woman clearly read Jesus' actions as motivated by sexual desire. Jesus comes across to them as every bit as sexual as the next man. Those of us who are the next man (or woman), who wonders if God has any clue what living with sexual desire is like, can therefore rest assured that Jesus' best friend felt sure that God does have a very clear idea, from his own experience, of what it is like.

John also suggests that Jesus had opportunity to act on his desires. The implication of the narrative is that he was reasonably sexually attractive. Although brushing him off initially, the Samaritan woman changes her mind and accepts what she has misread to be the sexual advances of a complete stranger. Not all men are sufficiently attractive that women will accept an offer of sex on first meeting; nor do they all come across as sufficiently safe to trust. The Samaritan distrusted Jesus at first and escaped the scene as soon as she felt the disciples were judging her. So why did she remain with Jesus until then – not least after he had spoken about her past and present? Somehow she felt safe with him. Jesus combined sexual attractiveness with being safe. He sounds like quite a nice guy.

John claims that he and others saw the glory of God in this. In the Gospel as a whole, people see the glory of God in Jesus giving his life for others on the cross. He can also be seen to put others before himself in his sexuality. At the well near Sychar he went without food, drink and sex because he was more concerned that the Samaritan woman should find life than he was that his sexual desires (or any other bodily appetites) be fulfilled. He put her needs before his own. His sexuality was marked by love.

In calling Jesus the 'saviour of the world', John contrasts Jesus' sexuality with that of other contemporary 'saviours' who were at best more fallible in their sexual expression and encounters. Where many of them expressed their power through their sexuality, Jesus expressed his self-sacrificial love.

None of this is to suggest that Jesus had little or no sex drive. The disciples and the Samaritan woman clearly thought otherwise. He simply had his sex drive under control. Readers may be sorely tempted at this point to assume that he managed this more easily than the rest of us because he was God incarnate. However, John will not let us put Jesus' self-control down to having divine powers. At the start of the story, he presents Jesus as exhausted and needing rest. He makes sure that we understand that Jesus had the same frail flesh that we do. We cannot play the God card here. Jesus exercised self-control over his sexuality in flesh as frail as ours.

Jesus' sexual unselfishness extends to his attitudes towards others. In telling this story John draws attention in another way to our tendency to transfer our unresolved sexual problems onto others. Craig Keener is probably right that ancient audiences would have judged the Samaritan woman to be sexually immoral.[143] John knew that people in his audience would have judged the woman, and many people today do the same. The debate about the reason for the woman being married five times proves as much. Readers supply reasons like divorce, levirate marriage, patriarchal oppression and serial adultery, and we are not always kind in the words we choose to describe her.[144] I offer no comment on what led to the end of her five marriages – except to note that neither John nor Jesus says anything about this in the narrative. Her past is past. Much as Jesus calls her into relationship with God which involves obedience to his commands, neither he nor John interrogate her past behaviour. The keynote of their attitude towards her is grace, and this may present some of us with a challenge.

Jesus' unselfish love has a healing effect on the woman. Her relationship history is central to her identity and she experiences shame around it. Something about the way Jesus speaks or comes across to her leaves her affirmed and accepted. Her actions demonstrate this. She shows no shame in telling her fellow townsfolk that Jesus has told her all about her relationship history, and this witness brings them to faith. Her sex life has become the locus of salvation and the vehicle of witness.[145] John challenges any who over-spiritualize salvation, as salvation is found here in messy sexual relationships and healing from the shame they bring. John's 'wrecking' the climax of the narrative underlines this point. True salvation does not avoid our physicality and sexuality but places the love of God there.

John springs one final surprise on us in the story. Sex and romance were major themes in ancient Greek, Roman and Jewish novels. The standard plot parts the lovers in an untimely manner and the rest of the story takes them through various adventures which finally lead them back together to live happily ever after as a married couple. In the story of the woman at the well, John sets up a betrothal narrative and hints at a budding relationship, and at one level we expect the romantic ending. Instead he offers a story of chastity and sexual healing. But surely that is the point. The sexuality of a truly loving person is no less real for abstaining for the benefit of another. As the Baptist put it in his marriage night metaphor, the real joy of sex lies in seeing the other find happiness.

4

Male intimacy

Just over halfway through his Gospel, John introduces as 'one of his disciples' a character whom he never names, identifying him later in the same sentence as the one 'whom Jesus loved' (John 13.23). He refers to this person explicitly five times (John 13.23; 19.26; 20.2; 21.7, 20), on each subsequent occasion calling him 'the disciple' or 'that disciple' or 'the other disciple', and qualifying this with the phrase 'whom Jesus loved' or 'whom he loved'. John clearly identifies this disciple as enjoying a special relationship with Jesus.[1]

John uses this character to say something about the intimacy of the love God the Father wants to share with humanity. He indicates that the Father and the Son love each other intimately and that the Son came into the world to invite everyone into the love they share. Jesus speaks of the disciples abiding in their love, and John uses the figure of the beloved disciple to show what the experience of entering the love of the Father and the Son looks like.[2] To underline the depth of the intimacy, he uses the language and imagery of an ancient Greek and Roman type of homoerotic relationship which in some circles was thought to be the closest one could ever get to perfect intimacy with another human being.

Using sexual relationships to explore and expound the nature of relationship with God and fellow religious believers can be tricky, as it can easily lead to misunderstanding and backlash. (Readers might not hear that John never envisaged Jesus or the beloved disciple engaging in homoerotic acts. Or they might hear this and find it offensive.) However, John seems to have been quite undeterred. Not only does he use a classic homoerotic model of relationship to explain the love of God, but he happily uses it to describe the nature of the love he (as beloved disciple) shared with Jesus his Lord, friend, brother and best mate, here on earth.[3]

Known by his intimacy with Jesus

John says something about the intimacy he shares with Jesus both when he enters and when he leaves the narrative. He introduces himself in the words 'he was reclining, one of his disciples, in the breast of Jesus, the one whom Jesus loved' (John 13.23). The words 'reclining . . . in the breast [or bosom or lap] of Jesus' translate the Greek *anakeimenos . . . en tō kolpō tou Iēsou*. As he asks the question Simon Peter wants him to put to Jesus, the disciple Jesus loved is described as reclining on the chest of Jesus, Greek *anapesōn . . . epi to stēthos tou Iēsou* (John 13.25). By using in these two verses the two terms *kolpos* (breast, bosom or lap) and *stēthos* (chest), John has chosen two different ways in Greek to draw attention to the same physical action: the disciple Jesus loved reclining in Jesus' chest. Later, when John talks of this disciple for the last time and speaks of rumours about his death, he again identifies the disciple as the one 'who reclined . . . on his chest', Greek *anepesen . . . epi to stēthos autou* (John 21.20). Thus, when the beloved disciple enters and exits the narrative, John identifies him as the one who reclined on the chest of Jesus. The image is significant and says something about the relationship between these two men.[4]

The reason the disciple Jesus loves reclines in his breast is because he is lying next to him at dinner. John 21.20 specifies as much, while the narrative of John 13 takes place at dinner. According to both Greek and Roman custom, people reclined on couches at table for dinner. At the time of the writing of the New Testament, the most common dining arrangement was the *triclinium*. Three couches were arranged around a table with three diners on each couch. Diners would recline with their heads facing the centre table and their feet facing outwards, making conversation easier.

John 13—17 gives few clues as to the arrangement of the diners, but the fact that the disciple Jesus loved reclines in Jesus' chest suggests that they are reclining on the same couch. Jesus gets up from the table in order to wash the disciples' feet (John 13.4–5), which is certainly compatible with the idea that the disciples are pictured as reclining on couches with their feet facing outwards. The disciples are also described as reclining in John 13.28 (literally 'but none of those reclining at the table . . .'). That whoever was going to betray Jesus would dip his bread into the dish at the same time as Jesus suggests they could reach the same dish, in turn suggesting some kind of arrangement like the *triclinium*.[5]

The fact that this disciple was reclining in Jesus' bosom has both social and emotional significance. Greek and Roman dining arrangements were socially stratified: in other words, the place you were given at the table suggested how important you were as a guest. Traditionally the places of highest honour at dinner were those nearest the host. We know that the social stratification of the average dining party was significantly undermined at this particular dinner. If anyone was to wash the feet of the guests, it would be a slave and not the host. In washing his disciples' feet so that they might dine more comfortably (John 13.3–12), Jesus takes the role of the slave before resuming his place at the table, where he seems to act as the host in leading the conversation.[6] After taking the role of a slave, moreover, he refers to himself as the disciples' lord and teacher (13.13–14). Although Jesus subverts the social stratification of customary dining arrangements, he maintains and underlines his status. So the disciple Jesus loved appears to have a place of honour, if not the place of highest honour – suggesting a special relationship between the two men.[7]

John identifies the disciple Jesus loved in terms of the readily understandable motif of an honoured guest, both when he introduces him and when he last mentions him in the narrative. He intends the audience to understand that this disciple is special to Jesus. Both in the way other disciples view his relationship with Jesus and in his physical proximity at dinner, this disciple is portrayed in the strongest possible terms as being intimate with Jesus.[8]

Reading (or misreading) the signs

These signals of the intimacy between Jesus and his beloved disciple could easily have been read by an ancient audience as suggesting a homoerotic relationship between the two men. Four aspects of John's portrayal could have given rise to this impression. First, the meal Jesus shares with his disciples looks quite like a Greek symposium. Second, at this meal, they talk of love. Third, Jesus' relationship with the beloved disciple looks like the relationship between a Greek teacher and his favourite. And fourth, one of the terms used to describe the beloved disciple lying in Jesus' chest – *kolpos*, breast, bosom or lap – would have evoked contemporary homoeroticism. Let us take these four elements in turn.

The supper as symposium

The arrangement of the disciples with their teacher, reclining on couches and talking into the night as they do in John 13—17, would bring the classical Greek drinking party or symposium to many minds in the ancient world.[9] The symposium traditionally took place after dinner, Greek *deipnon,* and was an all-male affair. The men would recline together on couches and drink freely. They would talk, discuss and debate. Entertainment might well include music and poetry. The participants were aristocratic and the symposia were events in which young men learned to take their place in society. They absorbed key cultural values and engaged in homoerotic bonding. The *Symposium* of Plato (roughly 429–347 BC) and that of Xenophon (roughly 430–354 BC) give us insights into the nature of this cultural tradition.[10]

By Roman times this Greek institution was sufficiently well known that gatherings which may not strictly have constituted a symposium might be seen as such. For example, in his novel *Leucippe and Clitophon,* Achilles Tatius portrays an all-male dining group discussing and debating the subject of love (Achilles Tatius, *Leucippe and Clitophon* 2.35–38). Clitophon, Clinias and Menelaus are chatting over brunch rather than during after-dinner drinks; nevertheless, the audience would have heard echoes of Plato and read this scene as a symposium.[11] Therefore, while there needs to be clear evidence that the supper Jesus shared with his disciples can be compared to a symposium, we do not need to find every aspect of a traditional symposium in John 13—17 to justify reading this text against such a cultural background.[12]

The conversation Jesus has with his disciples is an all-male affair set at and after dinner. The narrative begins 'during dinner', Greek *deipnou ginomenou* (John 13.2).[13] Jesus gets up to wash the disciples' feet 'from supper', Greek *ek tou deipnou* (13.4) and they seem to continue dining throughout most of John 13, as towards its end Jesus gives Judas the piece of bread dipped into the dish (13.30).[14] The discussion thus starts during the meal, differing from the classic symposium, but this does not constitute a significant departure from the classic form given that even Plato has Socrates introduce the conversation topic halfway through dinner (Plato, *Symposium* 175C–E). Besides which, the conversation in John 13—17 continues long after dinner, just as in the stereotypical symposium; there is nothing in John 13.31—17.26 to suggest that anyone is still eating.[15]

Nor should much be made of the fact that the disciples are not recorded as drinking heavily, as people did at symposia. This might be partly because early Church leaders discouraged drunkenness (e.g.

Rom. 13.13; 1 Cor. 5.11; 6.10; Gal. 5.21; Eph. 5.18; 1 Tim. 3.3; 1 Pet. 4.3), although John has already depicted Jesus turning vast amounts of water into wine at a wedding where people were expected to get drunk. However, John had no reason for recording that the disciples were drinking in order to depict this scene as a symposium. Plato and Xenophon make remarkably few references to anyone drinking in their *Symposia*. They prefer to record the conversation, as does John.[16] Besides which, if this were a Passover meal (as some but not all scholars contend), there would very likely have been plenty of wine.[17] Contemporary Jewish tradition instructs that even if it is necessary to fund this from charity, 'even the poorest Israelite' should drink 'no fewer than four cups of wine' (*m. Pesah.* 10.1). Possibly, Jesus' choice of the vine as a metaphor (John 15.1–11) indicates the presence of wine as he uses what he sees before him to illustrate his message for his disciples.[18]

Given that by the time of Jesus and John elements of the classic symposium had fused with other customs, the possible differences should not be overplayed. Greek and Roman audiences would most likely have heard Jesus' discussion with his disciples in John 13—17 either as a kind of symposium or at the very least as having elements of a symposium.[19]

Talking of love

At supper Jesus and his disciples talk about love, a topic which was popular at symposia.[20] Clitophon, Clinias and Menelaus likewise discuss the topic of love, arguing over whether men or women make better lovers (Achilles Tatius, *Leucippe and Clitophon* 2.35–38). Menelaus says young men are less complicated and better looking, and that Zeus only ever took the youth Ganymede to heaven to be with him eternally. He never took a woman. Clitophon counters that Zeus made a fool of himself for women and so must love them more – besides which, a woman's embrace and kiss are much softer and more pleasurable than that of a youth, particularly around orgasm. Menelaus responds that women only look good because of the make-up. You can also get physical with a guy you fancy by wrestling naked with him in the gym, without any need for a relationship.

In Plato's *Symposium* love is the main discussion topic. Phaedrus extols love as the highest blessing, especially that between a man and his younger male lover. Such love inspires people to great deeds, even to dying for the object of their love (Plato, *Symposium* 178A–180B). Pausanias speaks of the higher love which finds the enduring spiritual qualities of a person attractive and the lower love which finds itself attracted to someone's body, whether male or female, saying that the lower love leads to base behaviour whereas the higher love does only good. This higher love may find expression in sexual relationship but its purity guarantees that any such sexual relationship will be honourable (*Symposium* 180C–185C). Eryximachus follows with another speech on love.

Aristophanes continues the dialogue with his story about the origins of human love. Originally everyone was round, had two heads, four arms and four legs, and two sets of genitalia. Some people were male–male, some were female–female, and others were male–female. They conspired against the gods and Zeus decided to punish them by splitting them in two. As a result, they only had one set of genitals each and eagerly sought to be reunited with their other half. The male–males sought a male partner. The female–females sought a female partner. The male–females sought a partner of the opposite sex (*Symposium* 188C–193D). Aristophanes praises the male–males as seeking the best kind of love, that which is characterized by 'affection [Greek *philia*], intimacy [Greek *oikeitotēs*] and love [Greek *erōs*]'. Although these males did their duty in marrying and having children, their real loves were their intimate male friends (*Symposium* 192C). Agathon offers another speech which gives a wider perspective on love than intimate relationships between two individuals (*Symposium* 194E–197E).

Then Socrates speaks. In his speech on love he recollects a conversation he once had with a wise woman called Diotima. Love seeks beauty and goodness – first, and quite properly, in the physical beauty of young men. As understanding grows, love then seeks in the souls of young men beauty and the betterment of their own minds and souls. As love reaches yet further, it seeks beauty in knowledge and understanding. Finally, the true soul realizes that while beauty and goodness can be found in these things, none of them are beauty and goodness itself. At this point, love seeks only beauty and goodness and finds fulfilment in it (*Symposium* 210A–212A).

The applause following Socrates' speech is interrupted by the entrance of Alcibiades, who arrives drunk and tries to put Agathon off Socrates and reinstate himself as Socrates' favourite. The plan fails and more revellers interrupt the party, which continues long into the early hours with drinking and debate.

Xenophon, too, makes love central to his *Symposium*. Callias throws a party in honour of his young male lover Autolycus, who recently won at the pancratium, an athletic contest involving boxing and wrestling which required participants to be in peak physical condition (Xenophon, *Symposium* 1.2–4). All the guests are stunned by Autolycus' physical beauty, particularly Callias (*Symposium* 1.8–10). The party ensues with feasting, entertainments and conversation which culminate in Socrates speaking about love – partly inspired by Callias' clear devotion to Autolycus.

Although the conversation moves through various subjects, it returns from time to time to the topics of beauty and love. Socrates talks of what scents attract others (*Symposium* 2.4). Critobulus speaks of the power of male beauty to inspire others and of his particular devotion to his lover Cleinias (*Symposium* 4.10–22). Socrates berates Critobulus for his passion for Cleinias. Charmides then gets Socrates to admit that actually he has taken a fancy to Critobulus (*Symposium* 4.23–28). The entertainer at the symposium, a Syracusan, admits first to being jealous of his handsome young male dancer because other men admire him, and then to being his lover (*Symposium* 4.53–54). Socrates talks of two men put in touch with him by Antisthenes, and whose company he greatly desired (*Symposium* 4.63). Critobulus beats Socrates in a beauty contest, despite losing the arguments about who is more handsome (*Symposium* 5). Beauty and love are never off the agenda.

The party comes to a climax with Socrates' speech on love (*Symposium* 8). He compares love for the body and love for the soul, arguing that the latter is a better form of love. Bodily beauty fades and with it love for the body; it does not last and leads to many kinds of shameless behaviour. Love for the soul, however, genuinely seeks the benefit of the other person. Unlike love for the body, friendship does not need to fade and grows deeper and stronger with time. Even the gods preferred love for the soul over the body, says Socrates. Zeus left on earth the women whose bodies he desired; however, he took those whose souls he desired (like Ganymede and Heracles) to Olympus as immortals. Having begun the speech by admitting that he has always been in love with some man or other, Socrates ends by extolling friendship (Greek *philia*) as the best form of love (Greek *erōs*).

At their meal, too, John has Jesus talk to his disciples on the subject of love. Significantly, Jesus talks more about love here than anywhere else in the Gospels. In John, he uses love language at least five times as much as Matthew, Mark or Luke.[21] Of the 55 occurrences of 'love' in the Gospel's discourses, 34 occur in John 13—17, the high concentration of terms for love suggesting that the theme is more prominent in these chapters even than elsewhere in the Gospel. The chapters begin with love (John 13.1) and end with love (John 17.26). One of two Greek words for love (*agapaō* or *phileō*) or some related word occurs in each chapter of John 13—17. Love was clearly a central conversation topic at this supper, just as it was in Plato and Xenophon's *Symposia*.

The teacher's favourite

In identifying him as the disciple lying in Jesus' bosom and 'whom Jesus loved' (John 13.23), John introduces the beloved disciple in a way that seems to suggest Jesus was closer to him than to any other.[22] He accentuates their intimacy by comparing him with Peter, whom early Christian traditions held to be prominent among Jesus' closest disciples (e.g. Matt. 16.18).[23] When John introduces the disciple Jesus loved, Peter asks this disciple to enquire of Jesus something he himself seems too embarrassed to ask (John 13.24–25). Later, having found the tomb empty, the two disciples Mary Magdalene tells are Peter and the disciple Jesus loved. They run to the tomb but the disciple Jesus loved gets there first; he understands that Jesus has risen from the dead and believes before Peter does (John 20.1–9). Later still, when the disciples are fishing and the risen Jesus talks to them from the shore, the disciple Jesus loved recognizes him first and tells Peter that it is the Lord (John 21.7).[24] In such ways, John hints that he was more intimate with Jesus than Peter was.

Hearing the supper Jesus shares with his disciples as resembling a symposium and seeing Jesus identify himself as the teacher of his disciples (John 13.13–14), members of John's original audience are likely to have drawn connections with Socrates and his disciples. Just as Jesus talks to his disciples of love in John 13—17, Socrates talks to his disciples of love in both the *Symposia* of Plato and Xenophon. Just as Socrates takes centre stage in the conversation at these drinking parties, so Jesus appears to be at the heart of the discourse in the Gospel of John.[25] In the context of this all-male gathering of teacher and disciples, the question of homoeroticism arises. Within the Greek tradition the teacher often has a favourite; the teacher plays the *erastēs* (lover) and the student the *eromenos* (beloved). Socrates, for example, had many young lovers (e.g. Plato, *Symposium* 222B, 223A). Towards the end of Plato's *Symposium*, Socrates invites his new favourite Agathon to lie next to him (*Symposium* 222E–223B) when his old favourite Alcibiades tries to reinstate himself. John's description of the disciple Jesus loved reclining on his chest (John 13.23, 25)[26] looks very much like the beloved disciple playing the role of the Greek favourite disciple and lover.[27]

Encolpius

The very description of a disciple 'reclining . . . in the breast of Jesus', Greek *anakeimenos . . . en tō kolpō tou Iēsou* (John 13.23) would likely evoke notions of homoerotic liaisons in the minds of Greek and Roman audiences. The motif of reclining 'in the breast of' another was familiar in the ancient world and could carry homoerotic connotations. The Syrian poet Meleager (born 60 BC) uses the image of men lying in the chests of other men as an image of male homoerotic love (Meleager, *Anthology* 5.8, 130, 173).[28] The motif was sufficiently familiar, in fact, to have become the name of the main character in a contemporary Roman novel. Petronius takes the Greek words *en* (English 'in') and *kolpos* (English 'breast' or 'lap') and from them creates the name Encolpius. Although the name is officially Latin, the audience would have understood the Greek words and the homoerotic reference. Encolpius is the main character of Petronius' novel *Satyricon* and one who lives up to his name.

Briefly, by way of background, male homoeroticism was not quite the same in ancient Greece and Rome as in the contemporary West. Respectable free men within society were expected at some point to marry and have a family. However, in their youth it was neither unusual nor deemed indecent to have male lovers. An adult male might court a teenage lad to become his lover. In the classical Greek form of this relationship the older man would train the younger in the ways of society and pay him court with presents, while the younger man would offer the older man sexual favours. The older man would take the penetrative role and younger man the passive role in sex. (According to the classic Greek ideal, the partners practised intercrural sex, i.e. penetrating between the thighs. In practice, and beyond the confines of the original Greek ideal, there appears to have been quite a bit of creativity.) As young men became adult, they in turn would take on younger lovers and train them in the ways of the world in return for love. Men might have young male lovers alongside their wives in later life. It was considered indecent to remain the passive partner in adulthood, as being penetrated suggested weakness in the adult male; men who enjoyed the passive role and continued to allow themselves to be penetrated by other men were considered weak and effeminate. Nonetheless, there was nothing particularly strange or uncommon about men engaging in sex with other men in adult life.[29]

Encolpius comes across as someone who does seem to prefer sex with men. Although he has been, at some point, the lover of the beautiful woman Tryphaena (Petronius, *Satyricon* 113), he does not seem to be generally attracted to women. His companion Ascyltos claims Encolpius never was attracted to women (*Satyricon* 9). Encolpius experiences impotence at the prospect of making love to Circe (*Satyricon* 125–132) and Oenothea (*Satyricon* 133–138), despite their attempts to use magic to arouse him. As a student, he played younger lover to Ascyltos (*Satyricon* 9).

Encolpius' real love throughout the novel is his handsome young male companion Giton. Many people are attracted to Giton and this lively lad never seems to resist seduction. Every time Giton finds another lover, Encolpius becomes jealous and sullen (e.g. *Satyricon* 9–10, 79–92, 113). Petronius gives the impression that Encolpius too has had a number of male lovers: for example, the ship's captain Lichas (*Satyricon* 105), the son of Philomela (*Satyricon* 140) and probably also Eumolpus (*Satyricon* 140). Throughout the story, Petronius has Encolpius involved in some homoerotic escapade or other.

Petronius clearly chooses the name Encolpius for the main character of his novel on account of its homoerotic connotations. Even if he was writing for an educated audience, the fact that he could use Greek words to make up a Latin name with obvious homoerotic overtones suggests that together the Greek words *en* and *kolpos* signified something homoerotic to the Greek and Roman mind of the first century AD. Since John uses them to introduce the disciple Jesus loved, some in his audience almost certainly would hear homoerotic connotations.

John tells the story of Jesus' Last Supper with his disciples in ways that would evoke the homoeroticism of Greek and Roman culture. Placing the disciple Jesus loved in his chest at dinner where Jesus teaches portrays this disciple as the favourite of the teacher, and might easily have been read in terms of the homoerotic bonding of Socrates and his favourite disciples. The scene of a discussion about love at dinner between a teacher and his male disciples evokes the symposium which involved homoerotic bonding of male lovers. The language used to place the beloved disciple in Jesus' breast, *en tō kolpō tou Iēsou*, (John 13.23) also suggests homoerotic liaisons. Taken together, all this might suggest that John portrays Jesus as the *erastēs* or lover of the beloved disciple, and the love they share as belonging within the world of classical homoeroticism.[30]

Re-reading the signs (from heaven's perspective)

Although there are elements of the discourse and meal in John 13—17 which evoke aspects of the homoeroticism of the symposium, to assume that these similarities mean that John is suggesting homoerotic relationships between Jesus and his disciples overlooks some significant differences between the two. Using the intimacy of the homoerotic love tradition, John radically recasts the classical homoerotic ideal in order to say something about the love the Father shares with the Son and into which they both invite humanity. This radical transformation starts with the evocation, in the depiction of the disciple lying in Jesus' breast (John 13.23), of the love of the Son and the Father in whose breast he lies (John 1.18).

Signalling the difference

Although John takes in his account of the supper four motifs of classical homoeroticism, he does not develop them in ways typical of the classical tradition. The scene entirely lacks the flirtations between teacher and favourite found in the earlier *Symposia*. Xenophon has Socrates flirt with Antisthenes (Xenophon, *Symposium* 8.3–6) and Plato has Socrates flirt with Agathon (Plato, *Symposium* 222E–223B). The relationship of teacher and beloved disciple in John is very different.

As we have seen, in Plato's *Symposium* Aristophanes tells a charming tale of the origins of the sexual longings of what today would be called gay, lesbian and straight people (*Symposium* 188C–193D). Pausanias talks of the higher spiritual and lower sexual loves (*Symposium* 180C–185C). Socrates talks of the place of sexuality in finding goodness and beauty, the true goal of love (*Symposium*, 210A–212A). By way of stark contrast, although Jesus talks of love, John does not have Jesus and the disciples talk about sex or sexuality at all.

The words *en* and *kolpos* in the description of the disciple whom Jesus loved might have evoked the character of Encolpius from Petronius' *Satyricon*, characters like him or simply the culture he represented. Contemporary Greek and Roman novels were not short on homoerotic allusions and scenes, such as those in the *Satyricon* which reveal the connection between Encolpius' name and his character. Chariton hints at a homoerotic liaison between the hero Chaereas and his best mate, Polycharmus, by suggesting Polycharmus plays Patroclus to Chaereas' Achilles (Chariton, *Callirhoe* 1.5.2); Apuleius offers a ribald portrayal of the homoerotic predilections of the priests of the Syrian goddess (Apuleius, *Metamorphoses* 8.25–29). In contrast, nowhere in his Gospel does John give any hint of a sexual relationship between the beloved disciple and Jesus.[31]

The Father and the Son

Rather than defining the nature of the relationship of Jesus with the disciple he loved in terms of contemporary literary characters like Encolpius or their living counterparts in cities across the Roman empire, John chooses to compare their relationship to that of the Father and the Son. He uses the term 'breast', Greek *kolpos*, in only two places in his Gospel: of the beloved disciple lying in Jesus' breast (John 13.23) and of Jesus lying in the Father's breast (John 1.18).[32] This image of Jesus lying in the breast of the Father captures the intimacy of the Father and the Son. John clearly wants to emphasize the love the Son has for the Father (John 14.31) and the love the Father has for the Son (John 3.35; 5.20; 10.17; 15.9–10; 17.23–24, 26).[33] So he takes a poignant cultural image of intimacy and uses it to frame the relationship of the Father and the Son at the start of the Gospel. To understand the love shared by Jesus and John, we need to understand the love of the Father and the Son.

A different kind of divine love

Divine love was nothing new in the ancient world. Nor was the idea that gods might love human beings who lived in heaven alongside them. Zeus, the supreme god of the Greek pantheon, does precisely this with Ganymede, stolen from Troy and taken to live with the gods, where he serves as cupbearer to Zeus (Homer, *Iliad* 20.231–235), remaining Zeus' young lover eternally. The relationship of the Father and the Son might have been heard in similar terms: the Word becomes human and later ascends into heaven (John 20.17). The initial direction of travel may be different as the Son comes to earth, but ultimately he returns to the Father with whom he once shared great intimacy in heaven, and with whom he will share it again.[34]

However, there are clear differences between the Father and the Son and Zeus and Ganymede. Unlike Ganymede, who is taken into heaven without exercising any choice in the matter, Jesus acts in response to the Father's commands of his own free choice (e.g. John 10.17–18). The intimacy of the Father and the Son would not appear to be without parallel in the classical world; however, the looseness of any parallel with Zeus and Ganymede disallows the conclusion that their relationship is entirely like that of the Father and the Son.

The relationship of the Father and the Son differs from the one between Zeus and Ganymede in one particular respect: the relationship of Zeus and Ganymede is primarily sexual. John never suggests that there is anything remotely sexual about the relationship of the Father and the Son. The idea would be quite foreign to him as a Second Temple Palestinian Jew. The God of Israel did not engage in sexual intercourse. God had no partner. If anyone in Israel ever had thought that he did, then their theology was unorthodox.[35] Contemporary Jewish literature did not speculate about God's sexuality. Admittedly John was not averse to theological disagreement with his Jewish contemporaries – he clearly disagreed with them over the divinity of Jesus. However, as he spells out very clearly throughout the Gospel, the love shared by the Father and the Son was different in quality and expression from that shared between Zeus and Ganymede.

The lack of sexuality in the depiction of the relationship between Father and Son cannot be accounted for by appealing either to the spiritual nature of the Father (John 4.24), or presumably to that of the Son prior to his incarnation. John uses sexual imagery to describe spiritual realities elsewhere: as we have seen, he uses the graphic image of shouting at orgasm on consummating a marriage in describing the joy of John the Baptist at Jesus the messiah coming to claim his covenant bride (John 3.29).[36] The spiritual nature of the relationship of the Father and the Son does not then account for the absence of sexual imagery to describe it. Given his choice of a culturally homo-erotic image to depict their relationship, the lack of sexual language or imagery elsewhere in the Gospel to describe it suggests strongly that John did not conceive of any sexual aspect to their love. So, the love of the only begotten God and his Father in whose breast he lies is a world apart from the love of Encolpius, his real-life Greek and Roman models and their divine counterparts, Zeus and Ganymede.

The love of the Father and the Son

The love of the Father and the Son is mutual and pre-exists time. The Son knows the Father has loved him since before the creation of the world (John 17.24), while the Son lives or abides in the love of the Father (John 15.10). The love the Father shares with the Son seems to lie at the heart of their unity and intimacy (John 17.21–23). The Son abides in the love of the Father because he obeys the Father's commandments (John 15.10). However, the Son does not do so as a result of coercion. He freely chooses to obey the Father, who loves him for his willingness to give his life for others (John 10.17–18).

This love finds expression in the ministry of the Father and the Son, which also bears witness to their intimacy. The Son only does what he sees the Father doing, and the Father shows the Son what he does because he loves him (John 5.19–20). This includes giving the Son authority to judge and to call people back to life from the dead (John 5.21–29). The Father has placed this authority in the hands of the Son because he loves him (John 3.35–36). The Son follows his calling to the cross in order to demonstrate to the world his love for the Father (John 14.31), and prays for all who will believe in him that they may experience the love and intimacy that he shares with the Father (John 17.21–26).[37]

The Father and the Son love each other, although the Father seems to be the fount of love. John mentions quite frequently the love the Father has for the Son (John 3.35; 5.20; 10.17; 15.9–10; 17.23–24, 26), whereas he has the Son mention his love for the Father only once (John 14.31). The Son seems to respond in love to the love of the

Father and does so in willing obedience to him (John 15.9–10, 18). Their love is intrinsically missional, as their mission to save humanity both flows from and is an expression of their love.

The intimacy of the Father and the Son is then not sexual, but is one of deep mutual love which expresses itself in the sharing of their lives. The Father shares with the Son his authority even over life and death. The Son offers up his life for others out of love for the Father. The Son watches the Father constantly and the Father reveals to the Son all that he is doing. They both experience their love in mission to save humanity from death and sin. John pictures this in his final words of the prologue: 'the only begotten God who lies in the breast of the Father, this one made him known' (John 1.18). The Father and the Son share the deepest spiritual intimacy and the Son makes the love of the Father known to the world.

The Father, the Son and his disciples

The Father and the Son make their love known to the world in order to share that love with the world. Although the world does not recognize Jesus (John 1.10), he goes to the cross so that the world might see the love that he has for the Father (John 14.31). Jesus reveals the Father to those who are willing to believe in him so that they may experience the love with which the Father loves the Son (John 17.26). Jesus prays that, just as the Father and the Son are one in the intimacy and love they share, so those who believe in Jesus might experience the same unity and intimacy between themselves and know that the Son loves them as much as the Father loves the Son (John 17.22–26).

Jesus sees sharing this love with his disciples, and so living in them, as central to his calling (John 17.23, 26). John describes Jesus' going to the cross as loving his disciples to the end (John 13.1). Jesus teaches his disciples a new commandment, to love each other just as he has loved them (John 13.34–35; 15.12) and to demonstrate their love for him by keeping his commandments (John 14.15). If they love him and keep his commandments, they will know the love of the Father and the Son; they will live in the Son and he in them, and they will experience the intimacy of the Father and the Son (John 14.19–21, 23). Just as the Father has shared his love with the Son, so the Son shares his love with the disciples that they might live in his love. Just as the Son keeps the Father's commandments and lives in his love, so the Son invites his disciples to keep his commandments and live in his love and find perfect joy (John 15.9–11). John sees no contradiction between love and freedom, and obedience to the commands of another. The Son obeys the Father willingly and not under compulsion (John 10.17–18). Within their love there is both freedom and obedience. This is the model for the disciples. The Son makes them free (John 8.36) and they will obey his commandments as they live in his love.

These commandments include the new commandment to love one another (John 13.34), but they are not reduced to that one command. The language of commandments sounds like the covenant commands of the Old Testament, but John does not use the language of the LXX here.[38] Matthew has Jesus use the same language of keeping the commandments (Matt. 19.17), while Paul uses very similar language (1 Cor. 7.19).[39] The echoes of this covenantal language strongly suggest the commands are ethical or moral.[40] However, John has Jesus speak of his disciples keeping *his* commandments (John 14.15, 21; 15.10) not those of the law.[41]

Interestingly, John never records any of Jesus' ethical teaching.[42] However, he could hardly have written of Jesus' commands without some knowledge of them.[43] So he must have been aware of traditions of Jesus' ethical teaching such as we find in the Gospels of Matthew, Mark and Luke and in the Didache. His audience would already be familiar with them and know that John was referring to them. They were well enough known that he does not have to spell them out. John emphasizes free and willing obedience to the moral commands of Jesus as an identifying mark of the disciple's genuine love for the Son of God.

The Father and the Son, then, share a love which they do not express sexually but through giving themselves to each other and to the world in order to bring others life. The Father is the fount of love and gives good commands that result in life for all. The Son obeys his commands out of love and so offers life to the world. The disciples respond to this love and so find eternal life in the Son (e.g. John 6.68). The Son sets an example to the disciples. Just as he has loved and obeyed the Father, so they are to love and to obey the commands of the Son. In this way, they enter into the life and love of the Father and the Son.

The Son and the disciple he loved

The disciple Jesus loved exemplifies what it means to share in the love of the Father and the Son. The words used of the love between the Father and the Son and his disciples are the nouns *agape*, love (John 13.35; 15.9–10, 13; 17.26) and *philos*, friend (John 15.14–15), and the verbs *agapaō*, love (John 13.1, 34; 14.15, 21, 23–24, 28; 15.9, 12, 17; 17.23–24, 26) and *phileō*, love (John 16.27). These are the same two words which are used to identify the disciple whom Jesus loved: *agapaō* in John 13.23; 19.26; 21.7, 20, and *phileō* in John 20.2. The love which the Father and the Son promise to share with the disciples is the love Jesus shared with the beloved disciple. The love the beloved disciple shares with Jesus as he lies in his breast, Greek *en tō kolpō* (John 13.23) clearly mirrors the love the only begotten God shares with his Father as he lies in his breast, Greek *eis ton kolpon* (John 1.18). The nature of the love shared between Jesus and the beloved disciple is the same love that the Father and the Son share and long to share with all those who come to believe in the Son.

Given that there is nothing sexual about the love shared by the Father and the Son, there seems to be nothing to warrant reading the relationship of Jesus and the beloved disciple as sexual either. In fact, all the indications point in the opposite direction. Nowhere in John's narrative do Jesus and the beloved disciple do or say anything sexual to each other. The love of which Jesus speaks to his disciples finds expression in Jesus' commands rather than in the quest for beauty and truth. Given the centrality of lifelong marriage between a *man* and a *woman* as an expression of obedience to God's law in the sexual ethics of the Jesus traditions (e.g. Matt. 19.3–9; Mark 10.2–9),[44] it strains credibility to think that the Johannine Jesus was finding his way to beauty and truth through flirtatious sexual encounters with beautiful young men like the beloved disciple. (We do not even know whether the beloved disciple was beautiful – although if he was the apostle John, who was still alive towards the end of the first century, he was most likely fairly young.)[45] John indicates that their relationship is modelled after the love which the Father shares with the Son. Jesus loves the disciple and he responds in love and obedience.

The Gospel narrative reveals both these aspects of their relationship. When Jesus tells his disciples that one of them will betray him, the disciples seem to look around at each other in silence (John 13.22).

The fact that Peter gives the (silent) nod to the beloved disciple to ask Jesus the awkward question (13.24) suggests that the disciples perceived the beloved disciple as close to Jesus. That he does ask Jesus the question confirms this impression, as it suggests trust between the two men. John's reiteration that he is lying in Jesus' breast as he does so (13.25) underlines their intimacy.

The scene at the cross reveals not only something further of the intimacy and trust between the two men but also the willingness of the beloved disciple to obey the Son (John 19.25–27). This disciple stands near the cross with Jesus' mother, Mary the wife of Clopas and Mary Magdalene. Seeing his mother and his closest disciple standing beside her, Jesus gives them to each other as mother and son. His mother has a new son to look after her and his best friend has a duty to look after Jesus' mother. John remarks that the disciple took Jesus' mother into his home 'from that hour' (John 19.27). The obedience was total and immediate. And the obedience was offered within a relationship of love and trust.

The beloved disciple seems to know Jesus' mind. Having been told by Mary Magdalene that the stone has been rolled away from Jesus' tomb (John 20.2), Peter and the beloved disciple run to the tomb. Although the beloved disciple arrives before him, Peter enters first. He sees the grave clothes lying there. Like the other disciples, Peter does not understand what is going on, as they have not yet realized that Jesus is to rise from the dead (John 20.9). By contrast the beloved disciple sees the linen wrappings and believes (John 20.8). Somehow he was closer to Jesus than the others and knew him better. Their closeness meant that he had something more of the mind of Christ. And because he knew Jesus more intimately, he was able to discern what Jesus had meant and was now doing.

There may be one further hint that Jesus and John were relaxed in each other's company. It is John who recognizes Jesus first (John 21.7) when Jesus calls to Peter, Thomas, Nathanael, James and John and two others while they are fishing. The disciples are either naked or wearing very little.[46] Overjoyed at seeing Jesus, Simon Peter puts on his outer garment to jump into the sea to swim to him.[47] Putting on one's clothes to swim is foolish but Peter does not want to meet the Lord naked or in his underwear, even if working in this state of undress was common practice for Palestinian Jewish men. By including this detail, John highlights Peter's embarrassment about his nakedness before Jesus. (Accustomed to attending the Roman baths or Greek gymnasium, doubtless many in John's audience would find this an amusing narrative detail.) John does not mention any of the other disciples getting dressed, not even the beloved disciple to whom John as author draws specific attention. Writing for an audience influenced by Greek and Roman culture which had a more open attitude to public nudity, John may be hinting that he and the other disciples were physically more relaxed around Jesus than Peter was.

The Son shares his life with the beloved disciple just as the Father shares his with the Son. He seems to have been the disciple whose intimacy with Jesus was most marked – as John highlights in introducing his character and bidding him farewell from the narrative by reference to his physical intimacy with Jesus. In short, these two men loved each other.

Redefining male intimacy

If the relationship shared by Jesus and the beloved disciple followed so clearly the contours of the love of the Father and the Son, and was not in any way expressed or acted out sexually, why did John choose to frame its nature with such a sexually charged image? The points of contact with classical homoeroticism seem too clear to be accidental. There must have been something else about this classical ideal that John thought was characteristic of his relationship with Jesus, and more generally of the love of the Father and the Son which they wanted to share with the world.

The stripping of sexual encounters from the relationship was not entirely new. Pausanias describes relationships between male lovers which are focused purely on sexual gratification as base (Plato, *Symposium* 181B). Socrates claims that Diotima taught him that the pleasure of the contemplation of pure beauty was much greater than the experience of beauty in male lovers (*Symposium* 211C–212A). Pausanias highlights the beauty of lasting friendship as the real pleasure of this love (*Symposium* 181C–E). John's depiction of the relationship is more novel in that Jesus and the beloved disciple enjoy the closest intimacy with each other without making love. Pausanias assumes that lovemaking is part of the deal and that, provided all other motivations are pure, is perfectly acceptable (*Symposium* 184D). Within minutes of him telling his companions what he has learned from Diotima about the unalloyed pleasures of beauty without sex, Socrates is flirting with his ex-lover Alcibiades and his new boy Agathon.

Central to the classical Greek pederastic relationship was the idea that the teacher and his student sought truth and beauty, and that from their growing appreciation of these things would come a greater understanding of goodness and how to live the truly good life. But these do not seem to be ideas which John develops. Actually, he diverges from them. Unlike Socrates, the Johannine Jesus does not need to pursue truth, precisely because he himself is the truth (John 14.6). Socrates pursues truth but Jesus reveals truth, and their respective relationships with their disciples reflect this difference. Unlike Socrates, Jesus does not reason his way to an essentially intuitive understanding of the truth and the best way to act. Jesus trusts the Father and freely chooses out of love to do as the Father commands. Jesus loves his disciples and they are to choose to obey his commands out of their love for Jesus and each other. Socrates questions the commands of the gods and encourages the asking of questions to work out how to live the good life,[48] while Jesus teaches that life is found only in obedience to the commands of the Father and the Son. However, these differences do not explain what aspect of the classical Greek homoerotic relationship John wants to draw on in evoking this cultural model.

The answer must lie in something John has actually written (unless he has chosen for some reason to be deliberately obscure). The most obvious place to look for an answer is in the way he describes the relationship between Jesus and the disciple. Their relationship is marked by love and intimacy; the disciple is called 'the one Jesus loved'. The texts in which he enters and leaves the narrative depict him as lying in Jesus' chest – an image which denotes physical and emotional intimacy. By never portraying them as saying or doing anything sexual with each other, John strips their relationship of the sexual encounters of the classical Greek homoerotic friendship. John has also divested the relationship of any Socratic methods of learning about truth, the good life and ethics. What remains is the ideal of beautiful shared intimacy between two human beings who love each other passionately and devotedly.

John takes this model of passionate love and intimate friendship to describe the relationship of the Father and the Son into which they invite all humanity. It finds new content and direction in the belief that the one true God really loves humanity and can save it from all evil. This God of love models self-giving love, and invites humanity to participate in it both by enjoying the love of the Father and the Son and by sharing this love with other human beings. Loving behaviour is characterized by obedience to the commands of the Son, which are life-giving. And the love Jesus' disciples experience both with one another and with God is marked by passion and intimacy. Jesus and his beloved disciple model this renewed relationship of God and humanity into which the whole world is invited.

Love between men

John opens up about his relationship with Jesus in the second half of the Gospel. They were clearly best friends who shared a profound spiritual and emotional intimacy. John knew Jesus' mind and heart, while Jesus shared his family with John. They had complete trust in each other. John could not abandon his friend at the cross, even at the risk to his own life. Everyone knew that they were close. Within the narrative of the Gospel, John defines himself in terms of his relationship to Jesus. Commitment to another human being does not come a lot closer than that. John chooses an image of physical intimacy to express both the closeness of their relationship and his own identity. This image suggests that the physical touch they shared encapsulated something of their intimacy. The physical expression of their intimacy may not have been sexual, but it was clearly significant to John.

Using the Greek ideal of homoerotic relationships to give expression to the love they shared must have been a risky business. We know from Petronius' *Satyricon* and the satirical writings of Juvenal and Martial that homoerotic relationships were commonly lampooned in popular culture.[49] The Socratic ideal of the purest spiritual intimacy between two men who truly loved each other was often portrayed as a desperate façade for the pursuit of cheap sex among those who deemed themselves philosophers.[50] John's Jewish contemporaries were hardly likely to have been sympathetic to this model of relationship either, given the complete (or at least nearly universal) disapproval of homosexual activity in Second Temple Judaism.[51] Despite contemporary attempts to re-read Paul as not condemning homosexual activity, it would seem that early Christian churches also disapproved of such activity.[52] John may have been sailing close to the wind, but his choice of this Greek model for the intimacy he shared with Jesus would certainly have made an impression. Even though he empties it of homoerotic content, it is difficult to believe that there would not be some who found it hard to take.

Nonetheless John risks misunderstanding as he offers us insights into his friendship with Jesus. The ideal of friendship was sometimes lampooned as a cover for homoerotic sex, just as intimate friendships between men (and women) can often be misunderstood as closet homosexual relationships today. There are 'those who cannot conceive of Friendship as a substantive love but only as a disguise or elaboration of Eros', as C. S. Lewis complained. (In his view, people like this 'simply betray the fact that they have never had a friend'.)[53] As he further commented, 'kisses, tears and embraces [between men] are not in themselves evidence of homosexuality', as friends can do all these things without any sexual motivation.[54] John knew as much and enjoyed this kind of intimacy with Jesus. Why else define their friendship in terms of physical touch?

John does not simply risk misunderstanding. He challenges the *status quo*. To express their close relationship, John could have drawn comparisons between his friendship with Jesus and that of David and Jonathan. This would have made the point to an ancient Jewish audience successfully and without misunderstanding, while Greeks hearing his Gospel would simply have had yet another Jewish image to get their heads around. But John does not do this. He chooses the Greek homoerotic ideal to express the intimate love which bound the souls of these two men together, redefining it in terms of the divine love which Jesus shares with the Father. He challenges the Greek ideal, showing a better way of achieving its professed goal of the purest spiritual intimacy between two men. He tells his own story as testimony and holds up his friendship with Jesus as an invitation for others to experience the same.

John has good reason for doing this. His experience of the love of Christ has given him insight into the love the Father shares with the Son, and which they long to share with the whole world. He gives 'Greek' expression to this love, picturing the intimacy they share as being like that which he shared with Jesus at that meal – a moment so special to him that he identifies himself in terms of it. This love which the Father and the Son share is too good not to talk about it.

Arguably the whole Gospel is about this love. If the intimacy of passionate sexuality is the only image which gives adequate expression to its depths (even if this love does not express itself sexually), then John appears to have been willing to take the risk of disapproval in order to tell the world about it.

It would be easy to imagine devotees of Greek love criticizing John for limiting their sexual freedom by redrawing the lines of this love. It would be equally easy to imagine Jewish and Christian traditionalists objecting to what some might now worry sounded like a metrosexual Jesus. John could easily have offended them all. But the idea that God so loved the world that men could share this level of intimacy with one another physically, spiritually and emotionally was worth it all for John. He knew the beauty of this love first-hand. He also knew it was not limited to aristocratic free men (or male disciples), but that all could enjoy it – men and women, adults and children, slaves and free. And he wanted to share it.

5

Peter, Mary and the woman caught in adultery

There are other characters in John's Gospel worth studying with respect to our theme: not least Peter, Mary of Bethany, Mary Magdalene and the unnamed woman caught in adultery. While these figures may not tell us anything directly about Jesus' sexuality, suggestions have been made down the centuries about their relationships with Jesus which render it worthwhile taking a few pages to consider what we might learn (or not) from examining the way they interact with Jesus. In what follows I shall try to stick closely to the text of John rather than getting sidetracked into discussions of what novelists, church traditions and ancient religious teachers speculated might have been the case.

Something about Mary(s)

In recent years, unsuspecting members of the general public worldwide have been offered the idea that Jesus had some kind of sexual relationship with Mary Magdalene.[1] The roots of this speculation lie in an ancient text (probably third century AD) called the *Gospel of Philip*, which states

> As for the Wisdom who is called 'the barren', she is the mother [of the] angels. And the companion of the [. . .] Mary Magdalene. [. . . loved] her more than [all] the disciples [and used to] kiss her [often] on her [. . .]   (NHC II 3 63.30–35)[2]

The *Gospel of Philip* identifies Mary Magdalene as Jesus' companion (NHC II 3 59.6–11). Scholars trying to reconstruct the gaps in the text above tend to assume that it read that Jesus used to kiss her (i.e. Mary Magdalene) on the mouth often.[3] The *Gospel of Philip* also identifies Mary Magdalene with the disciple whom Jesus loved;[4] its author too suggests that Jesus kissed this disciple often.[5]

The question then is whether there is any evidence in the Gospel of John itself that Jesus ever had a romantic or sexual relationship with Mary Magdalene. One suggestion has been put forward. William Phipps reads John 20.17 as evidence of such a relationship. Standing near the empty tomb, Mary mistakes the risen Jesus for the gardener. When he calls her name (so identifying himself), she goes to hug him – or so it seems from his response. In Greek, his words are *mē mou haptou*, which most translators and commentators read as 'do not touch me' or 'do not cling to me'. On the basis that Paul uses the same Greek verb, *haptomai*, to refer to sexual intercourse (1 Cor. 7.1), Phipps suggests that John uses it with this meaning on the lips of Jesus here.[6] In other words, John relates that Jesus responds to Mary Magdalene with something like 'we must stop having sex'.[7]

This is the only place where John uses the verb *haptomai*. However, elsewhere in the NT it tends to mean 'touch' (without any sexual connotations) or 'light' a lamp or fire.[8] The nature of the discussion following 1 Corinthians 7.1 clearly determines that there the verb connotes sex. So, we have to ask whether anything in John suggests that Jesus might have been talking about sex with Mary Magdalene in the garden.

Prior to meeting Jesus in the garden, Mary only appears twice in the Gospel. We see her first near the cross where she stands with Jesus' mother and aunt, and Mary the wife of Clopas (John 19.25). She next appears on her way to the tomb only to discover it is empty, whereupon she announces to Peter and John that 'they' have stolen Jesus' body (John 20.1–2). When she makes this announcement, she refers to Jesus as 'the Lord' (20.2). From her use of this title and her presence at the cross we may assume that she is a committed follower of Jesus.[9] Earlier in the narrative, Jesus says to his disciples that they rightly call him 'teacher' and 'lord' (John 13.13), implying that they do indeed call him both these things. Therefore, Mary Magdalene's use of the same address (as well as calling him 'teacher' in John 20.16) suggests that she is his disciple. Nothing in either of these two earlier appearances suggests anything sexual about the relationship of Jesus and Mary Magdalene.

Nor does anything in the Gospel text suggest that Jesus was married.[10] Although Jesus does not make much of the sexual history of the Samaritan woman, his words to the effect that she is not married to her current man suggest that he does not approve of unmarried sex (John 4.17–18). In the resurrection story John portrays Jesus, the one who came to bring life, as having conquered death. So it is most unlikely that at this moment of triumph John would portray his hero as a hypocrite who turns out to have been having an illicit affair with Mary Magdalene all along. Nor it is likely that John would depict the first disciple to see the risen Christ bearing witness to his resurrection shortly after they have finished their affair.[11] For John the resurrection is good news, and so he is unlikely to taint its happening or announcement with the stain of a sex scandal between his hero and one of his disciples. While scholars debate the exact meaning and implications of Jesus' command *mē haptou mou*, there is some consensus that he is referring to Mary embracing or seeking to embrace him as the natural reaction of a disciple to the resurrection of her teacher.[12] Read within the context of the Gospel as a whole, nothing in these words suggests a sexual relationship between Jesus and Mary Magdalene.

Sjef van Tilborg has used the same scene to make a very different suggestion. Reading the scene in the garden as one of 'lovers getting together at the end of the novel', Tilborg expects to see Jesus and Mary fall into each other's arms. Mary stands outside the tomb weeping (John 20.11). She explains her tears to the angels as the result of not knowing where 'they' have taken her Lord (20.13). He calls her 'Mary' and she calls him 'teacher'; then she moves towards him to embrace him. At this point in the novel we would expect the lovers to come together, but instead Jesus says 'don't touch me' (20.17).[13] Tilborg concludes that Jesus is here showing unexpected coldness to Mary, which in turn indicates a lack of intimacy with women.[14] Coupled with his contention that Jesus had a relationship with the beloved disciple that was not unlike that of Socrates with his favourites, Tilborg suggests that John is indicating Jesus' behaviour to be consistent with having what might now be called homosexual inclinations.[15]

A major difficulty with this reading is that neither the Gospel as a whole nor this specific story provide any reason for thinking that this is a lovers' 'recognition scene'. The Greek novels generally introduce the lovers at the beginning, take them through a series of adventures and mishaps which threaten to thwart their love and then, through an equally convoluted (but entertaining) series of events, bring the lovers back together so we can all enjoy the recognition scene and the ensuing festivities.[16] None of these features are present in John. We do not even meet Mary Magdalene until the crucifixion and nowhere are she and Jesus presented as lovers, let alone thwarted lovers. In John 20 Mary consistently refers to Jesus as 'lord' (vv. 2, 13 and – perhaps ironically – 15) and 'teacher' (v. 16). As we have seen, John presents Mary as Jesus' disciple, not his lover.[17] Mary weeps just as Jesus has predicted that his disciples would weep on his disappearance (John 16.20), an action which clearly portrays her as Jesus' disciple and which does not require the unwarranted explanation that she was ever Jesus' lover.

While there may be nothing in John to suggest there was ever anything between Jesus and Mary Magdalene, the same cannot be said for Jesus and Mary of Bethany. John seems to hint that she is attracted to him, and that he is aware of this. Mary of Bethany, her sister Martha and their brother Lazarus were clearly very close friends of Jesus. John tells us that Jesus loved them (John 11.5). When Lazarus dies, Jesus raises him from the dead (John 11.1–44). The story is very moving, not least as it contains the only verse in the Gospels where Jesus weeps (John 11.35). However, John says something slightly odd in the introduction to this episode. Right at the start of the story, he identifies Mary of Bethany as the one who anointed the Lord with perfume and wiped his feet with her hair (11.2). Not only does this seem to play no great part in the narrative of the resurrection of Lazarus, but John does not tell the story of Mary anointing Jesus until after the raising of Lazarus (John 12.1–8). Possibly the story was so well known that people would recognize Mary by this identification.[18] But why draw attention to Mary? Why not identify Martha instead, possibly as the one who made the meal (Luke 10.38–42)? And why draw attention to Mary in this way, rather than as the one who sat and listened to Jesus?

Even if she is identified in this way, moreover, why not simply as the one who anointed Jesus? That would be enough to recall the episode. Why mention the expensive perfume and her wiping his feet with her hair? By including a detail in the Lazarus story which does not seem to fit, and at a point where it will worry the attentive reader, John upsets the equilibrium again, inviting us to look more closely at the episode to see what he might have put there for our consideration. This time he indicates we might want to read the story of the anointing first and then come back to the raising of Lazarus.

In John 12.1–8, Mary, Martha and Lazarus have invited Jesus around to dinner after he has raised Lazarus from the dead. Needless to say, Martha serves the meal (12.1–2). Mary takes a pound of extremely expensive pure nard and anoints Jesus' feet with it. She then wipes his feet dry with her hair. The perfume lingers and its scent fills the house (12.3). When Judas questions Mary's action in possibly wasting such expensive perfume, Jesus comes to her defence (12.4–8). The nature of his defence is puzzling. Literally Jesus says 'leave her alone, so as to keep it for the day of my burial' (12.7).

From the earliest times, readers have tried to fill in the gaps. Some early writers amended the wording to 'leave her alone, she has kept it for the day of my burial'.[19] Even this seems to point ahead to the day of Jesus' burial. But it seems odd as she has already used the perfume (v. 3) and so cannot keep it until the day of his burial.

Various suggestions have been made for making sense of the text. We might assume that the sentence ends at 'leave her alone' and the following sentence states tersely the purpose for which the perfume was originally bought.[20] Maybe John has not recorded the whole saying and we are to understand 'she bought this perfume to keep it for the day of my burial'.[21] In both cases we are to understand the action as prophetic of Jesus' death.[22] But this does not change the fact that the perfume was intended for an event which has not yet taken place. Some think Mary did not use the entire contents of the vase and the rest must be kept for his burial.[23] However, the text reads as if she used up the whole pound of nard. By 'keep', Jesus might have meant 'keep it in mind', so suggesting that Mary might want to remember what she did for Jesus when he was buried.[24] This suggestion is ingenious, but 'keep', Greek *tēreō*, does not normally mean this in the NT, which uses other terms for 'remember'.[25] Possibly Jesus means that rather than selling the perfume as Judas suggests, they should leave it on his feet and keep it there for his burial.[26] Given the importance John attaches to the death of Jesus, keeping the expensive burial perfume on Jesus' feet until his actual burial produces an inappropriately comical effect, not least as Mary appears to have wiped off quite a bit of it with her hair already. Neither does this explain the anointing of Jesus' feet rather than his whole body or head (as in Matt. 26.6; Mark 14.3).

No matter how we try to explain this passage, two points emerge: Jesus makes the response in Mary's defence; and this is Jesus' interpretation of the event, not necessarily one shared by Mary. Certainly, by the end of the story, the anointing is linked to Jesus' death and burial. The fact that John places the story after the plot to kill Jesus (John 11.47–53) underlines the anointing as one for burial. However, this does not mean that this was Mary's motive, or at least her only motive; it is Jesus' interpretation of her actions.

Three clues in the text suggest that something else might have been going on. First she anoints his feet. It was not normal to anoint feet,[27] so the detail calls for explanation. Possibly the anointing of the feet mirrors the foot-washing in John 13.[28] However, there are clear differences between these two accounts: anointing is not washing; oil is not water; and preparation for burial is not the same as exemplifying humble service. The connecting factor is feet and, given the differences, this does not seem a sufficiently strong link to read the one account in terms of the other. The explanation that Mary has anointed Jesus for burial still leaves a question mark hanging in the air, as the entire body would have been anointed for burial.[29] Feet are also a well-known euphemism for genitalia (e.g. Ruth 3.4, 7; 2 Sam. 11.8).[30] While Mary clearly anoints Jesus' feet (and no other body part), John might just be using this action to suggest a hint of sexual attraction.[31]

Two other details in the story point in the same direction.[32] The choice of 'perfume of nard', Greek *muron nardou*, is one of them. Beyond the account of the anointing in Mark 14.3, the only other place where nard occurs in the LXX or NT is the Song of Solomon (Sòng of Sol. 1.12; 4.13, 14). Within the Song of Solomon, the perfumes are clearly aphrodisiacs, as the young women adore the lover on account of them (Song of Sol. 1.3).[33] The detail of Mary wiping Jesus' feet with her hair also suggests something romantic. Within Second Temple Jewish culture a married woman who went around with her hair loose would have been deemed to contravene Jewish law and so her husband could divorce her (*m. Ketub.* 7.6). However, on her wedding day a woman might wear her hair loose and uncovered (cf. *m. Ketub.* 2.10).[34]

Taken on their own, none of these allusions amounts to very much. Taken together, the vague hint of genitalia, the use of a perfume associated only with lovers in the biblical tradition, and the wearing of one's hair in a manner appropriate to one's wedding day are less easy to dismiss. Most interesting is that in John's short account of her action, these three details are the only ones to which he draws attention. The coincidence would surely be too much. John drops three hints that Mary's action was motivated by some kind of romantic attraction.[35]

Re-reading the story of the raising of Lazarus, we notice that John introduces Mary using the exact same three details: perfume, feet and hair that has been let down. Either this is a remarkable coincidence or John is once again inviting us to read the narrative with an eye to what we might find there about romantic attraction between Mary and Jesus. There are various interesting details. When Jesus arrives, Mary stays at home while Martha goes out to greet him (John 11.20). After talking with Jesus briefly, Martha tells Mary that Jesus is calling for her (11.28). Possibly we are to understand that he has done so, but John does not say as much. Possibly Martha finds Mary's failure to come out to speak to Jesus uncomfortable and so tries to summon her to Jesus. John leaves the narrative open – except that he has suggested that Mary is attracted to Jesus.

When Mary meets Jesus, she tells him that if he had been there Lazarus would not have died (John 11.32). Given that the sisters had sent for Jesus' help in what seemed like good time (11.3) and it was Jesus who delayed (11.6), this sounds like a rebuke.[36] Note again that on meeting Jesus, Mary kneels at his feet (11.32). So far as we can tell, Martha did not (11.20). Why does John include all these details about the way Mary relates, and avoids relating, to Jesus at this point in the story? Given the hint he drops in v. 2, it makes sense to read the text as John suggesting that Mary was sufficiently close to Jesus to be making her disappointment in him felt. The allusion to feet in v. 32 might possibly constitute the subtlest of hints that romance lingers in the background, though I suspect this is a connotation too far. Nor does John state this, although to be fair, he does set up the narrative conditions in which his audience might draw such a conclusion.

John's next move is a master stroke of storytelling. When Jesus sees Mary weeping he loses his composure and he too begins to cry (John 11.33–35). Jesus doubtless feels sorrow at the loss of his friend Lazarus, but he seems to know that he will raise him from the dead (cf. 11.4, 40–44). Coupled with the fact that he does not cry (as far as we know) when he hears of Lazarus' death, his breaking down in v. 35 cannot be attributed solely to the loss of his friend. Neither does he weep (that John mentions) when he meets Martha, who was also grieving (as implied by the arrival of others to console the sisters in v. 19). Jesus begins to weep when he sees Mary and those with her weeping.[37] On seeing her weep, he becomes deeply distressed.[38] He is also shaken up inside.[39] Something about Mary's grief over the loss of her brother and all the other attendant emotions around his death affects Jesus deeply. There is a clear emotional connection between Jesus and Mary of Bethany.[40]

John does not fully define the nature of this connection. Having dropped three clear hints that Mary of Bethany was romantically attracted to Jesus, he invites the Gospel audience to read the pair's interactions in the light of these hints. By having him defend Mary against Judas' criticism of her action (John 12.4–8), and showing him moved to tears only when he sees Mary weeping, John suggests that Jesus has a soft spot for Mary. However, he makes no further comment about any feelings he may have had for her, and he gives no indication that there was ever any romantic liaison between them. John simply depicts her as occupying a particular place in his heart. She seems to have held a candle for him and he was not unfeeling towards her. That is as much as John suggests, and no more.

Lazarus, Thomas, Judas and Peter

In defending the reasonableness of reading the Bible with gay concerns in mind, Dale Martin suggests that Jesus had some kind of erotic emotional bond not only with the beloved disciple, but also with Lazarus, Thomas, Judas and Peter. His main argument is that it is as legitimate to read the biblical text with 'the gay imagination' as it is to read it within its historical context ('the historical imagination') or with reference to the early Christian interpreters of the text in the first few centuries AD ('the patristic imagination').[41] Consequently, he offers little more than brief comments justifying his reasons for reading homoerotic overtones to Jesus' relationships with these men. Given that the text may stand as a witness against some readings of the text but fully accept the possibility of others, these suggestions need to be assessed in the light of what the text says and does not say.

Martin notes that Jesus loved Lazarus and his two sisters (John 11.5) and asks the question 'perhaps a *ménage à quatre*?' He also notes that those who saw Jesus weep surmised that he must have loved Lazarus greatly (11.36).[42] There are some problems with this reading. First, John does not depict any *frisson* of sexual energy passing between Jesus and either Lazarus or Martha. The fact that he does indicate as much for Mary, on the other hand, suggests that John saw nothing sexual in the relationships with Lazarus and Martha. The verbs which he uses of the love Jesus has for Lazarus – *agapaō* (11.5) and *phileō* (11.36) – are the same as those used for the love of Jesus and the beloved disciple, and the Father and the Son.[43] John says nothing which would justify any reading of these relationships as sexually active. So he provides no support for reading Jesus as loving Lazarus sexually. However, these verbs suggest their love is marked by the intensity and intimacy of classical homoerotic love, and so in this sense John depicts Jesus' friendship with Lazarus as intimate. Given that the mission of the Father and the Son is to share this intimate love with all who will respond, that Jesus shares this quality of love with Lazarus need hardly surprise us. But it is not sexual.

Martin comments that 'Thomas is invited to penetrate holes in Jesus' body (John 20:24ff)'.[44] In favour of Martin's reading is the fact that Jesus invites Thomas to place his finger into the holes in his wrists and his hand into Jesus' side (John 20.27). The word 'hand' is a well-known euphemism for penis in Hebrew.[45] The nearest the LXX comes to using 'finger' with any sexual reference, however, is the advice the young men give King Rehoboam to assert his power, with the boast that his little finger was thicker than his father's loins (2 Chron. 10.10 LXX) – but even here the finger does not represent a penis. So the language John uses does not carry an erotic overtone. Moreover, the context clearly indicates that Jesus is inviting Thomas to confirm that his body bears the marks of crucifixion; nails would have been hammered through Jesus' wrists, and John records the piercing of Jesus' side with a spear (John 19.34). As the climax of the story demonstrates, Jesus' invitation and Thomas' actions are about belief in Jesus (John 20.27–29). Thomas, unlike Mary of Bethany, is on the same page as Jesus. Nothing in the context demands or suggests that a sexual overtone should be heard, and so reading the text in this way adds more than it clarifies. Given that John uses homoerotic motifs in developing his central theme of God sharing his love with the world, and that he uses none of them here, it is unlikely that he intended any such connotations to be heard. If he had done, he would surely have given his audience more clues, as he did in developing the relationship of Jesus and the beloved disciple.

Martin also reads homoerotic overtones into the betrayal: 'Jesus dips his "little piece" (*psōmion*) in the gravy and places it in the hand of Judas'.[46] This time Martin exercises a little too much gay imagination. The text does not say that Jesus places anything in Judas's hand. He simply gives him the morsel (John 13.26). And John says only that Judas received the morsel (13.30). Did he take it from Jesus' hand? From the table? From a plate? Did Jesus hand Judas the dish with the dipped morsel still in it? John leaves all these questions unanswered. The alleged homoerotic connotations of this text depend on the possible erotic connotations of the English phrase 'little piece'. The Greek word *psōmion* simply does not carry any homoerotic connotations in the LXX or Second Temple Jewish literature.[47] So the evidence counts against even the possibility of a homoerotic connotation to the Greek text.

Martin also suggests that there are homoerotic overtones to Jesus' relationship with Peter, claiming that in their final conversation 'Jesus flirts with Peter like a schoolgirl: "Do you *really* love me? Really? Really? Then prove it!" (John 21:15–19).' He adds to this the fact that Jesus washes his male disciples' feet, 'again taking time out for a special seduction of Peter (John 13:1–11)'.[48] Feet certainly can carry a homoerotic overtone. However, not every reference to the term needs to do so. It makes no sense, for example, in John 20.12 where hands and feet stand for the two ends of the body. The physical action of washing feet as the action of a servant makes perfect sense as precisely that. As to whether there is an erotic overtone to the action, nothing in the narrative (that I can see) demands or even suggests this. Unlike the narrative of Mary anointing Jesus' feet, we have no other clues in this story which might suggest such a reading. The text cannot be said to encourage it.

However, there may be an element of truth in Martin's suggestion that there is something in the air around Peter's final conversation with Jesus. The clue lies in what Peter does when they finish speaking. Seeing the beloved disciple, Peter asks 'Lord, what about him?' (John 21.21). Peter is implicitly comparing himself here with the beloved disciple.[49] In the dialogue between Jesus and Peter, John uses the two terms for love that he uses both when referring to the Father and the Son, and to Jesus and the beloved disciple.[50] The love of which they talk is the same love that the Father and the Son want to share with the world. That love has been characterized as having the same intimacy as the best of homoerotic friendships in the ancient Greco-Roman world. The fact that John identifies the beloved disciple in terms of his lying on Jesus' chest at dinner (21.20) supports a reading of that intimacy motif here. The beloved disciple shares this intimacy with Jesus. He stood at the cross. Peter did not. Does Peter really want to enter into this kind of intimate love with Jesus? It will involve his death.[51] Peter notices the disciple Jesus loved and makes the comparison.

John identifies this disciple by his physical intimacy with Jesus but uses the word 'chest', Greek *stēthos* rather than 'lap', Greek *kolpos*. He does not therefore use the word that carries all the homoerotic connotations, but still the motif of intimacy between two men is present. John may not portray Jesus flirting 'like a schoolgirl' but he does put the question of how deep the intimacy between Peter and Jesus is. We should not be surprised by this. John invites us all into the intimate love of the Father and the Son, and so to leave the Gospel with the question of how deeply one particular and rather famous disciple shares in this love might just get us as an audience thinking about our own relationship with Christ. But given the way that John uses the classical motif, it is intimacy rather than sexuality that hangs in the air around this conversation.

Sexual judgementalism: an addition

It would be difficult to end this discussion without some comments on the story of the woman taken in adultery. A woman, caught in the act of adultery, is brought to Jesus. Her captors ask Jesus if they should stone her, as the law commands. Jesus is silent for a while. Then he says that anyone who has committed no sins should cast the first stone. They leave her alone with Jesus (John 8.1–11).

The story does not address Jesus' sexuality directly. Nor does it seem to have formed part of the original Gospel. The earliest and most reliable manuscripts do not include it.[52] However, not only has it entered the lifeblood of the churches as one of the most enduringly popular Gospel stories, it also seems to be one of the more loved Gospel stories within secular cultures which have rejected (at least aspects of) Christianity. Although it was likely added by an early editor of the Gospel, it seems to say something about Jesus' attitudes towards sexuality which we have already found in John 4. I do not intend to ask or answer any questions about the canonicity or authority of this text, nor do I wish to enter into any speculation or argument about the historical reliability of the story. I will simply comment briefly on the basis that some early editor seems to have stuck it into the Gospel, and that it illustrates rather nicely something which John had already included in the original Gospel in his telling of the story of Jesus and the Samaritan woman at the well.

There are many elements of this story that are uncertain. No man is threatened with death, and it takes at least two to commit adultery. Have those condemning the woman simply let him escape?[53] Or has he been stoned already?[54] Are we to understand that Jesus has to choose between Roman law and Jewish law as the Romans had no death penalty for adultery and did not allow any other authority to exercise it without their sanction?[55] Or do we take Pilate's words 'take and crucify him yourselves' (John 19.6) to suggest that the Romans would permit this?[56] Or that the rule of Roman law was somewhat slack in this area of Pilate's Palestine? John does not tell us what Jesus wrote in the sand (John 8.6, 8).

We do know the woman was facing stoning. We know that she was charged with adultery and condemned under the Jewish law (Lev. 20.10; Deut. 22.22). We also know that the scribes and Pharisees wanted to hear Jesus' view on whether the woman should be stoned in accordance with the law of Moses. We are aware that Jesus saved her from stoning by giving an answer which did not seem to allow anyone there that day to carry out the sentence: 'let the one without sin [Greek *ho anamartētos*] cast the first stone at her' (John 8.7). The word *anamartētos* does not refer to sexual sin but to any sin. Some may have heard the reference to be primarily to sexual sin, and the context would permit such a reading; however, the word covers all manner of sin.[57] But the story does not fit the morally liberal Jesus who is sometimes preached from it. His parting words to the woman are 'sin no longer' (John 8.11). Again, the context might suggest a primarily sexual content to these words, but actually they have a wider meaning.[58] Jesus may not condemn her but he certainly instructs her to live life in obedience to his commands. It is not one or the other. It is both.

In itself the story tells us nothing about Jesus' sexuality. However, it does offer a couple of interesting parallels with the story of the woman at the well, a story which does explore his sexuality. Jesus says nothing to condemn the woman caught in adultery but accepts that she has committed adultery. He does not explore the whys and wherefores of the Samaritan's relationship history, but he does note that she is currently in a sexual relationship and unmarried. Jesus offers the woman caught in adultery another chance at life; he tries to offer the Samaritan woman the life God gives (*that* sort of 'living water'). The picture of Jesus as offering life and forgiveness to those who have made mistakes is underlined in this later story. It is sometimes suggested that unaddressed sexual aggression can lend vehemence to the views people hold on matters sexual, and indeed on other matters too. This does not seem to be the case with Jesus. John depicts him as able to forego his own sexual fulfilment and yet offer life, healing and a second chance to others who have made mistakes in their sex lives. The Jesus John presents in both these stories is not sexually judgemental, yet nor does he justify or gloss over mistakes. Jesus embodies an approachable holiness. He invites the broken into new life and calls them away from the sins that broke them and others in the first place. He makes the demand that we sin no longer, but he does so as our friend and brother.

Reflections

Those who have written on the subject have made many suggestions about Jesus' real or imagined romantic entanglements. In his novella, *The Escaped Cock*, D. H. Lawrence imagined the risen Christ putting ministry behind him in favour of the life-giving excitement of sexual love with a priestess of Isis. In *The Last Temptation of Christ* Nikos Kazantzakis famously pictured Jesus as being in love with Mary Magdalene but avoiding dragging her into his own violent destiny by breaking off the relationship. On the cross he wonders how it might have been. He dreams of the consummation of his relationship and marrying her, and after her early tragic death of marrying Mary of Bethany and her sister Martha. In his play *Corpus Christi* Terrence McNally explores the idea that Jesus was gay and had a brief relationship with Judas before moving to New York. Most recently, Dan Brown has given fictional life to the idea that Jesus had a relationship with Mary Magdalene. As we have seen, Dale Martin suggests that reading the Gospel texts with the gay imagination might open up many possibilities for reading Jesus in sexual relationship with others.

Examining these possibilities with reference to the Gospel of John has produced more negative than positive results. The text does not seem to be so easily persuaded of these ideas as some of its readers have been. It lends no support to the ideas that Jesus was in a relationship with Mary Magdalene, or had sexual encounters with any of Thomas, Judas, Peter or Lazarus – let alone a priestess of Isis. On the other hand, through its use of motifs and love language it does draw the intimacy that Jesus shares with Lazarus and which Peter might share with Jesus into the sphere of the Johannine rewriting of the script of Greek homoeroticism.

There is, however, one tiny glimmer of romance to which John draws our attention as audience. As Jo-Ann Brant has pointed out, three aspects of Mary's anointing of Jesus' feet suggest that she was motivated to do so out of romantic love for him. His defence of her against Judas' criticism and his weeping at Lazarus' grave only when he saw her weeping, taken together, suggest that he had a soft spot for her. If he did not, it is difficult to explain why his reaction to seeing her grief was so different from his reactions to the grief of others. Being deeply frustrated and all shaken up suggests a very strong reaction which itself hints at strong emotions behind the reaction – and all set off by Mary of Bethany. John tells us nothing much about their relationship, if indeed there was one. However, he leaves us in little doubt that God incarnate knew what it was to be romantically loved by a woman and to have affection for her.

6

Intimate Jesus

Coming back to our original question, how did God experience human sexuality? According to his friend and follower the apostle John, Jesus experienced it just the same way we do, in frailty and desire. Right at the start of his Gospel, John describes Jesus as the Word made 'flesh'. In its immediate context, that word suggests sexual desire. In the story at the well, Jesus' best friends clearly think him as capable of sexual desire as the next man. It is quite telling that in this same story, John offers one of his strongest images of Jesus' human limitations, depicting him as simply too tired to continue into town to get food and instead sitting down by the well. John deliberately brings out Jesus' experience of sexual desire in the frailty that is common to all of us. Those of us for whom questions about faith, sex and sexuality arise from our experience can heave a sigh of relief: the God whose commands we struggle with, and to whom we pray in and about our difficulties, understands sexual desire from experience. He is not only 'gentle and humble in heart' as he disciples us, but he has more than a rough idea of what we are going through.

Like his fellow disciples, John found this rather embarrassing at the time. The separation of sex from the sacred is not exclusively a Second Temple Jewish phenomenon. Many people even today find the idea of mixing God and sex uncomfortable. This discomfort tends to separate faith and sex in our mindset. It can lead to a rigorous sexual morality which separates us from our sexuality, or compartmentalizes our lives so that our sexual activity is not in synch with our sexual morality – or both. John too had a mental barrier separating sex from the sacred, but by the time he came to write the story, he understood that God had taken down this barrier in the incarnation. Knowing more of the love of God, his heart and mind were changed and he could see something of the glory of God in Jesus' sexuality. Exploring this sub-theme in his Gospel, he invites all of us who read and hear his words deeper into the love of the God who took on human sexuality for our healing.

Given the incarnation, it was all but inevitable that Jesus would be gendered male or female. Jesus was male, and in him God experienced exactly what it means to have a male mind and a male body. In the way John plays with and develops ancient stories and motifs of both the sexual desire of men for women and the sexual desire of men for other men, he depicts Jesus as male. However, John presents Jesus' sexuality in a way that suggests Jesus relates to all humanity (male and female) in his incarnation and his sexuality. Jesus became 'flesh' (men and women) rather than 'man'. Theologically and spiritually, Jesus experienced *human* sexuality. John makes the point to underline the fact that Jesus can identify with all of us, male and female, in the frailty of our sexual desire.

John pictures Jesus as not only attracted to women but also attractive to women. When they find him alone with the Samaritan woman at the well, the disciples are beside themselves with embarrassment. Without sharing a word, the questions going around their heads suggest they have all reached the same conclusion: that Jesus is up to some sort of sexual mischief. They could not have reached this conclusion if they did not think Jesus was attracted to women. After resisting what she thought were his sexual overtures, the Samaritan woman opens herself up to the possibility of a relationship with him. She would not have done so if she did not think he was attracted to her – not least in an ancient world where people were all too familiar with men whose preference was strictly for other men. The fact that she warmed to Jesus and began to explore the possibility of getting together with him suggests also that she found him attractive. Her relationship history is no reason to assume that she would take up with a man she found unattractive. That she initially gave him the brush-off gives us every reason to suppose she was quite capable of putting attempted suitors in their place if she wanted. John suggests that Mary of Bethany found Jesus attractive too. He also hints that he had a soft spot for her.

Although John explores his own friendship with Jesus through the lens of an ancient homoerotic ideal, he strongly suggests that Jesus was not sexually attracted to men. Given his use of the symposium motif, John had every opportunity to portray Jesus as attracted to young men. He does not do this. Instead he desexualizes the motif, using it to describe both his relationship with Jesus and the relationship of Jesus to the Father. He depicts the Father and the Son sharing a passionate emotional and spiritual intimacy. In the glimpses of his friendship with Jesus, he suggests they shared a similarly passionate intimacy. They knew each other's minds. The relationship was also gritty. John took up looking after Jesus' widowed mother at his death on the cross. Their love was not sexual but they loved each other all the same.

John encapsulates that intimacy in an image of physical intimacy and conviviality: lying in Jesus' chest at dinner. There is an edge to this image. John breaks with the ancient cultural norms: he takes power and sexual gratification out of the homoerotic ideal, replacing them with self-sacrificial love. By promoting emotional and spiritual intimacy among men, John may find himself in conflict with modern male stereotypes. The physical intimacy he depicts between himself and Jesus may also be something some contemporary men might find awkward. This is probably the most counter-cultural aspect of John's exploration of Jesus and ancient sexuality. Within our highly sexualized cultures, enjoying and expressing that kind of soul kinship and intimate friendship comes across to many as repressed homosexuality. But for John, it seems, too many men experience repressed friendship. So he runs the risk of misunderstanding, and depicts his close friendship with Jesus unashamedly because he wants to encourage others to experience and share this intimate and life-giving love of God.

John spells out that this intimate divine love reaches down into the whole of our humanity, including our sexuality. He depicts Jesus entering the complexity and confusion of our sexuality with the healing touch of divine love. The Samaritan woman experiences this salvation in her sexual relationships. Her testimony speaks of how he has reached into whatever difficulties she has experienced in her sex life. The fact that she loses her shame and can now speak boldly about her past embodies the very salvation to which she bears witness. John uses the everyday human experience of men and women attracted to each other and getting together to tell the story of salvation and to show that the salvation he brings embraces our passion, romance and sexuality. Nor does he limit this exploration to what we today call heterosexual relationships. His use of the classical homoerotic ideal demonstrates as much. Nothing sexual is beyond the healing touch and intimate love of the Christ who calls us into a relationship of love with him and with others, in which we freely obey his commands because we love him.

John does something quite daring here. This kind of theology was possibly as likely to upset just about everybody in the first century AD as it is today. Jews and Christians would most likely not have rejoiced in the use of well-known homoerotic images to describe the love of God. Some would not have been at all happy with the depiction of God as experiencing sexual desire – let alone in the frailty of the average human being. Many contemporary Greeks and Romans, and others influenced by their cultures, would not have enjoyed the limitation of their sexual freedom implicit in obedience to Jesus' commands. Most likely some found the idea of giving up sexual privilege and power for the sake of somebody else's fulfilment quite bizarre.

But John is no longer afraid to say it as he sees it. Something has changed since that day by the well. I suspect John Chrysostom was right: John now knew the love of Jesus so profoundly that he was simply not afraid to say that the intimate love of God in Christ embraces all, no matter who they are, and calls them to holiness of life and love. Given the antipathy of early Christianity to the homoeroticism of the contemporary Greek and Roman world, the depiction of his relationship with Christ in *the* homoerotic image of the ancient world must have come as a bit of a shock to at least some of his Christian contemporaries. It must also have been open to misunderstanding – but John seems to have been so overwhelmed with the love of Christ that he will take whatever theological risk he must to enable people not simply to see or understand but to experience this intimate love of Jesus. John wants to share the love he has found in and with Jesus Christ with others.

God experienced his human sexuality in love. This love meets people where they are and respects all, even those who have lost both self-respect and others' respect on account of their personal history. This love brings self-acceptance through divine acceptance, and thereby brings healing. This love is unafraid to speak God's commands into our lives ('go and sin no more'), but there is an approachable holiness about it that attracts people. In this approachable holiness Jesus walks with his disciples, wanting to share more of his love but waiting until they – we – are ready. He puts aside his own sexual needs and desires in order to meet the needs of others. He offers more than spiritualized salvation. John has Jesus offer salvation which reaches into the very depths of our being and genuinely heals – even our sexuality.

I began with the question: 'how did God experience human sexuality?' I am more than aware that there is more to say about the sexuality of God incarnate, not least because we have not even begun to look at the other Gospels. However, I am beginning to appreciate how John saw the glory of God in all this. I also mentioned that I undertook this study of a minor theme in the Gospel of John as a man of faith, and it is with faith that I would like to end. Initial reactions to the book suggest that some may find its subject matter, arguments and conclusions controversial. This I fully accept. However, whether or not any particular reader finds this or that aspect of the book acceptable, all Christian readers must surely agree on its main thesis: that in the incarnation, God experienced human sexuality in the person of Jesus Christ *and that those of us who espouse Christian faith must take this seriously in both our thinking about the faith and our practice of it.* Not to do so is surely to deny the incarnation, and that equally surely would be heresy. My hope is that we seek prayerfully what it means for our own sexuality that God has taken on frail flesh and lived in holiness and love – and that, as a result, our spirituality and relationships will be enriched.

Notes

Introduction

1 For discussion of these texts, and not least of the fact that the Evangelists had sex in mind here, and not simply the joining of two people into a new family bond, see William Loader, *The Septuagint, Sexuality, and the New Testament: Case Studies on the Impact of the LXX in Philo and the New Testament* (Grand Rapids: Eerdmans, 2004), pp. 80–6.

2 For a very reasonable defence of the view that Jesus was most probably single, see John P. Meier, *A Marginal Jew: Rethinking the Historical Jesus. Volume 1. The Roots of the Problem and the Person*, ABRL (New York: Doubleday, 1991), pp. 332–45.

3 In Palestinian Judaism in the first century AD, it seems less likely that Jesus could have woken up with a husband next to him, despite occasional suggestions that he might have been gay – see e.g. Hugh Montefiore, 'Jesus, the Revelation of God', in *Christ for Us Today: Papers from the Fiftieth Annual Conference of Modern Churchmen, held at Somerville College Oxford, 24-28 July, 1967*, ed. Norman Pittenger (London: SCM Press, 1968), pp. 108–10 – because there was no institution of marriage between men (or between women). Contemporary Jewish attitudes towards homoerotic actions were almost universally negative and some preferred to believe such things did not happen in their communities. As the Sages put it in later times, 'Israel is not suspected to this'; *t. Qidd.* 5.2; see Michael L. Satlow, *Tasting the Dish: Rabbinic Rhetorics of Sexuality*, BJS 303 (Atlanta: Scholars Press, 1995), p. 209. For a very thorough survey of Jewish attitudes towards homosexuality in this period, see the relevant sections in the works of William Loader, *Enoch, Levi and Jubilees on Sexuality: Attitudes towards Sexuality in the Early Enoch Literature, the Aramaic Levi Documents, and the Book of Jubilees*, Attitudes towards Sexuality in Judaism and Christianity in the Hellenistic Greco-Roman Era (Grand Rapids: Eerdmans, 2007); *The Dead Sea Scrolls on Sexuality: Attitudes towards Sexuality in Sectarian and Related Literature at Qumran*, Attitudes towards Sexuality in Judaism and Christianity in the Hellenistic Greco-Roman Era (Grand Rapids: Eerdmans, 2009); *The Pseudepigrapha on Sexuality: Attitudes towards Sexuality in Apocalypses, Testaments, Legends, Wisdom, and Related Literatures*, Attitudes towards Sexuality in Judaism and Christianity in the Hellenistic Greco-Roman Era (Grand Rapids: Eerdmans, 2011); *Philo, Josephus, and the Testaments on Sexuality: Attitudes towards Sexuality in the Writings of Philo and Josephus and in the Testaments of the Twelve Patriarchs*, Attitudes towards

Sexuality in Judaism and Christianity in the Hellenistic Greco-Roman Era (Grand Rapids: Eerdmans, 2011).

4 For example, D. H. Lawrence, *The Escaped Cock* (Isle of Skye: Aquila, 1982); Terrence McNally, *Corpus Christi* (New York: Grove Press, 1998); and most famously Nikos Kazantzakis, *The Last Temptation of Christ*, trans. P. A. Bien (New York: Simon & Schuster, 1960). For an exploration of the sexuality of Jesus in art, see Leo Steinberg, *The Sexuality of Christ in Renaissance Art and in Modern Oblivion*, 2nd edn (Chicago: University of Chicago Press, 1996).

5 William E. Phipps, *Was Jesus Married? The Distortion of Sexuality in the Christian Tradition* (New York: Harper & Row, 1970). See also William E. Phipps, *The Sexuality of Jesus: Theological and Literary Perspectives* (New York: Harper & Row, 1973); *The Sexuality of Jesus* (Cleveland, OH: Pilgrim Press, 1996). For a very fair appreciation and critique of his arguments, see Meier, *Roots of the Problem*, pp. 332–45.

6 E.g. E. P. Sanders, *Jesus and Judaism* (London: SCM Press, 1985); John Dominic Crossan, *The Historical Jesus: The Life of a Mediterranean Jewish Peasant* (Edinburgh: T&T Clark, 1991); N. T. Wright, *Christian Origins and the Question of God. Vol. 1. Jesus and the Victory of God* (London: SPCK, 1996); Dale C. Allison, *Jesus of Nazareth: Millenarian Prophet* (Minneapolis: Fortress, 1998) and *Constructing Jesus: Memory, Imagination and History* (London: SPCK, 2010); James D. G. Dunn, *Christianity in the Making. Vol.1. Jesus Remembered* (Grand Rapids: Eerdmans, 2003); Maurice Casey, *Jesus of Nazareth: An Independent Historian's Account of His Life and Teaching* (London: T&T Clark, 2010). The same is true of the four volumes of John Paul Meier's *A Marginal Jew*, ABRL (New York: Doubleday, 1991–2009).

7 Morton Smith, *Clement of Alexandria and the Secret Gospel of Mark* (Cambridge, MA: Harvard University Press, 1973), p. 185.

8 Karen L. King, 'Jesus said to them, "My wife . . .": A New Coptic Papyrus Fragment', *HTR* 107 (2014), p. 133.

9 On the *Secret Gospel of Mark* as a modern creation, see Stephen C. Carlson, *The Gospel Hoax: Morton Smith's Invention of Secret Mark* (Waco, TX: Baylor University Press, 2005); Peter Jeffery, *The Secret Gospel of Mark Unveiled: Imagined Rituals of Sex, Death and Madness in a Biblical Forgery* (New Haven: Yale University Press, 2007). On the *Gospel of Jesus' Wife* as a forgery, see Leo Depuydt, 'The Alleged *Gospel of Jesus' Wife*: Assessment and Evaluation of Authenticity', *HTR* 107 (2014), pp. 172–89; Hershel Shanks, 'The Saga of "The Gospel of Jesus' Wife",' *BAR* 41.3 (2015), pp. 54–9.

10 Dale B. Martin, 'Sex and the Single Saviour', in *Sex and the Single Saviour: Gender and Sexuality in Biblical Interpretation* (Louisville: Westminster John Knox, 2006), pp. 91, 94.

11 Martin, 'Single Saviour', pp. 100–2, although for all the openness of his 'nonfoundational hermeneutical world' he still seems to presuppose the importance of critical methodologies and critical readings of texts.

12 Preached at the Conference of Anglican and Ecumenical Institutes of Theological Training in the UK. I dare not say which year or who hosted – let alone who preached. The facial expressions of one Old Testament scholar in the congregation were, however, entertainingly memorable.

13 See e.g. the cautionary comments of Phyllis Trible, *God and the Rhetoric of Sexuality* (London: SCM Press, 1978), p. 202. Similarly, Janeth Norfleete Day, *The Woman at the Well: Interpretation of John 4:1–42 in Retrospect and Prospect*, BibInt 61 (Leiden: Brill, 2002), p. 149.

14 E.g. Lyle Eslinger, 'The Wooing of the Woman at the Well', in *The Gospel of John as Literature: An Anthology of Twentieth-Century Perspectives*, ed. Mark W. G. Stibbe (Leiden: Brill, 1993), pp. 165–82; and on the beloved disciple, Sjef van Tilborg, *Imaginative Love in John*, BibInt 2 (Leiden: Brill, 1993).

15 So e.g. R. Alan Culpepper, *Anatomy of the Fourth Gospel: A Study in Literary Design*, FF (Philadelphia: Fortress, 1983); Jeffrey Lloyd Staley, *The Print's First Kiss: A Rhetorical Investigation of the Implied Reader in the Fourth Gospel*, SBLDS 82 (Atlanta: Scholars Press, 1988).

16 Culpepper, *Anatomy*, pp. 151, 233.

17 For a defence of this view (with references to relevant patristic texts), see D. A. Carson, *The Gospel according to John*, Pillar New Testament Commentary (Eerdmans: Grand Rapids, 1991), pp. 68–87. For authorship by disciples of John on the basis of his testimony, see e.g. Rudolph Schnackenburg, *The Gospel according to John, volume 1: Introduction and Commentary on Chapters 1–4*, trans. Kevin Smyth, HThKNT (New York: Herder, 1968), pp. 75–104; Craig S. Keener, *The Gospel of John: A Commentary*, 2 vols (Peabody, MA: Hendrickson, 2003), pp. 82–115. For something closer to the majority perspective, see J. Ramsey Michaels, *The Gospel of John*, NICNT (Grand Rapids: Eerdmans, 2010), pp. 5–24, 37–8. Those who disagree with my assumptions are free to reframe any insights I might offer within the framework of the more commonly held view that John was written late in the first century AD by an otherwise unidentified Christian author.

18 Hence I cannot approach John as pure narrative. If we only read John as a narrative which contains all the information necessary for its interpretation, then the implied author clearly wants to frustrate the implied readers by pointing out that they can only express their love for Jesus by obeying his commands at the same time as withholding knowledge of his commands from them. This seems an unnecessary reading and out of keeping with the relationships of love which, according to the Gospel, the Father and Son wish to establish with all people. It makes

more sense to assume that everybody in John's audience already knew what Jesus' commands were.

19 For brief statements of arguments used by many modern scholars against the originality of chapter 21, see C. K. Barrett, *The Gospel According to St John: An Introduction with Commentary and Notes on the Greek Text*, 2nd edn (London: SPCK, 1978), pp. 567, 576–7; Rudolph Schnackenburg, *The Gospel According to John, volume 3: Commentary on Chapters 13–21*, trans. David Smith and G. A. Kon, HThKNT (New York: Crossroad, 1982), pp. 341–51; Ernst Haenchen, *John 2: A Commentary on the Gospel of John Chapters 7–21*, trans. Robert W. Funk, Hermeneia (Philadelphia: Fortress, 1984), pp. 229–30. For a recent short statement in favour of reading John canonically (i.e. including chapter 21), see Michaels, *John*, pp. 1020–4.

20 Danna Nolan Fewell and Gary A. Phillips in 'Drawn to Excess, or Reading Beyond Betrothal', *Semeia* 77 (1997), pp. 23–58, offer a stark warning on this score in their critique of betrothal narrative readings of John 4. For an irenic if brief response, see Jo-Ann A. Brant, 'Hammering Out a Response from One Mennonite's Perspective', *Semeia* 77 (1997), pp. 285–90.

1 Asking the question

1 Schnackenburg (*John 1–4*, p. 443) argues that the second question must be '*what* are you talking about with her?' rather than '*why* are you talking with her?' because the Greek word *ti* is used in both questions, and since they are in parallel the suggestion is that *ti* must mean the same in both. However, *ti* occurs in a (parallel) question and statement in John 18.21 in which it means 'why?' in the question and 'what' in the statement, as Schnackenburg (*John 13–21*, p. 228) recognizes. So parallel usage in phrases even in the same verse is no guarantee of the same meaning. Given that the disciples are questioning Jesus' motives in the question 'What are you after?', it makes most sense to translate the parallel question '*why* are you talking with her?' as this gets to the heart of the matter, Jesus' motives.

2 Similarly, Calum M. Carmichael, 'Marriage and the Samaritan Woman', *NTS* 26 (1980), p. 335.

3 Between them, commentators who remark on Jesus not talking to a woman draw attention to the following texts by way of explanation: Sir. 9.1–9; *m. 'Abot* 1.5; *m. Sot.* 3.4; *b. 'Erub.* 53b; *b. Qidd.* 70a; *'Abot R. Nat.* 2.1d; and more generally the book of Proverbs. See e.g. J. H. Bernard, *A Critical and Exegetical Commentary on the Gospel According to St. John*, 2 vols, ICC (London: T&T Clark, 1928), p. 152; E. C. Hoskyns, *The Fourth Gospel*, ed. Francis Noel Davey, 2nd edn (London: Faber and Faber, 1947), p. 245; Wilbert F. Howard and Arthur John Gossip,

The Gospel According to St. John, IB 12 (Nashville: Abingdon, 1952), pp. 529–30; William Hendriksen, *The Gospel of John* (London: Banner of Truth Trust, 1954), p. 170; Raymond E. Brown, *The Gospel according to John 1–12*, AB 29 (New York: Doubleday, 1966), p. 173; John Marsh, *Saint John*, PNTC (London: Penguin, 1968), p. 221; J. N. Sanders and B. A. Mastin, *The Gospel According to John*, BNTC (London: Black, 1968), pp. 141, 149; Schnackenburg, *John 1–4*, pp. 442–3; Rudolph Bultmann, *The Gospel of John: A Commentary*, trans. G. R. Beasley-Murray (Oxford: Blackwell, 1971), p. 193; Barnabas Lindars, *The Gospel of John*, NCB (London: Oliphants, 1972), p. 193; Birger Olsson, *Structure and Meaning in the Fourth Gospel: A Text-Linguistic Analysis of John 2:1-11 and 4:1-42*, ConBNT 6 (Lund: Gleerup, 1974), p. 156; Barrett, *St John*, p. 240; Lesslie Newbigin, *The Light Has Come: An Exposition of the Fourth Gospel* (Grand Rapids: Eerdmans, 1982), p. 55; F. F. Bruce, *The Gospel of John: Introduction, Exposition and Notes* (Grand Rapids: Eerdmans, 1983), p. 112; Ernst Haenchen, *John 1: A Commentary on the Gospel of John Chapters 1–6*, trans. Robert W. Funk, Hermeneia (Philadelphia: Fortress, 1984), p. 224; Teresa Okure, *The Johannine Approach to Mission: A Contextual Study of John 4:1-42*, WUNT 31 (Tübingen: J. C. B. Mohr, 1988), p. 133; Carson, *John*, p. 227; J. Eugene Botha, *Jesus and the Samaritan Woman: A Speech Acts Reading of John 4:1-42*, NovTSup 65 (Leiden: Brill, 1991), p. 160; Charles H. Talbert, *Reading John: A Literary and Theological Commentary on the Fourth Gospel and Johannine Epistles*, Reading the New Testament Series (London: SPCK, 1992), p. 112; Thomas L. Brodie, *The Gospel According to John: A Literary and Theological Commentary* (Oxford: Oxford University Press, 1993), p. 224; Leon Morris, *The Gospel according to John*, rev. edn, NICNT (Grand Rapids: Eerdmans, 1995), pp. 242–3; Gail R. O'Day, *The Gospel of John*, NIB 9 (Nashville: Abingdon, 1995), p. 565; Bruce J. Malina and Richard L. Rohrbaugh, *Social-Science Commentary on the Gospel of John* (Minneapolis: Fortress, 1998), pp. 100–1, 105 ; G. R. Beasley-Murray, *John*, 2nd edn, WBC 36 (Nashville: Nelson, 1999), p. 62; Francis J. Moloney, *The Gospel of John*, SP 4 (Collegeville, MN: Liturgical Press, 1998), p. 134; Colleen M. Conway, *Men and Women in the Fourth Gospel: Gender and Johannine Characterization*, SBLDS 167 (Atlanta: Society of Biblical Literature, 1999), p. 111; Gary M. Burge, *John*, NIV Application Commentary (Grand Rapids: Zondervan, 2000), p. 155; Keener, *John*, pp. 596–7; Andreas J. Köstenberger, *John*, BECNT (Grand Rapids: Baker Academic, 2004), pp. 158–9; Herman C. Waetjen, *The Gospel of the Beloved Disciple: A Work in Two Editions* (London: T&T Clark, 2005), p. 176; Andrew T. Lincoln, *The Gospel according to St John*, BNTC (London: Continuum, 2005), p. 178; John F. McHugh, *A Critical and Exegetical Commentary on John 1–4*, ICC (London: T&T Clark, 2009), p. 289; Urban C. von Wahlde, *The Gospel and Letters of*

John, volume 2: Commentary on the Gospel of John, ECC (Grand Rapids: Eerdmans, 2010), pp. 186–7; Michaels, *John*, pp. 257–8; Frederick Dale Bruner, *The Gospel of John: A Commentary* (Grand Rapids: Eerdmans, 2012), p. 279. Luise Schottroff, 'The Samaritan Woman and the Notion of Sexuality in the Fourth Gospel', in *'What Is John?' Volume II: Literary and Social Readings of the Fourth Gospel*, ed. Fernando F. Segovia, SBL Symposium Series 7 (Atlanta: Scholars Press, 1998), p. 166, suggests that we should not read sayings like *m. 'Abot* 1.5 as background here, as John 4 clearly recalls Genesis 24 where Abraham's servant talks to Rebekah. However, she presents no evidence to suggest that the pre-servers of the tradition found in *m. 'Abot* 1.5 would have thought it appropriate to emulate the behaviour of Abraham's servant. This is important, as contemporary authors did sometimes feel it necessary to explain the untoward behaviour of even their greatest forebears. Joseph married the daughter of Potiphera, priest of On, an Egyptian god and so an idol (Gen. 41.45) – an embarrassing fact which the author of *Joseph and Aseneth* thought needed explaining. Elisabeth Schüssler Fiorenza, in *In Memory of Her: A Feminist Theological Reconstruction of Christian Origins* (London: SCM Press, 1983), p. 326, suggests that the disciples are shocked 'that Jesus converses and reveals himself to a woman' and stay silent so as not to question his egalitarian agenda. Given that Peter does question Jesus' washing his feet in John 13, this is most unlikely.

4 E.g. Bernard, *St John*, p. 152; Hoskyns, *Fourth Gospel*, pp. 245–6; Howard and Gossip, *St. John*, p. 530; Hendriksen, *John*, p. 170; Brown, *John 1–12*, p. 173; Marsh, *Saint John*, p. 221; Sanders and Mastin, *John*, p. 149; Schnackenburg, *John 1–4*, pp. 442–3; Bultmann, *John*, p. 193; Lindars, *John*, p. 193; Olsson, *Structure*, p. 156; Barrett, *St John*, p. 240; Merrill C. Tenney, *The Gospel of John*, Expositor's Bible Commentary (London: Pickering & Inglis, 1981), p. 57; Newbigin, *Fourth Gospel*, p. 55; Culpepper, *Anatomy*, p. 116; Haenchen, *John 1*, p. 224; Gerard Sloyan, *John*, Interpretation (Louisville: Westminster John Knox, 1988), pp. 50–7; Botha, *Samaritan Woman*, p. 160; Talbert, *Reading John*, p. 112; Mark W. Stibbe, *John*, Readings (Sheffield: JSOT Press, 1993), pp. 62–70; Morris, *John*, pp. 242–3; O'Day, *John*, p. 568; Malina and Rohrbaugh, *John*, pp. 100–1, 105; Beasley-Murray, *John*, p. 62; Conway, *Men and Women*, p. 122; Burge, *John*, p. 155; Lincoln, *John*, p. 178; Waetjen, *Beloved Disciple*, p. 176; Mark Edwards, *John*, Blackwell Bible Commentaries (Oxford: Blackwell, 2004), p. 58; Jerome H. Neyrey, *The Gospel of John*, NCBC (Cambridge: Cambridge University Press, 2007), pp. 95–7; McHugh, *John 1–4*, p. 289; von Wahlde, *Gospel of John*, pp. 186–7; Bruner, *John*, p. 279.

5 For one such cryptic statement, see e.g. Jo-Ann A. Brant, *John*, Paideia (Grand Rapids: Baker Academic, 2011), p. 87, who says that 'what the disciples witnessed is unspeakably shameful' without explaining why.

6 So Bruce Milne, *The Message of John,* BST (Leicester: Inter-Varsity Press, 1993), p. 86.

7 Schottroff, 'Notion of Sexuality', p. 167.

8 Bruce, *John,* p. 112; Köstenberger, *John,* p. 159.

9 Carson, *John,* p. 227. John Bligh, 'Jesus in Samaria', *HeyJ* 3 (1962), p. 336, suggests on the basis of the disciples' reaction in v. 27 that the woman stood before Jesus 'wanting, perhaps only half-consciously, marriage'. Much as I think she did by v. 15, the disciples' questions are addressed to Jesus and not the woman.

10 Some early Greek texts (codex Sinaiticus and codex Bezae) actually spell out that the disciples were addressing their unspoken questions to Jesus by adding the Greek word *autō* ('to him'). None add the Greek for 'to her' (*autē*). So Michaels, *John,* p. 258 n. 101. Olsson (*Structure,* p. 157) argues similarly that context demands both questions are directed towards Jesus. So also Okure, *Mission,* p. 134.

11 Keener, *John,* p. 621. Similarly, Tenney, *John,* p. 57.

12 Moloney, *John,* p. 134. Similarly, Okure, *Mission,* p. 134. Brodie (*John,* p. 224) suggests that the disciples perceive the 'whiff of scandal'. Similarly, William Loader, *Sexuality and the Jesus Tradition* (Grand Rapids: Eerdmans, 2005), pp. 40–1. F. Scott Spencer, 'Feminist Criticism', in *Hearing the New Testament: Strategies for Interpretation,* ed. Joel B. Green, 2nd edn (Grand Rapids: Eerdmans, 2010), pp. 314–15, all but suggests the same thing.

13 The similarities between Proverbs and Ben Sira are probably due to Ben Sira drawing on Proverbs 7. See Patrick W. Skehan and Alexander A. di Lella, *The Wisdom of Ben Sira,* AB 39 (New York: Doubleday, 1987), pp. 218–19.

14 George Foot Moore, *Judaism in the First Centuries of the Christian Era: The Age of the Tannaim, volume 2* (Cambridge, MA: Harvard University Press, 1927), p. 269. Moore cites various passages in support of this view and, along with Strack-Billberbeck, *Kommentar zum Neuen Testament aus Talmud und Midrasch,* 6 vols (Munich: Beck, 1922–1961), is one of the two sources generally used by commentators to find their rabbinic texts explaining why rabbis ought not to talk to women.

15 So I cannot agree with Adele Reinhartz' comment that 'allusions to the biblical betrothal type scene draw the reader's attention to the gendered identity of the earthy (*sic*) Jesus as a man, only to undo it yet again', 'Gospel of John', in *Searching the Scriptures, Volume Two: A Feminist Commentary,* ed. Elisabeth Schüssler Fiorenza (London: SCM, 1995), p. 572.

16 Similarly, Botha, *Samaritan Woman,* p. 161, who notes that if the disciples' motivation for silence had been reverence for the master, then one wonders why John mentions it now. He insists that John's comments on the disciples' thoughts require explanation. John does this precisely

to invite the audience into the disciples' questions and ask about Jesus' sexuality, as argued above.

17 On ancient Greek and Roman sexuality, see particularly Eva Cantarella, *Bisexuality in the Ancient World*, trans. Cormac Ó Cuilleanáin, 2nd edn (New Haven: Yale University Press, 2002). See also Kenneth J. Dover, *Greek Homosexuality*, rev. edn (Cambridge, MA: Harvard University Press, 1989); David M. Halperin, *One Hundred Years of Homosexuality and Other Essays on Greek Love*, New Ancient World (London: Routledge, 1990).

18 It will not be possible for those who do not accept that this Gospel was written by John the Apostle to accept the explanation given above for John's inability to avoid the question of the sexuality of Jesus. However, it should still be more than possible to follow the general lines of my perspective in reading John. The so-called Fourth Gospel was written in Greek, and therefore for Greek speakers, in some part of the Roman empire which was infused with Greek and Roman culture. The subculture of the public baths and the Greek gymnasium was a prevalent element of the culture of the empire. Whoever wrote this Gospel wrote it within that culture and for people who were familiar with that culture. Almost inevitably he or she wrote the Gospel, and the audience read or heard it, with that culture in mind, and so would almost certainly draw connections between Jesus' incarnation and his sexuality.

19 So e.g. Bultmann, *John*, pp. 697–9; Barrett, *St John*, p. 575; Brown, *John 1–12*, p. viii; Bruce, *John*, pp. 395–6; Brodie, *John*, pp. 571–2; Brant, *John*, p. 11; Bruner, *John*, pp. 1198–9. I offer no comment here on whether the Gospel is designed to bring people to faith in Christ (e.g. Carson, *John*, pp. 87–95, 661–3) or to confirm their faith in Christ (e.g. Brown, *John 1–12*, p. viii) or both (e.g. Barrett, *St John*, p. 26) as this does not alter my main point that exploring the sexuality of Jesus is not its chief purpose. For similar reasons, I take no issue with the view that an original Gospel including chapter 21 might soften the case for John 20.30–31 being the 'definitive statement of purpose for the gospel as a whole' (Michaels, *John*, p. 1024) or that the exact nature of the belief John wrote to encourage changed in the various editions which lie behind the present text (von Wahlde, *Gospel of John*, pp. 873–7).

20 In line with ancient tradition (Irenaeus, *Against Heresies* 3.16.5, 8; Dionysius of Alexandria in Eusebius, *Ecclesiastical History* 7.25.6; Tertullian, *Against Praxeas* 15; *Antidote for the Scorpion's Sting* 12), I read 1 John as also written by John the Apostle. See also e.g. Colin G. Kruse, *The Letters of John*, Pillar New Testament Commentary (Grand Rapids: Eerdmans, 2000), pp. 9–14; Robert W. Yarborough, *1–3 John*, BECNT (Grand Rapids: Baker Academic, 2008), pp. 5–25. Many scholars, e.g. Georg Strecker, *The Johannine Letters: A Commentary on 1, 2, and 3 John*, trans. Linda M. Maloney, Hermeneia (Minneapolis: Fortress,

1996), pp. xxxv–xlii; John Painter, *1, 2, and 3 John*, SP 18 (Collegeville, MN: Liturgical Press, 2002), pp. 44–51 do not ascribe authorship of this epistle to anyone in particular, preferring an unstated author in the putative Johannine circle of churches.

2 Word become flesh

1 For discussions of the various possibilities for interpreting the 'Word', see Brown, *John 1–12*, pp. 519–24; Schnackenburg, *John 1–4*, pp. 481–93; McHugh, *John 1–4*, pp. 7–9, 91–6.

2 John states that 'the Word was God', or in Greek *theos ēn ho logos* (1.1). The correct translation of this phrase has been much disputed. Because there is no equivalent to 'the' before the word 'god' in Greek, some have translated the phrase 'and divine was the Logos', e.g. Haenchen (*John 1*, p. 108, citing in evidence Origen, *Commentary on the Gospel of John* 2.2.13–15. If this had been John's meaning he would much more likely have written *theios ēn ho logos*, as *theios* is the normal Greek word for divine (Carson, *John*, p. 117). So it is unlikely that John was saying the Word was divine rather than God. The fact that John did not write *ho theos* leaves open the question of whether he could have meant that the Word was one god among others rather than the one true God, as the word *theos* on its own would normally be translated 'a god'. The order in which John places the words *theos ēn ho logos* counts against this suggestion. Where predicate nouns like *theos* ('God') have no article like *ho* ('the'), they should still be understood as specific (e.g. Schnackenburg, *John 1–4*, pp. 234–5; see also the article of E. C. Colwell, 'A Definite Rule for the Use of the Article in the Greek New Testament', *JBL* 52 (1933), pp. 12–21. So when he claims that the Word was God, John intends the reader to identify the Word with the one true God of Israel. John has a very good reason for not using the article *ho*. If he had done, grammatically he would have stated that the Word alone was God and that no other was God (Barrett, *St John*, p. 156). This would have been a flat contradiction of what he says twice elsewhere in the same opening statement, that the Word was with God. This implies that God and the Word are not identical but have distinct identities. What is more, the ending of the prologue makes it quite clear that John is happy to use *theos* without the article to refer to the one true God of Israel. He writes 'nobody has seen God', or in Greek *theon oudeis heōraken pōpote* (1.18). Again, *theos* occurs without the article. Within the ancient world, it would be absurd to claim that nobody had ever seen a god, as Greek and Roman myths contain many stories of gods appearing to human beings, particularly heroes. The idea is a peculiarly Jewish one, stemming from God's words to Moses that nobody can see God and live (Exod. 33.20). So, in making the statement that no one has seen

God, John is thinking of this story about God speaking to Moses and is using the word *theon* without the article to refer to the one true God of Israel. John wants to identify the Word with the one true God of Israel. However, he does not wish to suggest that they are exactly identical.

3 So e.g. Barrett, *St John*, p. 151. The LXX (or Septuagint) was the first translation of the Old Testament, originally written in Hebrew and then translated into Greek.

4 Barrett (*St John*, p. 151) believes that probably the words *en archē* also recall Proverbs 8.22–31.

5 I use the term 'Second Temple Judaism' as convenient shorthand for the culture of Judaism in the period from 500 BC to around AD 200. I recognize the shortcomings of the term, not least that Second Temple Judaism was varied rather than monolithic and different groups within it disagreed over many issues. However, the term is useful for referring to Judaism in this period and to the common beliefs of Jews, for example that there was only one God – although see, for example, Peter Hayman, 'Monotheism – A Misused Word in Jewish Studies?' *JJS* 42 (1991), pp. 1–15. However, very few scholars would agree with him that Judaism was not fundamentally monotheistic in this period.

6 For the date of the Wisdom of Solomon, see David Winston, *The Wisdom of Solomon*, AB 43 (New York: Doubleday, 1979), pp. 20–5. For a brief description of Wisdom herself, see Winston, *Wisdom*, pp. 42–3.

7 For the date of Sirach, see Skehan and di Lella, *Sirach*, pp. 8–16.

8 Skehan and Di Lella, *Sirach*, p. 333.

9 Brown, *John 1–12*, p. 17; Köstenberger, *John*, pp. 49–50; von Wahlde, *Gospel of John*, p. 16; Francis J. Moloney, *Love in the Gospel of John: An Exegetical, Theological, and Literary Study* (Grand Rapids: Baker Academic, 2013), p. 110 n. 25.

10 E.g. Lindars, *John*, p. 99; Bruce, *John*, p. 45. Other suggestions have been made but do not have the same support from the Gospel itself. Brant (*John*, pp. 36–7) suggests the image of a mother or nurse with a child, on the basis that the same words for 'in the breast of' (Greek *eis ton kolpon*) are found in Num. 11.12 LXX and Ruth 4.16 LXX to refer to mothers and nurses carrying children at their breasts. Lindars (*John*, p. 99) and others (Bruce, *John*, p. 45; von Wahlde, *Gospel of John*, p. 16) note that the same words are used of Lazarus lying in Abraham's bosom (Luke 16.22). The same words are used of the sexual intercourse of Abram and Hagar (Gen. 16.5 LXX). Lindars (*John*, p. 99) notes a similar usage in Deut. 13.7 LXX, although this text does not use exactly the same words.

11 Brown, *John 1–12*, p. 218; Carson, *John*, p. 250; Lincoln, *John*, p. 202. For this image to work, it does not matter whether an ancient proverb lies behind Jesus' usage of it or not.

12 Translating the Hebrew text rather than the LXX.

13 For a brief overview of the *egō eimi* sayings in John, see Brown, *John 1–12*, pp. 533–8, or Rudolph Schnackenburg, *The Gospel According to John, volume 2: Commentary on Chapters 5–12*, trans. Cecily Hastings, Francis McDonagh, David Smith and Richard Foley, HThKNT (London: Burns and Oates, 1980), pp. 79–89.

14 Lincoln (*John*, p. 178) who also notes the similarity with Isa. 45.19 LXX, *egō eimi kurios lalōn* ('I am the Lord speaking . . .'). Similarly Köstenberger, *John*, p. 158.

15 So e.g. Keener, *John*, p. 673; Lincoln, *John*, pp. 218–19. For a full discussion of the mythological background to the text, see John Paul Heil, *Jesus Walking on the Sea: Meaning and Gospel Functions of Matt 14:22-33, Mark 6:45-52 and John 6:15b-21*, AnBib 87 (Rome: Biblical Institute Press, 1981), esp. pp. 37–56, 77–9. For a recent defence of reading these NT texts against the background of the divine warrior, see Andrew R. Angel, '*Crucifixus Vincens*: The "Son of God" as Divine Warrior in Matthew', *CBQ* 73 (2011), pp. 299–317.

16 For a brief introduction to the questions relating to the identification of 'the Jews' in John, see John Ashton, *Understanding the Fourth Gospel* (Oxford: Clarendon, 1991), pp. 131–7.

17 So e.g. Schnackenburg, *John 5–12*, p. 224; Lincoln, *John*, p. 276; Michaels, *John*, p. 536.

18 So e.g. Brown, *John 1–12*, p. 348; Schnackenburg, *John 5–12*, pp. 199–202; Lincoln, *John*, p. 269.

19 Technically the first phrase is grammatically genitive and means '*of* our Lord and God'. Many commentators hear this echo, e.g. Sanders and Mastin, *John*, pp. 437–8; Lindars, *John*, p. 615; Sloyan, *John*, p. 226; Moloney, *John*, pp. 539–40; Brodie, *John*, p. 571; Edwards, *John*, p. 198; Keener, *John*, pp. 1211–12; Köstenberger, *John*, p. 580; Lincoln, *John*, p. 503; Bruner, *John*, p. 1192. Grudgingly, Brown (*John 13–21*, p. 1047) recognizes the parallel. However, others do not, e.g. Schnackenburg, *John 13–21*, p. 333 (without giving a reason). Warren Carter in *John and Empire: Initial Explorations* (New York: T&T Clark, 2008), pp. 71–2, 195–6, downplays these parallels in order to argue that they cannot serve as evidence of the persecution of the Johannine community. While this may be thin evidence on which to posit persecution, the parallels of 'our/my Lord and God' remain quite stark despite the fact that Martial and Suetonius write in Latin and John writes in Greek.

20 For an overview of possible situations into which the Gospel was written (including Docetism), see Brown, *John 1–12*, pp. lxvii–lxxix. For a recent discussion of John as challenging docetic Christology, see Udo Schnelle, *Antidocetic Christology in the Gospel of John: An Investigation of the Place of the Fourth Gospel in the Johannine School*, trans. Linda M. Maloney (Minneapolis: Fortress, 1992).

21 The book of Tobit can be found in the Apocrypha, which can itself be found in many Bibles. For an introduction to the book of Tobit, see Joseph A. Fitzmyer, *Tobit*, CEJL (Berlin: de Gruyter, 2003), pp. 3–58.

22 So e.g. Barratt, *Saint John*, p. 231.

23 Andrew R. Angel, *Angels: Ancient Whispers of Another World* (Eugene, OR: Cascade, 2012), pp. 52–3; David Goodman, 'Do Angels Eat?' *JJS* 37 (1986), pp. 160–75.

24 Interestingly John does not leave this as evidence of Jesus' humanity. Rather he states that Jesus said this in fulfilment of Scripture (John 19.28). This seems to be in line with his portrait of Jesus being in control of his own betrayal and crucifixion, which underlines Jesus' teaching that he goes to his death voluntarily and not under compulsion (John 10.18). Similarly, e.g. Brown, *John 13–21*, pp. 907–9; Haenchen, *John 2*, p. 193.

25 Such commentators include Brown, *John 13–21*, p. 948; Schnackenburg, *John 13–21*, p. 289; Carson, *John*, p. 623. For an overview of modern speculation about the event's deeper significance, see Brown, *John 13–21*, pp. 948–52; and for patristic interpretation, see B. F. Westcott, *The Gospel According to Saint John* (London: John Murray, 1908), pp. 284–6.

26 For an overview of scholarly discussion, see Brendan Byrne, 'Beloved Disciple', *ABD* 1, pp. 658–61.

27 Note that the words imply conflict wherever they occur in the LXX: Judg. 11.12; 1 Kings 17.18; 2 Kings 3.13; 2 Chron. 35.21; 1 Esd. 1.24 (similarly Mark 5.7; Luke 8.28). This counts strongly against any benign interpretation which attempts to soften the impact of these words, e.g. Morris, *John*, p. 159; Köstenberger, *John*, pp. 94–5; Lincoln, *John*, p. 127; McHugh, *John*, p. 181; Michaels, *John*, pp. 143–5. Brown (*John 1–12*, p. 99) suggests that 2 Kings 3.13 and Hos. 14.8 use these words to signal disengagement but Elisha's retort in 2 Kings 13.4 instead suggests hostile dismissiveness, and Hos. 14.8 does not use these words at all. Schnackenburg (*John 1–4*, pp. 327–9) translates 'what would you have me do?' but as Carson (*John*, pp. 170–1) notes, this translation is 'groundless'. For simple acceptance of the harshness of the words, see Moloney, *John*, p. 71; Brant, *John*, pp. 56–7.

28 I can only disagree with the well-known view of Ernst Käsemann in *The Testament of Jesus: A Study in the Gospel of John in the Light of Chapter 17*, trans. Gerhard Krodel, NTL (London: SCM Press, 1968), pp. 4–26, esp. pp. 9–10, that John downplays the humanity of Jesus in favour of his divine glory. If this had been his aim, he would surely have included only the more noble and heroic aspects of Jesus' human actions (e.g. caring for his mother in his death) and eliminated the scenes where Jesus does things which seem beneath the divinity of the one true God of Israel (e.g. arguing with his mother and siblings), these being actions more suited to the com-

ical presentation of the pagan gods by an author like Ovid than to a serious presentation of the divine glory in human form.

29 E.g. Brown, *John 1–12*, p. 12; Marsh, *Saint John*, p. 107; Sanders and Mastin, *John*, p. 78; Lindars, *John*, p. 92; Carson, *John*, p. 126; Morris, *John*, p. 89; Moloney, *John*, p. 45; Beasley-Murray, *John*, p. 13; Köstenberger, *John*, pp. 39–40; Lincoln, *John*, p. 103; McHugh, *John 1–4*, p. 47; Michaels, *John*, p. 72.

30 John Calvin, *Commentary on the Gospel According to John. Volume 1*, trans. William Pringle, Calvin's Commentaries vol. 18 (Grand Rapids: Baker Books, 2009), p. 45.

31 Brant, *John*, p. 34.

32 See also, Bernard, *St John*, p. 18; Hoskyns, *Fourth Gospel*, p. 147; Brown, *John 1–12*, p. 12; Marsh, *Saint John*, p. 107; Sanders and Mastin, *John*, p. 78; Lindars, *John*, p. 72; Bruce, *John*, p. 39; Carson, *John*, p. 126; Morris, *John*, p. 89; Beasley-Murray, *John*, p. 13; Keener, *John*, p. 404; Köstenberger, *John*, p. 40; Lincoln, *John*, p. 103; McHugh, *John 1–4*, p. 47; Michaels, *John*, p. 72.

33 E.g. Morris, *John*, p. 89; Lincoln, *John*, p. 104; McHugh, *John 1–4*, p. 47; Michaels, *John*, p. 72.

34 Calvin, *John*, p. 45.

35 Lindars (*John*, pp. 93–4) and Barrett (*St John*, p. 164) see the philological connection, drawing the conclusion that *sarx* in v. 14 must be read in the light of *sarx* in v. 13 to refer to the frailty of the flesh, but completely miss the connotation of sexuality. Of all the commentators I have consulted on this point (Barrett, Beasley-Murray, Bernard, Brant, Brodie, Brown, Bruce, Bruner, Bultmann, Burge, Carson, Edwards, Haenchen, Hendriksen, Hoskyns, Howard and Gossip, Keener, Köstenberger, Lightfoot, Lindars, Marsh, McHugh, Michaels, Moloney, Morris, Newbigin, Neyrey, O'Day, Perkins, Reinhartz, Schnackenburg, Sloyan, Stibbe, Tenney, von Wahlde, Waetjen, Westcott) they are the only ones to note the connection.

36 So also Morris, *John*, p. 90; Köstenberger, *John*, p. 40.

37 Not all of these are villains as two of them (the Samaritan woman and the man born blind) come to believe (John 4.39; 9.38). So it is not even possible to argue that John avoided the term *anthrōpos* in John 1.14 on account of any connotations of lack of understanding or rejection of Jesus.

38 E.g. Brown, *John 1–12*, pp. 32–5; Schnackenburg, *John 1–4*, pp. 269–70; Carson, *John*, pp. 127–8; Morris, *John*, pp. 91–3; McHugh, *John 1–4*, pp. 55–8; Michaels, *John*, pp. 79–80.

39 On the glory of God being manifest in Jesus' life and works generally, see Moloney, *Love*, pp. 40–54, 92–6, 152–7.

40 Loader, *Philo, Josephus and Testaments*, pp. 321, 356.

41 Loader, *Enoch, Levi and Jubilees*, pp. 276–80.

42 Loader, *Dead Sea Scrolls*, pp. 10–28, 366.
43 See further Loader, *Enoch, Levi and Jubilees*, pp. 275–85; Loader, *Philo, Josephus and Testaments*, pp. 356–7; William Loader, *Making Sense of Sex: Attitudes towards Sexuality in Early Jewish and Christian Literature* (Grand Rapids: Eerdmans, 2013), pp. 75–104.
44 See further Andrew R. Angel, 'From Wild Men to Wise and Wicked Women: An Investigation into Male Heterosexuality in Second Temple Interpretations of the Ladies Wisdom and Folly', in *A Question of Sex? Gender and Difference in the Hebrew Bible and Beyond*, ed. Deborah W. Rooke, Hebrew Bible Monographs 14 (Sheffield: Sheffield Phoenix, 2007), pp. 148–9.
45 Roland E. Murphy, 'Wisdom and Eros in Proverbs 1–9', *CBQ* 50 (1988), pp. 600–3; Bruce K. Waltke, *The Book of Proverbs Chapters 1–15*, NICOT (Grand Rapids: Eerdmans, 2004), pp. 278–83, 369–70; Tremper Longman III, *Proverbs*, BCOTWP (Grand Rapids: Baker Academic, 2006), pp. 149–51, 187.
46 Loader, *Philo, Josephus and Testaments*, pp. 92–3. For a positive assessment of the place of pleasure in procreation in Philo, see Loader, *Philo, Josephus and Testaments*, pp. 56–60.
47 Angel, 'Wild Men', 149; Loader, *Philo, Josephus and Testaments*, pp. 70, 81–3.
48 The Greek here literally translates 'for I was resolved to do her', which standard translations like NRSV render 'for I was resolved to live according to wisdom'.
49 Angel, 'Wild Men', pp. 152–8; Ibolya Balla, 'Ben Sira/Sirach', in William Loader, *The Pseudepigrapha on Sexuality: Attitudes towards Sexuality in Apocalypses, Testaments, Legends, Wisdom, and Related Literature*, Attitudes towards Sexuality in Judaism and Christianity in the Hellenistic Greco-Roman Era (Grand Rapids: Eerdmans, 2011), pp. 395–6. See further J. A. Sanders, *The Psalms Scroll of Qumran Cave 11 (11QPsa)*, DJD 4 (Oxford: Clarendon, 1965), pp. 79–85; Takamitsu Muraoka, 'Sir. 51:13–20: An Erotic Hymn to Wisdom?' *JSJ* 10 (1979), pp. 166–78; Celia Deutsch, 'The Sirach 51 Acrostic: Confession and Exhortation', *ZAW* 94 (1982), pp. 400–9; and the non-erotic reading of Isaac Rabinowitz, 'The Qumran Hebrew Original of Ben Sira's Concluding Acrostic on Wisdom', *HUCA* 42 (1971), pp. 173–84.
50 Balla, 'Ben Sira', p. 396.
51 Admittedly only in the LXX, as 11Q5 XXI has no clear equivalent to Sir. 51.20b LXX. For the reference to ritual purity practices here, see Deutsch, 'Acrostic', p. 406.
52 Against e.g. Reinhartz ('Gospel', 565), who assumes that the Word is 'a nongendered entity' like God who became male for 'one relatively short moment in an ongoing, ungendered existence'. This misses the female gender of the figure of Wisdom throughout Jewish tradition.

53 The Greek words are *ho opisō mou erchomenos*. If this person were female,
John would need to have said *hē opisō mou erchomenē*. Translations
regularly use the words 'he' or 'him' in vv. 1–14 but the Greek words
in these verses may also be translated 'it'. The reason the Greek uses
the masculine *autos* is because *ho logos* (the Word) is masculine. As the
Word is not grammatically masculine in English, there is no reason to
translate 'he' or 'him'. Similarly, nothing in any of the verbs in vv. 1–14
indicates that the Word is male as opposed to grammatically masculine.
So they could also be translated with 'it'. Nor does the word *monogenēs*
('only begotten') which Luke uses of Jairus' daughter (Luke 8.42).

54 On flesh as a euphemism for penis, see Moshe Greenberg, *Ezekiel
1–20*, AB 22 (New Haven: Yale University Press, 1983), p. 283; Moshe
Greenberg, *Ezekiel 21–37*, AB 22A (New Haven: Yale University Press,
1997), p. 480.

55 For a general review of *sarx* in the LXX, see Eduard Schweizer and Friedrich
Baumgärtel, 'σάρξ, σαρκικός † σαρκινός', *TDNT* 7, pp. 105–10.

56 I would like to thank Maureen Marshall for drawing my attention to
this point.

3 A Samaritan bride and her Jewish groom

1 That is, much despised by their Second Temple Jewish neighbours.

2 For an exposition of the standard plot of the betrothal type scene, see
Robert Alter, *The Art of Biblical Narrative*, 2nd edn (New York: Basic
Books, 2011), pp. 61–78.

3 So e.g. Mary Margaret Pazdan, 'Nicodemus and the Samaritan
Woman: Contrasting Models of Discipleship', *BTB* 17 (1987), pp. 145–8;
Craig Koester, 'Hearing, Seeing and Believing in the Gospel of John',
Bib 70 (1989), pp. 333–6; Stibbe, *John*, p. 62; Winsome Munro, 'The
Pharisee and the Samaritan in John: Polar or Parallel?' *CBQ* 57 (1995),
pp. 710–28, esp. p. 711; Conway, *Men and Women*, p. 106; R. Alan Culpepper, *The Gospel and Letters of John*, Interpreting Biblical Texts (Nashville: Abingdon, 1998), p. 139; Neyrey, *John*, p. 88; McHugh, *John
1–4*, p. 217; Cornelis Bennema, *Encountering Jesus: Character Studies
in the Gospel of John* (Milton Keynes: Paternoster, 2009), pp. 75–93.

4 James H. Charlesworth, in *The Historical Jesus* (Nashville: Abingdon,
2008), p. 83, suggests that the marriage at Cana may have been Jesus'
own, but has not to date offered a full justification for his view.

5 So e.g. O'Day, *John*, p. 565; McHugh, *John 1–4*, pp. 191–4. For a
fuller statement of the theme, see Jocelyn McWhirter, *The Bridegroom
Messiah and the People of God: Marriage in the Fourth Gospel*, SNTSMS
138 (Cambridge: Cambridge University Press, 2006).

6 Similarly, e.g. Jerome H. Neyrey, 'Jacob Traditions and the Interpretation
of John 4:10-26', *CBQ* 41 (1979), p. 426; Staley, *First Kiss*, p. 93; Paul

D. Duke, *Irony in the Fourth Gospel* (Atlanta: John Knox, 1985), p. 101; Sandra Schneiders, *The Revelatory Text: Interpreting the New Testament as Sacred Scripture* (San Francisco: HarperSanFrancisco, 1991), pp. 186–99; Loader, *Jesus Tradition*, pp. 40–1.

7 Cf. Charlesworth, *Historical Jesus*, p. 83.

8 E.g. Carson, *John*, p. 169; Brant, *John*, p. 56.

9 Even if she is part of the wider family, as Neyrey (*John*, p. 67) suggests, she has received an invitation to the wedding (John 2.1–2), implying she is a guest, not the host.

10 So e.g. NRSV. The fact that elsewhere in the Bible these words are always spoken to an enemy (or putative enemy) counts against translating them 'what concern is that to you and to me?' Jesus does not draw a line between the situation on one side and his mother and himself on the other. Similarly, Olsson, *Structure*, pp. 36–9. Many commentators wish to soften the harshness of his address (e.g. Brown, *John 1–12*, p. 99; Schnackenburg, *John 1–4*, pp. 327–9; Morris, *John*, p. 159; Köstenberger, *John*, pp. 94–5; Lincoln, *John*, p. 127; McHugh, *John*, p. 181; Michaels, *John*, pp. 143–5. Refreshingly, others have conceded that Jesus uses this language to distance himself from his mother (e.g. Moloney, *John*, p. 71; Brant, *John*, p. 57).

11 J. Duncan M. Derrett, *Law in the New Testament* ((London: Darton, Longman & Todd, 1970), pp. 228–46), suggested that Jesus and his disciples turned up without the contribution of wine they should have made and that this lack of traditional courtesy lies behind his mother's determination to make him put things right. This would certainly heighten the comedy, but sadly nothing in the text supports the suggestion (so Barrett, *St John*, p. 191; Moloney, *John*, p. 71).

12 Brant (*John*, p. 58) interprets the humour similarly although she focuses on his maintaining his honour outwardly through staying silent rather than on what might have been going through his head. Michaels, *John*, p. 152, rightly points out that we can only wonder what his reaction was. However, I find his suggestion that the groom keeps silent and takes credit for the 'good wine' when the master of ceremonies has just insulted what was most likely the best wine he could afford a little short of the whole story. For this reason, I cannot agree with Malina and Rohrbaugh, *John*, p. 69 either when they claim that Jesus 'honors the bridegroom'. He saves his face publicly, perhaps, but not without cost to his self-esteem and so to his dignity and honour.

13 So e.g. Staley, *First Kiss*, pp. 89–90; McWhirter, *Bridegroom*, p. 49; McHugh, *John 1–4*, p. 193; Michaels, *John*, p. 152. Similarly, Olsson, *Structure*, p. 88.

14 John links the stories by use of the cognate words 'purification', Greek *katharismos* (John 2.6; 3.25), and 'decrease', Greek *elattousthai* (John 3.30) and 'the inferior [wine]', Greek *ton elassō* (John 2.10). These are

the only places in the Gospel where such cognate words appear. So, Brown, *John 1–12*, p. 153.

15 McHugh, *John 1–4*, p. 193.

16 John Chrysostom suggested that John the Baptist moves from figurative language to plain speech part way through the parable and so the 'voice of the bridegroom' should be understood to refer to the teaching of Jesus (*Homilies on St John* 29.3). Augustine seems to interpret the voice similarly (*Tractates on the Gospel of John* 13.12–16). They are unlikely to be correct, however. In these verses, John the Baptist clearly speaks in the first person when speaking of himself and in the third person when he speaks as best man within the metaphor. The best man hears the 'noise of the groom' and so the meaning of the *phōnē* must be sought within the metaphor.

17 Brown, *John 1–12*, p. 152. I use the term 'marriage attendant' rather than 'best man' as the rabbinic *shushbinin* (or 'marriage attendants') did not have the same role as 'best men' today; see Michael L. Satlow, *Jewish Marriage in Antiquity* (Princeton: Princeton University Press, 2001), p. 175.

18 Westcott, *John*, p. 60; Bernard, *St John*, p. 131; Brown, *John 1–12*, p. 152 possibly; Barrett, *St John*, p. 223 possibly.

19 Carmichael, 'Marriage', pp. 333–4. He cites in evidence Isa. 66.10, where 'rejoice greatly' unmistakably refers to rearing children. However, the suckling of infants is not the same as childbirth. The difference between the images does not permit the use of Isa. 66.10 as background for reading John 3.29. The Baptist uses marriage imagery (bride and groom rather than husband and wife), and so pictures the friend standing around at the marriage ceremony or some attendant ritual when he hears the voice of the groom and rejoices. The friend would hardly have stood around until the happy couple had progeny.

20 Schnackenburg, *John 1–4*, p. 416 (drawing on *b. Ketub.* 12a among other later texts); Barrett, *St John*, p. 223 possibly; Derrett, *Law*, p. 230; Beasley-Murray, *John*, p. 53; McHugh, *John 1–4*, p. 251.

21 Joachim Jeremias, 'νύμφη, νυμφίος', *TDNT* 4, pp. 1099–106, esp. p. 1101, using the same rabbinic texts. Following the general lines of this and the previous suggestion: Lindars, *John*, p. 167; Lincoln, *John*, p. 161; Michaels, *John*, p. 219.

22 Satlow, *Jewish Marriage*, pp. 162–80. Sjef van Tilborg, *Imaginative Love*, pp. 76–7, suggests that Hellenistic customs constitute a more likely cultural background than Jewish for John 3.29, as Greek weddings had only one bridegroom whereas Jewish weddings had two, and John only mentions one. Though interesting, this does not make the exact nature of the voice or noise of the groom any clearer. Nor does McWhirter's contention in *Bridegroom*, pp. 50–6, that the background is not the rabbinic role of the bridegroom or the Song of Solomon LXX but Jeremiah

LXX (Jer. 7.32–34; 16.9; 25.10; 33.10–11; Baruch 2.23). That the voices of bridegrooms are heard in these texts does not explain what they are doing or why.

23 Satlow, *Jewish Marriage*, p. 175.
24 For evidence of these elements of weddings in Second Temple Judaism, see Satlow, *Jewish Marriage*, pp. 168–80.
25 *b. Ketub.* 7b–8a.
26 On the many biblical allusions in this text and its sexual overtones, see Satlow, *Jewish Marriage*, pp. 53–66, 164.
27 William Loader, in *Sexuality in the New Testament: Understanding the Key Texts* (London: SPCK, 2010), p. 37, makes this suggestion – unless I seriously misconstrue his words 'ecstatic shout on consummating the marriage' and he means something more like Schnackenburg suggests!
28 Similarly, McHugh, *John 1–4*, p. 193.
29 Should John the Apostle or the author of the Fourth Gospel have made the saying up, the point still applies in modified form. None of Matthew, Mark or Luke chose to have John the Baptist or any other character in the narrative describe Jesus in quite such sexually intimate terms.
30 Following the many scholars who read this story as playing with either the betrothal narrative form or elements of a particular OT betrothal narrative – notably, Isaac and Rebekah (Gen. 29.1–20) – e.g. Bligh, 'Jesus', p. 332; Sanders and Mastin, *John*, pp. 140–1; Olsson, *Structure*, p. 172; Carmichael, 'Marriage', pp. 332–46; Culpepper, *Anatomy*, p. 136; Duke, *Irony*, p. 101; Staley, *First Kiss*, pp. 98–103; Brodie, *John*, pp. 217–19; Eslinger, 'Wooing', pp. 165–82; Stibbe, *John*, pp. 68–9; Reinhartz, 'Gospel', p. 572; Munro, 'Pharisee', p. 721; Brant, 'Husband Hunting', p. 211; Jean K. Kim, 'A Korean Feminist Reading of John 4:1-42', *Semeia* 78 (1997), p. 110; Schneiders, *Revelatory Text*, p. 187; Conway, *Men and Women*, pp. 108–9; Burge, *John*, p. 142; Keener, *John*, p. 586; Köstenberger, *John*, p. 148; Lincoln, *John*, p. 170; Loader, *Jesus Tradition*, p. 40; Waetjen, *Beloved Disciple*, p. 162; McWhirter, *Bridegroom*, p. 59; Neyrey, *John*, p. 91; Michael W. Martin, 'Betrothal Journey Narratives', *CBQ* 70 (2008), pp. 505–23; McHugh, *John 1–4*, p. 267; C. Clifton Black, 'Rhetorical Criticism', in *Hearing the New Testament: Strategies for Interpretation*, ed. Joel B. Green, 2nd edn (Grand Rapids: Eerdmans, 2010), p. 181; Kevin J. Vanhoozer, 'The Reader in New Testament Interpretation', in Green (ed.), *Hearing the New Testament*, p. 277; Spencer, 'Feminist Criticism', p. 308; Michaels, *John*, p. 237; von Wahlde, *Gospel of John*, p. 171 (ambivalently); Alter, *Biblical Narrative*, pp. 61–70. See also Moloney (*John*, p. 121) for influence of Jacob traditions but not betrothal narrative form. Gail R. O'Day in *Revelation in the Fourth Gospel: Narrative Mode and Theological Claim* ((Philadelphia: Fortress, 1986), pp. 131–2 n. 49)

argues that while John 4 may allude to betrothal narratives, it is not modelled on them because two key elements (the drawing of water and the betrothal) are absent. This argument misses the point. John deliberately has Jesus forego meeting bodily needs (food, water and sex) in order to develop his Christology, and the betrothal (and marriage) does take place in the conversion of the citizens of Sychar. In her commentary, O'Day (*John*, p. 565) accepts that John creatively reworks the betrothal narrative type. Okure (*Mission*, pp. 87–8) admits 'no real parallels' between OT betrothal narratives and John as it now stands. This is an unacceptable claim given that: (a) Jesus travels to a foreign land; (b) he meets a woman by a well; and (c) he asks for a drink. Her further protest that John radically reverses some of their key functions simply reasserts a central observation of most narrative critics of this text: that John develops the type for his own purposes. She suggests that Joshua 24 forms the best OT background to John 4 (Okure, *Mission*, p. 90). However: (a) the strongest link, Shechem, disappears with the preferred reading of Sychar in John 4.5; (b) the themes 'God as giver' and 'so worship God' are present thematically in many other covenant texts (e.g. Exod. 20.1–17; Deuteronomy) and creation texts (e.g. Gen. 1; Ps. 104). Even if Joshua 24 were in the background, this would not demonstrate that betrothal narratives are not also. Fewell and Phillips ('Beyond Betrothal', pp. 23–31) express strong ethical disapproval of, if not anger at, various betrothal narrative readings. However, they offer no critique of the formal evidence for betrothal narratives or for reading John 4 as one, and they proceed to read John 4 alongside Genesis 24 themselves. Conway (*Men and Women*, p. 108) also shows concern at using the betrothal type to inform a negative assessment of the woman's character but also sees the force of the argument for the type and recollection of Genesis 29. Andrew E. Arterbury in 'Breaking the Betrothal Bonds: Hospitality in John 4', *CBQ* 72 (2010), pp. 63–83 argues that the betrothal narrative form does not exist and that these stories are simply examples of ancient hospitality narratives. The chief difficulty with his argument is that he does not consider the possibility that betrothal narratives may be a subset of hospitality narratives or use hospitality narrative form. Such an explanation accounts for all his evidence and explains what his thesis does not: why some of these hospitality narratives follow a similar pattern which ends in betrothal and involves meeting at water sources. Furthermore, two of his key pieces of evidence for hospitality narratives (Homer, *Odyssey* 6.110–332; 15.403–54) involve finding husbands and women and so look more like betrothal than hospitality narratives. Rather, as Jo-Ann A. Brant notes in *Dialogue and Drama: Elements of Greek Tragedy in the Fourth Gospel* (Peabody, MA: Hendrickson, 2004), pp. 247–8, the dialogue is 'a comic treatment of

the [betrothal] type-scene that plays with the elements of marriage'
rather than slavishly imitating them.

31 We cannot read very much from the time of day. Some are tempted
to suggest that only suspect women would turn up at the well at such
an hour, e.g. Brant, 'Husband Hunting: Characterization and Narrative
Art in the Gospel of John', *BibInt* 4 (1996), pp. 212. However, Rachel
turned up at her well in broad daylight (Gen. 29.7) and she had impeccable credentials as a bride-to-be. Possibly John simply wants to recall
this betrothal narrative (so Eslinger, 'Wooing', p. 175) not least as he
makes multiple allusions to Jacob, e.g. vv. 5, 6, 12 (Lincoln, *John*, p.
172). Nor is it necessary to assume by using the Roman 'clock' that the
woman came to the well in the early evening (so Culpepper, *Anatomy*,
p. 219). Most commentators do not follow him in this and a Jewish
author writing a Jewish betrothal narrative set in Palestine about the
Jewish messiah seems more likely to use the Jewish 'clock', even if he
is writing for a religiously and culturally mixed audience in Hellenistic
Ephesus. Besides which, the evidence for Culpepper's suggestion is
questionable (see Carson, *John*, pp. 156–7). Nor is it necessary to identify the woman as a water bearer (so Schottroff, 'Notion of Sexuality',
pp. 165–6) to rescue her from slanders resulting from going to the well
at noon. Defences which have no basis in the text do not rehabilitate her
reputation effectively anyway.

32 Alter, *Biblical Narrative*, pp. 62–3; Staley, *First Kiss*, p. 100; Eslinger,
'Wooing', p. 167.

33 Alter, *Biblical Narrative*, pp. 61–70. On John 4.1–42, see Staley, *First
Kiss*, pp. 100–1. Black ('Rhetorical Criticism', pp. 181–2) suggests that
John plays with the betrothal narrative form similarly.

34 In the light of these similarities, I cannot agree with Lindars' assertion
(*John*, pp. 179–80) that despite the reminiscences of Gen. 24.10–27 and
29.1–12 'there is no hint of literary allusion'.

35 Similarly, Conway, *Men and Women*, pp. 111–12.

36 At least in the way in which some among the covenant people expected.
Arguably, Jesus is bringing back together the whole covenant people
by wooing back the lost ten tribes of northern Israel (so e.g. Waetjen,
Beloved Disciple, pp. 162–3; McHugh, *John 1–4*, p. 267).

37 As Botha (*Samaritan Woman*, p. 108) notes. This fact counts against
the possibility of drawing any conclusions from the comparative Jewish
material collated by Olsson, *Structure*, pp. 162–73, in which the well
was associated with God's saving work for his people, wisdom and the
law. In John 4, water from the woman's well needs replacing by Jesus'
living water, so the living water, not the well, is identified with God's
saving work and Jesus/wisdom/*logos*.

38 Eslinger, 'Wooing', pp. 168–9; Brant, 'Husband Hunting', p. 214. On
these images in the Hebrew text, see also Michael V. Fox, *Proverbs*

1–9, AB 18A (New York: Doubleday, 2000), pp. 199–202; Longman, *Proverbs*, p. 161.

39 Brant, 'Husband Hunting', p. 214. The Greek phrase *apostolai sou* renders the Hebrew *shelakhayikh*, which has been emended and interpreted variously as 'shoots', 'channel', 'branches', 'products' and even 'javelins'; see Marvin Pope, *Song of Songs*, AB 7C (New Haven: Yale University Press, 1977), pp. 490–1. Whatever the exact image, the meaning seems reasonably clear in that the beloved speaks of the charms of his beloved. On these images more generally in the Hebrew text, see Roland E. Murphy, *The Song of Songs*, Hermeneia (Minneapolis: Fortress, 1990), pp. 160–1; Richard S. Hess, *Song of Songs*, BCOTWP (Grand Rapids: Baker Academic, 2005), pp. 146–52.

40 Alter, *Biblical Narrative*, p. 62; Eslinger, 'Wooing', p. 170.

41 Similarly, Longman, *Proverbs*, p. 430; Michael V. Fox, *Proverbs 10–31*, AB 18B (New Haven: Yale University Press, 2009), p. 739.

42 For example, Rachel is introduced as a virgin whom no man had known (Gen. 24.16). She and the daughters of Midian are introduced as the daughters of their fathers, i.e. not yet married and 'belonging' to a husband.

43 Similarly, Botha, *Samaritan Woman*, pp. 105–12; Brant, 'Husband Hunting', pp. 212–13.

44 When Abraham's servant arrives in Nahor the daughters of the inhabitants are all coming out to the well to draw water, as is their custom in the evening (Gen. 24.11–13). Jacob reaches the well where he meets Rachel to find a number of shepherds already there (Gen. 29.3–4). When Moses arrives at the well in Midian the seven daughters of Jethro come to draw water (Exod. 2.16).

45 Carmichael ('Marriage', p. 336) argues that the Greek *dos moi piein* ('give me to drink') deliberately avoids using the word 'water' (Greek *hudōr*) so as to give Jesus' request a sexual connotation. Given that water in various forms carried a sexual connotation in Hebrew poetry (e.g. Prov. 5.15; Song of Sol. 4.15), this argument is not persuasive, as including the term could just as easily achieve the same effect. Within the context of a betrothal narrative type story the request is certainly ambiguous. The ambiguity is only resolved later on where John clearly intends the audience to hear the covenant marriage of the Lord God to the Samaritans. Alan Watson, in *Jesus and the Jews: The Pharisaic Tradition in John* (Athens, GA: University of Georgia Press, 2012), pp. 29–37, builds on Carmichael's suggestion, offering his own highly sexualized reading which differs from Carmichael's. He invites the reader to decide between them on the basis of plausibility (Watson, *Pharisaic Tradition*, pp. 51–2). His framework for reading the text, that the woman deliberately chooses to travel to this well to seduce men (Watson, *Pharisaic Tradition*, pp. 29–33) though plausible is not

compelling. She could equally have chosen the well because she wanted to avoid others or even because she rather liked the spot. Watson bases his reading on what the text does not say, which is more often than not a precarious procedure.

46 Similarly, Eslinger, 'Wooing', p. 176 n. 3; Conway, *Men and Women*, p. 113. It is precisely this emphasis which contradicts those like Robert Gordon Maccini, 'A Reassessment of the Woman at the Well in John 4 in the Light of the Samaritan Context', *JSNT* 53 (1994), pp. 38–9, who suggest that the disciples are shocked that Jesus, as a Jew, would talk to a Samaritan.

47 Some interpretations of the text (e.g. NRSV) read this as a comment of the narrator. The original Greek text had no punctuation and so does not indicate who is speaking – the woman or the narrator. I have opted for the woman (like e.g. Michaels, *John*, p. 229) as she is already speaking and these words make sense on her lips. Either way, there is nothing incompatible with my overall reading of this text.

48 So David Daube, 'Jesus and the Samaritan Woman: The Meaning of *sugchraomai*', *JBL* 69 (1950), pp. 137–47. So also e.g. Bligh, 'Jesus', p. 333; Brown, *John 1–12*, p. 170; Barrett, *St John*, p. 232; Carson, *John*, p. 218; Michaels, *John*, pp. 239–40. Carmichael ('Marriage', p. 336 n. 16) sees no reason not to assume a double meaning with sexual overtones.

49 BDAG 953–4; LSJ 1668.

50 Similarly, Eslinger ('Wooing', p. 177 n. 1) notes that *sugchraomai*, as an intensive form of *chraomai*, would refer to sexual intercourse – citing LSJ 2002 and arguing that the betrothal narrative context demands such a reading.

51 Similarly, Brant ('Husband Hunting', p. 213) although I do not read the woman's resistance as being on account of the contemporary Jewish attitude towards Samaritan women or wishing to conceal her past. If she thought that she should be considered a perpetual menstruant (m. Nid. 4.1), she would not have considered what she thought was his offer in vv. 14–15. If she had wanted to conceal her past, she surely would have made more of an effort. She tells the truth in v. 17 and comes clean immediately in v. 18. I suspect she is trying to protect herself.

52 Hence I read slightly differently from Eslinger ('Wooing', pp. 176–9), who believes that the narrator leads the audience to think that she flirts with Jesus. While I fully agree that double meanings underlie the conversation, I read her response to suggest that at least initially she tries to brush off what she reads as his flirtation.

53 Jesus uses similar words, 'the one talking to you' (Greek *ho lalōn soi*), also citing Isaiah (e.g. Isa. 52.6 LXX) in John 4.26 to make the same point that he is God who brings salvation to her. Similarly, O'Day, *Narrative Mode*, pp. 59–60.

54 McHugh, *John 1–4*, p. 269; cf. Friedrich Büchsel, 'δωρεά', *TDNT* 2, p. 167. Neyrey notices that there were later rabbinic traditions which speak of the well as a gift ('Jacob Traditions', pp. 423–4), so John might assume his readers would also hear Jesus' statement as suggesting his gift is better than the gift of the well.

55 The giving of gifts to lovers or would-be lovers was a commonplace motif in ancient Greek and Roman literature – e.g. Clinias' gift of a horse to his young lover (Achilles Tatius, *Leucippe and Clitophon* 1.7) or Tibullus' gifts to his mistress (Tibullus 2.4) or the miserable Naevolus (Juvenal, *Satires* 9) whose patron has stopped making him 'love' gifts – and so a Greek audience could very easily have heard this.

56 See also e.g. Gen. 26.19 LXX.

57 See also the ritual atonement of a house that had previously been the site of a leprous disease (Lev. 14.50–52 LXX); the testing of a woman accused of adultery (Num. 5.17 LXX); and the cleansing of people who have touched a dead body (Num. 19.17 LXX).

58 E.g. Black, 'Rhetorical Criticism', p. 178. On the life-giving nature of the waters of salvation in Zech. 14.8, see Carol L. Meyers and Eric M. Meyers, *Zechariah 9–14*, AB 25C (New York: Doubleday, 1993), pp. 434–5. On living waters as symbolic of salvation in Jer. 2.13, see William L. Holladay, *Jeremiah 1*, Hermeneia (Philadelphia: Fortress, 1986), p. 92.

59 On living water bearing sexual connotations here, see Murphy, *Song*, pp. 160–1; Hess, *Song*, pp. 150–2. For useful discussions of some of the connotations of 'living water', see Brown, *John 1–12*, pp. 178–80; Olsson, *Structure*, p. 213; Barrett, *St John*, pp. 233–4; McHugh, *John 1–4*, pp. 273–9. However, these discussions offer scant attention to Song 4.15 LXX and ignore the clear connotations of the erotic usage of these words in this context.

60 So Eslinger, 'Wooing', pp. 168–70; Brant, 'Husband Hunting', p. 214; Lincoln, *John*, pp. 173–4; Vanhoozer, 'Reader', p. 277. Watson (*Pharisaic Tradition*, p. 32) suggests that 'living water' could connote semen – 'what water could be more alive?' Beyond obvious responses like 'seas full of plankton' there lies the serious fact that the LXX never uses 'living water' in this way. Eslinger ('Wooing', p. 170) puts it nicely: 'literary devices such as euphemism and double entendre are suggestive, not explicit, and demand flexibility from the reader in reception of the suggestion.' Conway (*Men and Women*, p. 108) believes that the argument for 'drinking, water, wells, and fountains' carrying 'sexual undertones' is 'convincing' but relies too heavily on the reader to pick the undertones up. This does not make sense given her own assumption (*Men and Women*, pp. 109–10) that the reader will be aware of the cultural background of Jewish conflict with the Samaritans and so pick up on the tensions underlying v. 9, or indeed be aware of the betrothal

narrative form which Conway believes the author employs. More importantly, John may write things which not all in the audience will pick up and still write the story with his assumptions in mind. John (or the implied author) seems to be sufficiently aware of Second Temple Judaism and its writings to be aware of the different connotations of 'living water' and employ them in his narrative.

61 So e.g. Bligh, 'Jesus', pp. 334–5; Barrett, *St John*, p. 233; Carson, *John*, pp. 218–19; Keener, *John*, pp. 604–5 (all with reference to Jer. 2.13). See Lincoln (*John*, p. 255) for justification for reading the living water as flowing from Jesus rather than the believer, and Carson (*John*, pp. 323–5) for a presentation of the opposing view.

62 For discussions of the possibilities, see Brown, *John 1–12*, pp. 327–9; Barrett, *St John*, pp. 328–39; Schnackenburg, *John 5–12*, pp. 155–7; Carson, *John*, pp. 326–8; Keener, *John*, pp. 725–8.

63 Alan Watson (*Pharisaic Tradition*, p. 32) reads this response as full of sexual innuendo. He reads 'well' as referring to her genitalia and 'bucket' as referring to his. She suggests that he is not properly equipped for the task and that she is too much of a woman for him as a result. Watson assumes that her cajoling him in this way would make him want to prove himself a real man with her – in other words, this is a 'come-on'. This seems unlikely. Not only does he provide no evidence that these words were ever used with such connotations in Jewish tradition, but a bucket seems an intrinsically unlikely metaphor for a penis given its shape (at least 'hand' and 'foot' are well attested as euphemisms for penis in biblical and extra-biblical literature). In the LXX buckets and drawing (Greek *antlēma* and *antleō*) either refer to drawing water (Gen. 24.13, 20 LXX) or are used as a metaphor for salvation (Isa. 12.3 LXX). In the light of this fact, Watson's argument that buckets go up and down wells just as penises go up and down vaginas and that the woman must therefore be referring to his penis and her vagina seems less than compelling.

64 This explains why she does not raise the subject of sex explicitly. The unsuspecting reader (like Botha, *Samaritan Woman*, pp. 126–38) might not get the sexual innuendo until vv. 15–16 where it becomes much more obvious. However, just because the reader does not get the innuendo immediately it does not mean that the character does not, or that the reader might not pick it up later on in the narrative. John is a good storyteller.

65 Similarly, Spencer, 'Feminist Criticism', p. 309. Unlike Eslinger ('Wooing', pp. 178–9) and Brant ('Husband Hunting', p. 214) I do not read this as comparing Jesus to Jacob in order to challenge Jesus' masculinity, because I cannot see a reference to the fertility of Jacob in v. 12b. As well as his sons, it mentions Jacob himself and his cattle, neither of which betoken his sexual prowess. Eslinger alleges that John

makes this allusion by ordering 'well, sons, and flocks' to reflect the order they appear in Genesis 29—30 ('Wooing', p. 179). To make this work, he ignores that the woman's order is really 'himself, sons and flocks' (v. 12b) and that the Genesis narrative does not describe Jacob's opening of the well or growing of the flocks as resulting from his masculinity (and Genesis describes the difficulties that Jacob and Leah experience in conceiving). So, rather than seeing a sexual put-down here, I see a straight put-down.

66 A simple search of the LXX reveals that the exact phrase *pēgē hudatos hallomenou zōēn aiōnion* occurs nowhere. The phrase *pēgē hudatos* occurs most often with reference to a physical well of running or spring water (Lev. 11.36 LXX; Deut. 8.15 LXX; Josh. 15.9 LXX; 18.15 LXX; 2 Kings 3.19, 25 LXX) as does the phrase *pēgē tou hudatos* with reference to a specific well (Gen. 16.7 LXX; 24.13, 43 LXX; Judith 7.12; 12.7). As Jesus uses the idea of a spring of bubbling water metaphorically, none of these are of any particular use in elucidating his meaning as they use the terms literally. Metaphorical uses include those which allude to sexual relationships and activities (Prov. 5.18 LXX) and to salvation (Isa. 35.7 LXX; Jer. 2.13 LXX). Of all these references the only one to use the word 'life' (Greek *zōē*) is Jer. 2.13 LXX, making it the most likely LXX text for elucidating the background of Jesus' words. Similarly, Waetjen, *Beloved Disciple*, p. 166.

67 E.g. Barrett, *St John*, p. 234; Brown, *John 1–12*, p. 178; Schnackenburg, *John 1–4*, p. 430; Lincoln, *John*, p. 174; McHugh, *John 1–4*, p. 272.

68 So e.g. Brown, *John 1–12*, pp. 178–9. I translate 'grace instead of grace' as this seems to be the more natural meaning of the Greek term *anti*; cf. Maurice Casey, *Is John's Gospel True?* (London: Routledge, 1996), p. 67. However, this does not suggest that the law was bad. Quite the opposite, John calls it 'grace'.

69 Similarly, Eslinger, 'Wooing', p. 180; Brant, 'Husband Hunting', p. 215. Botha (*Samaritan Woman*, pp. 141–2) suggests that the absence of the address 'sir' (Greek *kurie*) in v. 17 indicates a distancing from Jesus (as the address indicates an attitude of humble respect) and so proves she cannot have sexual designs on him. First, she uses *kurie* to begin her rebuff in vv. 11–12 which is neither humble nor respectful. Second, just because she withdraws in v. 17 does not mean she was not opening up in v. 15 to what she thought were Jesus' sexual advances. What he said to her in v. 16 was enough to put anyone off. Stephen D. Moore, in 'Are There Impurities in the Living Water that the Johannine Jesus Dispenses? Deconstructionism, Feminism, and the Samaritan Woman', *BibInt* 1 (2003), pp. 205–27, suggests that in v. 15 the woman desires water which is both spiritual and literal, deconstructing Jesus' binary opposition of spiritual and physical and, in showing herself smarter than him, deconstructing also the binary opposition of male

and female. Besides the implausibility of John constructing a parody of Jesus, making him the victim of Johannine irony, Moore fails to take account of the sexual (and ritual) connotations of 'living water', which fully explain the woman's response in v. 15 and render his suggestions unnecessary. On another note, I cannot find any support in the LXX or the narrative of John 4 for the suggestion that the woman thought Jesus was offering her 'such a stupendous orgasm that she would never need sex again' (Watson, *Pharisaic Tradition*, p. 32). Again, Watson rests his interpretation on conjecture, which in the light of the actual LXX allusive use of 'water' and 'well' vocabulary to hint at sexuality (rather than specifying particular acts and body parts) loses plausibility.

70 I freely admit here to trying to interpret the words and actions of the Samaritan woman so as to understand her character. However, I do so on the basis of what I think I have already read out of the text and so do not feel too guilty in the wake of the scathing attack on interpretations of John 4 by Fewell and Phillips ('Beyond Betrothal', pp. 23–31), not least as they import things into their reading which are clearly not in the narrative, e.g. that she is 'in a state of economic and social dependence' ('Beyond Betrothal', p. 40). John says nothing of this. For all we know, she could be a wealthy widow with a lover who draws her own water. We might surmise that she would more likely have a slave do this if she were wealthy, and so assume her economic dependence on the man she lives with, but these are no less assumptions than those held by the scholars they critique. For further critique of sexism in readings of John 4, see Schottroff, 'Notion of Sexuality', pp. 157–62.

71 Commentators note the disconnect between vv. 15 and 16, e.g. Bernard, *St John*, pp. 142–3; Carson, *John*, p. 220; Moloney, *John*, p. 131; J. Eugene Botha, 'John 4.16: A Difficult Text Speech Act Theoretically Revisited', in *The Gospel of John as Literature: An Anthology of Twentieth-Century Perspectives*, ed. Mark W. G. Stibbe (Brill: Leiden, 1993), pp. 183–4; Waetjen, *Beloved Disciple*, p. 168; Lincoln, *John*, pp. 174–5. I follow those who see the various connotations of 'living waters' as supplying the connection (e.g. Eslinger, *Wooing*, p. 166; Watson, *Pharisaic Tradition*, p. 30). Carmichael ('Marriage', p. 332) seeks to explain the disconnects and subject changes from water to worship (John 4.15–20) by their connection through the common theme of rebirth (e.g. waters of rebirth), recreation and the original creation of man and woman. But these alleged themes seem to me to lie *too* deeply behind the narrative to supply a convincing connection. Some ironic readings suggest that Jesus, the narrator and the reader all know that they are talking about the life that Jesus brings but the Samaritan woman still thinks they are talking about water (e.g. Duke, *Irony*, pp. 101–3; O'Day, *Narrative Mode*, pp. 49–92, esp. 60–1). Such readings do not eliminate the problem of an uneven narrative, as within the narrative the woman still experiences the

conversation as disjointed. Furthermore, they create other problems: (1) why does the Word who came to make his own those who were not (John 1.10–13) offer salvation to this woman in incomprehensible riddles? (2) how does such an action exhibit the love of the Father and the Son which the author assumes lies behind the mission of the Son? If the only word play is 'living water' = salvation or water, then the irony suggests that the Son mocks this woman by talking in ways that keep salvation beyond her understanding for most of the conversation. This presents a very different God incarnate from the God of love the author claims to present, as this God seems to be toying with the woman, which comes across as nasty (similarly, Kim, 'Korean Feminist', pp. 111–12). Botha's speech-act reading (*Samaritan Woman*, pp. 140–1), in which the narrative character Jesus talks riddles and then inexplicably changes the subject, raises all the same questions. Some object further to such readings on the grounds of sexism, as they portray the woman as a simple fool (e.g. Schottroff, 'Notion of Sexuality', pp. 161–2; Spencer, 'Feminist Criticism', p. 314). Okure (*Mission*, pp. 106–7) suggests that vv.15 and 16 are linked by: (a) a catchword link; (b) Jesus' desire to continue the conversation as it is his missionary labour; (c) the role reversal of Jesus now offering water and the woman wanting it. However, (c) does not link v. 15 with v. 16 but reverses the position in v. 7b. Jesus' desire to continue the conversation does not explain away either the nastiness of the irony he employs (*if* he is simply talking above her ability to understand) or the disjunction. It simply makes Jesus a slightly odd evangelist, and the catchword link a bad join in a strange conversation. None of these difficulties exist if we assume that 'living water' = salvation or sex or cult or water, as the woman is intelligently alert to the connotations from the moment she enters the scene and good reasons are supplied for her to make the assumptions she does (e.g. boy meets girl at well suggests sexual connotations, prophetic insight suggests religious connotations – on which last point see further below).

72 Eslinger, 'Wooing', p. 180, although I maintain that the woman only softened to what she perceived were his advances in John 4.15. Before that point she was not interested. She was not entertaining 'carnal misconceptions' and may well not have been offering herself up for adultery in v. 15 either. She may have been hoping to leave the man who has not married her, marry Jesus and live happily ever after.

73 Similarly, Brant, 'Husband Hunting', p. 215.

74 So e.g. Eslinger, 'Wooing', p. 180; Keener, *John*, p. 606.

75 Scholars who comment on this tend to read Jesus' words as gently affirming: so e.g. Carson, *John*, p. 221; Köstenberger, *John*, p. 152; Munro, 'Pharisee', p. 718; Michaels, *John*, p. 247; Brant, *John*, p. 85. O'Day (*Narrative Mode*, p. 67) reads it as 'biting sarcasm'. John Chrysostom (*Homilies on John* 32.2) reads them as a reproof.

76 Similarly, John Chrysostom, *Homilies on John* 32.2.

77 Similarly, Day, *Woman*, pp. 179–80; Spencer, 'Feminist Criticism', pp. 309–10; Jennifer Wright Knust, *Unprotected Texts: The Bible's Surprising Contradictions About Sex and Desire* (New York: HarperOne, 2011), pp. 237–8. Some read the reference to five husbands to be symbolic of Samaritan idolatry, as 2 Kings 17.24 records that the Assyrians repopulated Samaria with people from five nations who brought seven foreign gods. In his retelling, Josephus reduces the number of gods to five (*Jewish Antiquities* 9.14.3§287). Some of these see the reference to the multiple relationships as symbolic of the idolatry of Samaritan religion (e.g. Westcott, *John*, p. 71; Bligh, 'Jesus', p. 336; Marsh, *Saint John*, p. 214; Schneiders, *Revelatory Text*, p. 190; Brodie, *John*, p. 223; Waetjen, *John*, pp. 169–71; McHugh, *John 1–4*, pp. 281–2). Barrett (*St John*, pp. 235–6) and Brown (*John 1–12*, p. 171) see it as possible. Others see a more general overtone of idolatry here (e.g. Newbigin, *Fourth Gospel*, p. 52; Lincoln, *John*, pp. 175–6). This reading does not fully convince because: (1) 2 Kings 17.24 records seven gods not five and we cannot guarantee that John would have preferred the tradition in Josephus over that in 2 Kings; (2) Samaritanism at the time of Jesus and John was not syncretistic but based on Torah; (3) the imagery of legal marriages for idolatry and adultery for true worship would be at the very least odd in Second Temple Judaism and early Christianity; and (4) the Samaritans followed the idolatrous gods simultaneously, whereas the woman had her five husbands consecutively (similarly, Bernard, *St John*, pp. 143–5; Schnackenburg, *John 1–4*, p. 433; Sanders and Mastin, *John*, p. 144; Lindars, *John*, pp. 186–7; Bruce, *John*, p. 107; Haenchen, *John 1*, p. 221; Okure, *Mission*, pp. 108–13; Carson, *John*, pp. 232–3; Moloney, *John*, pp. 131–2; Morris, *John*, p. 235; Beasley-Murray, *John*, p. 61; Keener, *John*, p. 606; von Wahlde, *Gospel of John*, p. 174; Michaels, *John*, p. 247). Add to this John's invitation in v. 27 to read the text in terms of sexuality and it is not possible to maintain Schneider's reading (*Revelatory Text*, pp. 188–94) of the woman's five husbands as purely symbolic. Laurence Cantwell, in 'Immortal Longings in Sermone Humili: A Study of John 4.5-26', *SJT* 36 (1983), pp. 73–86) takes this debate as an opportunity to debunk historical critical readings of this text in favour of a moving meditation, placing the Samaritan woman in the culture of a tenement block in South Glamorgan, Wales. However, his own reading is no less full of judgements about the text and the woman – e.g. 'imprisoned by the private immoralities of her past life' ('Immortal', p. 83), only his are based on personal preference rather than historical data and falsifiable interpretation. I am sticking with the standard scholarly methods, whatever their shortcomings, as they seem more objective.

78 E.g. Hendriksen, *John*, pp. 164–5; Marsh, *Saint John*, pp. 214–15; Bultmann, *John*, p. 188; Newbigin, *Fourth Gospel*, p. 52; Duke, *Irony*,

p. 102; Sloyan, *John*, p. 54; Moloney, *John*, p. 127; Morris, *John*, p. 234; Neyrey, *John*, p. 90. I prefer not to quote some of the less pleasant things said about her, and it is unnecessary as strong responses have already been made (e.g. Fewell and Phillips, *Beyond Betrothal*).

79 Culpepper, *Gospel*, pp. 141–2. The Greek *sou* ('your') is in the emphatic position, drawing attention to 'your' and so meaning something like 'is not *your* husband', i.e. he belongs to somebody else.

80 E.g. Bernard, *St John*, p. 143; Lightfoot, *Commentary*, p. 134; Brown, *John 1–12*, p. 171; Schnackenburg, *John 1–4*, p. 433; Lindars, *John*, p. 186; Barrett, *St John*, p. 235; Haenchen, *John 1*, p. 221; Carson, *John*, p. 221; Beasley-Murray, *John*, p. 61; Burge, *John*, p. 145; Keener, *John*, pp. 606–8; Edwards, *John*, p. 56; Köstenberger, *John*, p. 152; Lincoln, *John*, p. 175.

81 Pheme Perkins, *The Gospel according to St. John: A Theological Commentary*, Herald Scriptural Library (Chicago: Franciscan Herald Press, 1978), p. 55.

82 Köstenberger, *John*, pp. 152–3.

83 E.g. Westcott, *John*, p. 71; Sanders and Mastin, *John*, p. 144; Bruce, *John*, p. 107; Schottroff, 'Notion of Sexuality', pp. 163–4; Waetjen, *John*, p. 169.

84 O'Day, *John*, p. 567; Lincoln, *John*, p. 175; Michaels, *John*, p. 247 n. 66. Note in this regard the story of the woman who married seven brothers, Mark 12.18–23.

85 Munro, 'Pharisee', p. 718.

86 Keener, *John*, pp. 606–7.

87 See e.g. Sanders and Mastin, *John*, p. 144; Spencer, 'Feminist Criticism', p. 310; Brant, *John*, pp. 82, 85.

88 Here I will admit to being appreciative of the caution expressed by Fewell and Phillips ('Beyond Betrothal') in interpreting the character of this woman, not least in terms of urging readers not to demonize her.

89 So Conway, *Men and Women*, p. 117; Kim, 'Korean Feminist', p. 112; Day, *Woman*, pp. 179–80. Robert Kysar, *John: The Maverick Gospel*, 3rd edn (Louisville: Westminster John Knox, 2007), p. 180, also notes that we are not told why she has had five husbands.

90 Similarly, Schottroff, 'Notion of Sexuality', p. 164. So, by way of response to Fewell and Phillips ('Beyond Betrothal'), the text itself does seem to indicate that she now has a sexual relationship with a man outside the matrimony her culture saw as necessary and divinely ordained for sexual activity. Similarly, as the most natural reading assumes that *anēr* (Greek 'man' or 'husband') will retain the same meaning throughout v. 18a, Köstenberger's suggestion (*John*, pp. 152–3) that the woman has had five men (Greek *andras*, v. 18aα – i.e. she was not married to them) and that the person she now lives with is not her husband (Greek *anēr*, v. 18aβ) is mistaken.

91 Similarly Botha, *Samaritan Woman*, p. 142; Bruner, *John*, p. 260.

92 Haenchen (*John 1*, p. 221) puts the Evangelist's silence on the reasons for her situation down to his choosing not to speak of 'lawless and

vulgar' matters. This might be more convincing if John did not tip the wink in v. 27 that he wants us to re-read the narrative in terms of Jesus' sexuality. John is not the prude Haenchen makes him out to be.

93 Kim ('Korean Feminist', pp. 112–13) suggests the reason is because the Samaritan woman is merely a foil for Jesus' revelation. Taking this cue from O'Day (*Narrative Mode*), Kim suggests that the text and the narrative Jesus victimize the Samaritan woman by effectively silencing her story and devaluing her. Reading O'Day as mistaken, I cannot agree with Kim. From the moment she was asked for a drink and then offered living water, the woman has read the encounter in terms of her own story and been in control of her side of the conversation.

94 I fully accept that I may be 'psychologizing' here, but I want to stress that I only do so on the basis of ambiguity in the meaning of the key words in this text, 'living waters'. Given that almost all (if not all) commentators accept that the ambiguity of the connotations of this phrase is key to unlocking the coherence of the text, I would want to defend my 'psychologizing' by pointing out that it has a solid basis in the text and the meanings of its key words.

95 With respect to the abrupt change in conversation, I am highly appreciative of the critiques of ironic readings such as that of e.g. Duke (*Irony*, pp. 101–3) and O'Day (*Narrative Mode*) made by Fewell and Phillips in 'Beyond Betrothal', pp. 24–5 (see also Schottroff, 'Notion of Sexuality', pp. 161–2), who object to assuming the woman is stupid. Although anyone could respond to their concerns by pointing out that stories can involve unintelligent characters, nothing in the text indicates that this woman is obtuse. Quite the opposite, it presents her as alert to cultural resonances and the nuances of multivalent idioms like 'living waters'.

96 Similarly, Brant, *John*, p. 85.

97 Again, most commentators note a disjunction in the conversation, generally explaining it as the woman's attempt to change the topic in embarrassment or to save face (so e.g. Bernard, *St John*, p. 145; Hendriksen, *John*, pp. 165–6; Marsh, *Saint John*, p. 216; Eslinger, 'Wooing', pp. 180–1; Morris, *John*, p. 236; Köstenberger, *John*, p. 153; Bruner, *John*, p. 261), and some attempt to explain why she chose the topic of worship. Bultmann (*John*, p. 189) simply dismisses the question. Westcott (*John*, p. 71) claims that 'no question could appear more worthy of a prophet's decision than the settlement of the religious centre of the world' but offers no evidence in support of this conjecture (similarly, Bernard, *St John*, p. 145; Schnackenburg, *John 1–4*, p. 434; Sanders and Mastin, *John*, p. 145; Lindars, *John*, pp. 187–8; Carson, *John*, p. 222; Botha, *Samaritan Woman*, pp. 143–4; Moloney, *John*, p. 128; Beasley-Murray, *John*, p. 61; McHugh, *John 1–4*, p. 284; Michaels, *John*, p. 248). Barrett (*St John*, p. 236) dismisses the suggestion on the basis of lack of evidence but offers no other. O'Day (*Narrative Mode*, pp. 67–8)

assumes that they stand on or near a Samaritan holy place which brings the topic to mind, but nothing in the text indicates that this prompted the woman to change the subject to holy places. Bruce (*John*, p. 108) suggests that as she is talking to a prophet 'the conversation must take a religious turn' (similarly Okure, *Mission*, pp. 114–15). However, this does not explain why she chose a cultic topic, which is more a priestly than a prophetic concern. Keener (*John*, p. 610) conjectures that he is 'the prophet' (cf. Deut. 18.18, which the Samaritans called the *Taheb*). However, if this were so she would not continue arguing with him or assume the messiah was another as she does in v. 25, or still be doubting he was the messiah in v. 29. Given that (almost) all commentators accept that John plays with the meanings of 'living waters', there is no need to look any further than the ambiguity provided by the connotations of this phrase to explain the change of topic.

98 Picking up on a theme that John as narrator has already introduced in Jesus' prophecy of the destruction of the Temple and its replacement by his body (John 2.19–22). So e.g. Barrett, *St John*, p. 237.

99 Similarly, Eslinger, 'Wooing', p. 181.

100 Similarly, McHugh, *John 1–4*, p. 288.

101 Similarly e.g. Bernard, *St John*, p. 151; Brown, *John 1–12*, pp. 172–3; Schnackenburg, *John 1–4*, p. 442; Lindars, *John*, p. 191; O'Day, *Narrative Mode*, pp. 72–4; Botha, *Samaritan Woman*, p. 153; Keener, *John*, p. 620; Lincoln, *John*, p. 178; Waetjen, *Beloved Disciple*, pp. 174–6; McHugh, *John 1–4*, p. 288; Brant, *John*, p. 86. Barrett (*St John*, p. 239) and Carson (*John*, p. 227 n. 1) comment that this instance of *egō eimi* is not 'theologically loaded'. In view of the theme of the marriage of God to his people running throughout this section and the similarity to Isa. 52.6 LXX, I cannot agree.

102 So McHugh, *John 1–4*, pp. 267, 288–9. The Samaritans were not Gentiles, strictly speaking, but the descendants of the ten northern tribes of Israel. They were regarded as apostate by the Jews. However, OT prophecies (e.g. Hos. 2.14–23; 14.4–7) and contemporary predictions (e.g. 4 Ezra 13.39–50 – although this text specifies nine tribes of the northern kingdom) looked forward to the return of the ten tribes and their being brought back into covenant relationship with God. John appears to develop the idea in this narrative.

103 The 'surely not' (Greek *mēti*) of v. 29 demonstrates that she has not yet accepted the revelation of v. 26 that he is the messiah. So, unlike most commentators (e.g. Okure, *Mission*, p. 135), I do not read v. 26 as the climax to the dialogue but as an aborted climax. The real conversation could now have begun, if the disciples had not interrupted it.

104 Schneiders (*Revelatory Text*, p. 192) proposes that the disciples' silent question 'what are you seeking?' witnesses to their concern that Jesus may be choosing a woman to fulfil the missionary role they believe

belongs to men. However, nothing in the context supports this interpretation. The disciples do not ask about the missionary role of the
woman in John 4.31–38. If anything, these verses affirm the missionary
call of the disciples and Jesus says nothing of any missionary role for the
woman. Nor does he attempt to recruit her as a missionary anywhere
in the dialogue. The text stands as a witness against Schneiders' reading
here, and the unasked questions of the disciples strongly indicate that
they suspect Jesus of some inappropriate sexual motive.

105 See 1 Cor. 1.18–31 for an example of an early Christian proclaiming this
kind of classic spiritual message.

106 For example, she may have left it because she knew she was coming back
(so e.g. O'Day, *Narrative Mode*, p. 75). She may have left it for Jesus or
the disciples to take a drink (so e.g. Barrett, *St John*, p. 240). Perhaps
John uses this motif to signify that she now does not want ordinary
but living water (so e.g. Brown, *John 1–12*, p. 173; Botha, *Samaritan
Woman*, pp. 162–4). Interesting though they are, none of these specula-
tions gain support from the text. The 'therefore' counts against reading
the woman leaving her water jar as her accepting living water, as does
the *mēti* in v. 29b, on which see below.

107 Its place in the narrative counts against it referring back to v. 26 (against
Okure, *Mission*, p. 136).

108 Spencer, 'Feminist Criticism', pp. 314–15.

109 This must be heard alongside any claim like that of Kim ('Feminist
Reading', p. 113) that the woman receives no approval from Jesus, her
people or even the author. She receives disapproval neither from nor
within the text, whereas Jesus does. Moreover, Jesus may well mean to
affirm her in his words 'you have spoken rightly' (v. 17).

110 Similarly Carson, *John*, p. 228; Keener, *John*, p. 622.

111 Similarly Carson, *John*, p. 228.

112 Similarly e.g. Neyrey, *John*, pp. 94–5; Duke, *Irony*, p. 103.

113 Famously, Joseph decides to drop Mary quietly when he discovers she is
pregnant (Matt. 1.19). Whatever anyone makes of the historicity of the
Matthean birth narrative, the fact that the narrative makes sense in this
culture makes the point.

114 Similarly, Schottroff, 'Notion of Sexuality', p. 164.

115 Here I disagree with Schottroff ('Notion of Sexuality', p. 164) on two
counts: (1) John does present evidence that the woman is ashamed of
her past, namely in her evasion in v. 17; (b) John gives no evidence that
she frees herself from the judgement of others through this encounter
but hints that, somehow, something Jesus said removes her shame –
suggesting strongly that it is Jesus, not the woman, who removes the
shame.

116 Here I disagree with Kim. The Samaritan woman is not placed in anything like the 'triple jeopardy' of the Korean woman Kim describes

('Korean Feminist', p. 117). Something in her conversation with Jesus releases her entirely from the shame she experienced and so liberates her. On the basis of evidence from Craig R. Koester ('"The Savior of the World" (John 4:42)', *JBL* 109 (1990), pp. 675–6), Kim argues that as a Samaritan she was a victim of colonial powers, a victimization only repeated by the text of John 4, which silences her voice and experience as a victim of colonialism ('Korean Feminist', pp. 113–14, 118). Despite his own conclusions, the evidence Koester presents ('Savior', 675–6) clearly presents Samaritans as identified with foreign colonists, not as the local victims of colonists (Josephus, *Jewish Antiquities* 9.14.3§288–291) as both he and Kim suggest. If anything, this would indicate that the Samaritan woman ought to be identified as a foreign colonist and so as an oppressor; see the similar reading of Sisera's mother in Katherine Doob Sakenfeld, 'Whose Text Is It?' *JBL* 127 (2008), p. 13.

117 BDAG 649.

118 Some commentators accept the force of *mēti* but still read nascent faith: so e.g. Brown, *John 1–12*, p. 173; Schnackenburg, *John 1–4*, p. 444; Barrett, *St John*, p. 240; O'Day, *Narrative Mode*, p. 76; Carson, *John*, p. 228; McHugh, *John 1–4*, p. 290; Brant, *John*, p. 87. Bernard (*St John*, p. 152) agrees but notes that John 18.35 and 21.5 use the same term and expect the answer 'no' (although John 21.5 uses *mē ti*). The only other places John uses *mēti* (John 8.22; 18.35) support the suggestion that a negative answer is expected (against Lindars, *John*, p. 193).

119 Some commentators assume that her testimony is far from perfect because it only speaks of her relationship history and does not proclaim that Jesus is messiah (e.g. Lightfoot, *Commentary*, p. 127; Morris, *John*, p. 250). John's point is precisely that the reality of the salvation the messiah brings is found in her testimony concerning Jesus speaking into her broken sex life. This is what brings the Samaritans to faith. This point seems to be missed even by those who explore the apostleship of the Samaritan woman, e.g. Sandra M. Schneiders, 'Women in the Fourth Gospel and the Role of Women in the Contemporary Church', *BTB* 12 (1982), pp. 39–40.

120 This bears both similarities to and differences from Bultmann, who claims (*John*, p. 201) that faith comes from the encounter but that it is impossible to give a definitive dogmatic statement of the proclamation. John seems to illustrate here that faith comes through an encounter with Christ and pictures it coming through Christ speaking into the concrete realities of our ordinary lives in all their dysfunctionality and brokenness.

121 In disagreement with Kim ('Feminist Reading', p. 113), who does 'not find any important role for the Samaritan woman as a revealer of Jesus, a missionary, or a disciple' (a conclusion which calls into question the arguments of e.g. Schneiders, 'Women'; Okure, *Mission*), the story of

the Samaritan woman's sex life becomes both the locus and the vehicle of salvation. John embodies salvation in her person and continuing story, which makes her absolutely central to the text because Jesus' work as saviour does not take place apart from her. Note also that Jesus does not tell her story and so use her for his witness. She tells her own story. No one tells her to do this. Jesus tells her to call her husband, not her people. She chooses to witness to Christ (before she has even fully accepted what he has been trying to tell her about himself and his mission). Neither the text, Jesus nor John victimizes this woman.

122 Similarly, Eslinger, 'Wooing', pp. 167, 181. Given that bringing people to faith is Jesus' food, the betrothal banquet motif continues to the end of the story and clearly includes the many coming to faith in vv. 39–42 (as suggested by e.g. Lincoln, *John*, p. 181). The townspeople's request that Jesus stay with them in v. 40 clearly echoes the invitation of the suitor in betrothal narratives to stay with the family (Botha, *Samaritan Woman*, p. 183).

123 Similarly, Botha, *Samaritan Woman*, pp. 174, 180; O'Day, *John*, p. 569.

124 So e.g. Okure, *Mission*, p. 152; McHugh, *John 1–4*, p. 293.

125 So e.g. McHugh, *John 1–4*, p. 293.

126 Talbert, *Reading John*, p. 116.

127 Schottroff ('Notion of Sexuality', pp. 167–8) argues that the Samaritan's question in v. 11 assumes that Jesus has already had a drink. However, her question implies the opposite (if anything) as she asks why he is asking for a drink, not why he accepts water from her. Moreover, the conversation up to v. 15 turns on Jesus' request and makes little sense if it has already been satisfied – no reason for text, no opportunity for subtext.

128 See the brief review in Koester, 'Savior', pp. 665–8. The title never occurs in the writings of Josephus and only once in those of Philo (Philo, *On the Special Laws* 2.198). It occurs three times in the *Testaments of the Twelve Patriarchs* but quite likely as a result of Christian editing of these documents (T. Levi 10.2; 14.2; T. Benj. 3.8). For the likely Christian provenance of these occurrences, see H. W. Hollander and Marinus de Jonge, *The Testaments of the Twelve Patriarchs: A Commentary*, SVTP 8 (Leiden: Brill, 1985), pp. 65, 160, 169, 420.

129 Similarly, Brown, *John 1–12*, p. 175; Schnackenburg, *John 1–4*, p. 458; Barrett, *St John*, p. 244; Haenchen, *John 1*, p. 226; Carson, *John*, p. 232; Morris, *John*, p. 251 n. 98; Lincoln, *John*, p. 181; Keener, *John*, pp. 627–8; McHugh, *John 1–4*, p. 296; Neyrey, *John*, p. 99; Bruner, *John*, p. 285. Bernard (*St John*, pp. 162–3) demurs, but provides no plausible reason for ignoring the resonance Gentiles would hear given the usage in Hellenistic culture.

130 E.g. Deut. 32.15 LXX; 1 Sam. 10.19 LXX; Esth. 5.1 LXX; Judith 9.11; 1 Macc. 4.30; 3 Macc. 6.29, 32; 7.16; Pss. 23.5 LXX; 24.5 LXX; 26.1, 9 LXX; 61.3, 7 LXX; 64.6 LXX; 78.9 LXX; 94.1 LXX; Wisd. 16.7; Sir. 51.1; Pss. Sol. 3.6; 8.33;

16.4; 17.3; Mic. 7.7 LXX; Hab. 3.18 LXX; Isa. 12.2 LXX; 17.10 LXX; 45.15, 21 LXX; 62.11 LXX. Only comparatively rarely does the LXX use *sōtēr* of a human being (Judg. 3.9, 15 LXX; 12.3 LXX; Neh. 6.27 LXX; Esth. 8.12 LXX).

131 Werner Foerster and Georg Fohrer, '† σωτήρ', *TDNT* 7, pp. 1003–21; Carter, *John and Empire*, p. 188.

132 Jove and Jupiter are Roman names for Zeus, and Juno is the Roman name for Hera.

133 Foerster and Fohrer, *TDNT* 7, pp. 1006–12.

134 For example, albeit ironically, of Ptolemy I Soter (Josephus, *Jewish Antiquities* 12.1.1§1–11) and Antiochus IV Epiphanes (Josephus, *Jewish Antiquities* 12.5.5§257–262). He also uses it of Herod the Great and Augustus Caesar (Josephus, *Jewish War* 1.32.2§625).

135 For a summary of the evidence, see Koester, 'Savior', pp. 666–7.

136 For the deification of Vespasian, see Guy Edward Farquhar Chilver and Barbara Levick, 'Vespasian', *OCD* 1544.

137 On this whole episode, see Loader, *Philo, Josephus and the Testaments*, pp. 315–16.

138 Foerster and Fohrer, *TDNT* 7, p. 1010 – although the words are not exactly the same as John 4.42, which has *sōtēr tou kosmou.*

139 Josephus also gives instances of self-styled saviours or those hailed quite wrongly as saviours, e.g. Eurycles whom Herod called his 'saviour' (Josephus, *Jewish War* 1.26.4§530), the terrorists who hailed themselves the 'saviours' of Jerusalem (Josephus, *Jewish War* 4.3.5§146), and Simon bar Giora, who was greeted as 'saviour' of Jerusalem (Josephus, *Jewish War* 4.9.11§575).

140 Hercules is simply the Roman name for the Greek hero Heracles.

141 Foerster and Fohrer, *TDNT* 7, p. 1005.

142 To Megara, Omphale and Deianira. On becoming a god, he married Hebe the goddess of youth.

143 Keener, *John*, p. 607.

144 One of the stronger descriptions I have found among the commentators was 'this specimen of matrimonial maladjustment'. I omit the reference quite deliberately.

145 In this sense, I agree with Moore ('Impurities') that John does not allow the precedence of the spiritual to denigrate the physical and material.

4 Male intimacy

1 Similarly, e.g. O'Day, *John*, p. 729. For brief overviews of the beloved disciple, see Brown, *John 1–12*, pp. xcii–xcviii; Barrett, *St John*, pp. 116–19; Carson, *John*, pp. 472–3; Keener, *John*, pp. 84–9.

2 As Moloney (*Love*) demonstrates.

3 Again, I am assuming that John the Apostle both wrote the Gospel and identifies himself with the beloved disciple of the narrative. Those who disagree may wish to attribute this to an unknown Christian of the first

century AD who is identified as the author and as the beloved disciple by the final redactor of the Gospel. Either approach can accommodate the observations I make about reading John within its ancient Greek environment.

4 Similarly, Lindars, *John*, p. 638; Carson, *John*, p. 681; Beasley-Murray, *John*, p. 409; Köstenberger, *John*, p. 601. Others – e.g. Brown, *John 13–21*, p. 1109, Bruce, *John*, p. 407, Lincoln, *John*, p. 520 and Michaels, *John*, p. 1050 – note how John 21.20 recalls John 13.25 but do not mention how the motif of intimacy marks the entrance and exit of the beloved disciple. Some, e.g. Moloney, *John*, p. 560, assert that recalling the words of John 13.25 in John 21.20 is clumsy, as the beloved disciple appears in v. 7 of the narrative. However, this is to miss the point that John makes by identifying the beloved disciple as the one who reclined on Jesus' breast as this figure enters and exits the narrative (similarly, von Wahlde, *Gospel of John*, p. 897).

5 So e.g. Brown, *John 13–21*, p. 574; Morris, *John*, pp. 555–6; von Wahlde, *Gospel of John*, p. 606.

6 On the implied servitude of Jesus' washing his disciples' feet, see Keener, *John*, pp. 904–7.

7 Similarly, Bernard, *St John*, p. 471; Schnackenburg, *John 13–21*, p. 29; Sanders and Mastin, *John*, p. 313; Lindars, *John*, p. 458; Barrett, *St John*, p. 446; Morris, *John*, p. 556; Witherington, *John's Wisdom*, p. 239; Moloney, *John*, p. 383; Keener, *John*, pp. 915–16; Köstenberger, *John*, p. 415; Waetjen, *Beloved Disciple*, p. 334; von Wahlde, *Gospel of John*, p. 606. Against Carson (*John*, p. 473), who asserts the unlikelihood of the disciples ever reclining 'according to rank' in the light of the foot washing. But they wash no feet, Jesus does. Other Gospels (e.g. Mark 10.35–45) suggest that rank was very important to them. So we have every reason to believe that they would recline to dine according to rank. Greek and Roman audiences would assume this unless otherwise told and John says nothing to the contrary, so they would have heard him this way.

8 Schnackenburg, *John 13–21*, pp. 29, 368; Lindars, *John*, pp. 458, 638; Carson, *John*, p. 681; Moloney, *John*, p. 387; Conway, *Men and Women*, p. 181; Köstenberger, *John*, p. 601; Brant, *John*, p. 285.

9 For the reading of John 13—17 in the light of the symposium, see George L. Parsenios, *Departure and Consolation: The Johannine Discourses in Light of Greco-Roman Literature*, NovTSup 117 (Leiden: Brill, 2005), pp. 31–5, 111–49. Further to what I suggest below, Parsenios suggests (pp. 112–22) that John presents Judas in the role of 'the unwelcome dinner guest' who he suggests was a stock figure of ancient symposia. He engages with the growing consensus that John 13—17 should be read in the light of testamentary literature – see e.g. Francis J. Moloney, *Glory not Dishonour: Reading John 13–21* (Minneapolis: Fortress, 1998),

pp. 5–7 – arguing for reading this section of John in the light of the Greek symposium. Even if there are elements of this tradition, testamentary literature does not explain the facts that John 13—17 takes place during and after dinner, forms a conversation with a revered teacher as the key figure rather than a monologue, and has love as its predominant theme.

10 Oswyn Murray, 'Symposium', *OCD*, p. 1418. For details of other ancient texts (fragmentary and otherwise) preserving elements of symposia, see Parsenios, *Departure*, pp. 33–4.

11 Helen Morales, *Vision and Narrative in Achilles Tatius' Leucippe and Clitophon*, Cambridge Classical Studies (Cambridge: Cambridge University Press, 2004), p. 52; John F. Makowski, 'Greek Love in the Greek Novel', in *A Companion to the Ancient Novel*, ed. Edmund P. Cueva and Shannon N. Byrne, Blackwell Companions to the Ancient World (Oxford: Wiley Blackwell, 2014), p. 496.

12 Parsenios, *Departure*, pp. 33–5.

13 A variant reading, 'supper having ended' (Greek *deipnou genomenou*) has the support of many manuscripts and versions (including the very early P[66]). Also in support of this reading is the fact that it is the more difficult, as it is harder to reconcile with the idea that dinner seems to continue in vv. 4, 26–27. Indeed, some (e.g. Barrett, *St John*, p. 439) reject the reading precisely because the alternative fits the context better. However, v. 4 might use 'from dinner' in the sense of Jesus getting up from the dinner table after eating had finished and the little morsel Jesus gives to Judas in vv. 26–27 might be an after-dinner snack. After all, Niceratos, Charmides and Socrates discuss having a few onions to go with their wine during the *Symposium* (Xenophon, *Symposium* 4.7–9). Accepting this reading would make the case for reading John 13—17 as a symposium even stronger. Incidentally, I can see no evidence in John for identifying the dish into which Jesus dips the morsel as *ḥaroseth*, a sweet dish made of fruit and nuts eaten at Passover (so e.g. Barrett, *St John*, p. 447 – oddly, as he denies this is a Passover meal; Carson, *John*, p. 474), as you should dip twice, once in salt water and then in *ḥaroseth*, according to the Passover *Haggadah*. The Mishnah also mentions dipping twice (*m. Pesaḥ.* 10.4–5) and *ḥaroseth* (*m. Pesaḥ.* 2.8). If this was a Passover meal, Jesus could just as easily have dipped the morsel into salt water. Against any association with Passover dipping, see Schnackenburg, *John 13–21*, p. 30.

14 Parsenios, *Departure*, pp. 120–4.

15 Parsenios (*Departure*, pp. 123–4) suggests that the departure of Judas marks the separation of the *deipnon* and the symposium, as only after this does Jesus begin in earnest his speech on love.

16 So Parsenios (*Departure*, pp. 129–34, 148), who suggests that John, like Plato and Xenophon, played down the theme of feasting and drinking in order that the audience/their readers might concentrate on the feast

of words from the great teacher which they present in their writings. As Parsenios observes here, John is hereby closer to the symposia of Plato and Xenophon than are the dinner of Trimalchio in Petronius' *Satyricon* or Lucian's *Lexiphanes*. This is central to his argument that John uses the symposium motif to present a feast of Jesus' words not simply for contemporary Christians but for believers down the succeeding centuries (*Departure*, pp. 142–9, 154).

17 Scholars disagree over whether the meal was a Passover celebration or not (see discussion in Schnackenburg, *John 13–21*, pp. 33–7). In favour of a Passover, see e.g. Carson, *John*, p. 475; Keener, *John*, pp. 900–1. Against such a reading, see Barrett, *St John*, p. 435; Waetjen, *Beloved Disciple*, p. 327. Whatever the meal John records, he presents it in the form of a symposium.

18 Or, as Brant (*John*, p. 207) asserts, 'Jesus' emphasis on the imagery of the vine provides an abundance of metaphorical wine.'

19 Reading the scene as a symposium are e.g. Tilborg, *Imaginative Love*, pp. 133–7; Witherington, *John's Wisdom*, pp. 231–4; Malina and Rohrbaugh, *John*, p. 227; Lincoln, *John*, p. 366; Parsenios, *Departure*, pp. 111–49, 154; Brant, *John*, p. 207. Similarly, Keener (*John*, p. 900) reads the meal in terms of the customs of a Hellenistic banquet. In a recent study of meals in John, Esther Kobel, *Dining with John: Communal Meals and Identity Formation in the Fourth Gospel and its Historical and Cultural Context*, BibInt 109 (Leiden: Brill, 2011) reads the theme of eating in this Gospel in the light of meals in the Qumran community, the Therapeutae, Haburoth, the early Christian community and the mystery cults. Interestingly, she does not explore the symposium as background to eating in John except to note it as part of the general background to meals in the Greco-Roman world (*Dining*, p. 295). This is a pity as the customs she does study do not compare easily to the meal in John 13—17: the Qumran community held their meals in almost complete silence (Josephus, *Jewish War* 2.8.5§133); the meals of Therapeutae, the Haburoth and the early Christians were mixed rather than male-only gatherings. She notes just two possible connections with John 13—17 and the mysteries: the 'striking parallel' between Jesus the vine in 15.1 and Dionysus as the personification of the vine (*Dining*, p. 230); and Judas consuming the morsel Jesus hands him (John 13.27) as parallel to the ritual consumption of the raw flesh of the bull in Dionysian mystery rites. However, the vine saying more likely results from the OT image of Israel as the vine (Ps. 80.14–15) – e.g. Moloney, *John*, p. 422 – and possibly the wine on the table before him. As for the second suggestion, the evidence for this Dionysian ritual is highly disputed (as Kobel admits) and nothing in the text of John 13 suggests that Jesus hands Judas raw flesh, let alone anything signifying or recalling pagan mystery rites.

20 Parsenios, *Departure*, pp. 113–14.

21 The two most frequent terms for love in the Gospels are the Greek term *agapaō* and related words, and *phileō* and related words. Matthew uses *agapaō* (and related words) 12 times, 8 of those in discourses or conversations on love (Matt. 5.43–46, four times; 19.19; 22.37–39, twice; 24.12). He uses *phileō* and related words eight times but only twice in conversations on love (Matt. 10.37, twice). Mark uses *agapaō* and related words eight times, including four times in discussions of love (Mark 12.30–31; 12.33 twice each). He uses *phileō* and related words twice but not in a discourse on love. Luke uses *agapaō* and words related to it 16 times, 10 of which are in discussions of love (Luke 6.27, 32, twice, 35; 7.47, twice; 10.27; 11.42). He uses *phileō* and related words 23 times, partly because he uses the word 'friend' (Greek *philos*) so often, but never once in a discourse on love. John uses *agapaō* and related words 44 times, 36 of which are in discussions on love: John 3.16, 19, 35; 5.42; 8.42; 10.17; 13.34 (three times), 35; 14.15, 21 (four times), 23 (twice), 24, 28, 31; 15.9 (three times), 10, 12 (twice each), 13, 17; 17.23 (twice), 24, 26 (twice); 21.15, 16. He uses *phileō* 19 times, 13 of which are in discourses on love (John 5.20; 12.25; 15.13, 14, 15, 19; 16.27 (twice); 21.15, 16, 17 (three times)). This means that John uses *agapaō* and *phileō* and related words in discussions of love 55 times compared to ten in Matthew, four in Mark and eight in Luke.

22 So e.g. Schnackenburg, *John 13–21*, p. 29.

23 Additionally, his name occurs as the first in the list of the disciples (Matt. 10.2; Mark 3.16–17; Luke 6.14), where the inner circle of Peter, Andrew, James and John head the list of the Twelve. Jesus invites this inner circle (Peter, James and John especially) into parts of his ministry and self-revelation from which other disciples are excluded (Matt. 17.1–9; 26.37; Mark 5.37; 9.2–9; 13.3–37; 14.33; Luke 8.51; 9.28–36). Outsiders also seem to recognize Peter as a leader among the disciples (Matt. 17.24). Matthew, Mark and Luke often have Peter speak on behalf of all the disciples (e.g. Luke 18.28).

24 For a moderate reading of any possible rivalry between Peter and the beloved disciple, see e.g. Schnackenburg, *John 13–21*, pp. 29–30; Barrett, *St John*, pp. 116–17; Michaels, *John*, pp. 19–20.

25 Admittedly, unlike the other guests attending the symposia of Plato and Xenophon, none of the disciples offers any viewpoint on love in John 13—17. Instead, the disciples make comments and ask questions which Jesus answers. The difference need not be pressed. This is typical of the whole Gospel tradition, where only the authoritative teaching voice of Jesus is heard, in contrast to rabbinic tradition where many teaching voices are heard – see Samuel Byrskog, *Jesus the Teacher: Didactic Authority and Transmission in Ancient Israel, Ancient Judaism and the Matthean Community*, ConBNT 24 (Stockholm: Almqvist & Wiksell,

1994), esp. pp. 396–8) – so we ought not to be surprised to find a modification of the symposium tradition at this point.

26 For a satire of the custom of male teachers having young lovers, see Petronius, *Satyricon* 85–87. The fact that this works as satire suggests the custom was sufficiently well-known for Petronius' audience to get the joke.

27 Tilborg (*Imaginative Love*, pp. 78–9) similarly reads the beloved disciple against the background of the teacher's favourite in Greek philosophical traditions. While this possibility seems to occur to few commentators, some (e.g. Keener, *John*, p. 917; Moloney, *Love*, p. 33 n. 55) register Tilborg's arguments and evidence, but without much discussion by way of response.

28 Tilborg, *Imaginative Love*, p. 90. Similarly Schottroff, 'Notion of Sexuality', pp. 177–8.

29 See further Cantarella, *Bisexuality*, pp. 17–48, 120–54. See also Dover, *Greek Homosexuality*, for the classic exposition of the classical Greek form of these relationships.

30 Tilborg, *Imaginative Love*, p. 109.

31 So also Tilborg, *Imaginative Love*, p. 80.

32 Reading the one verse in the light of the other: Sanders and Mastin, *John*, p. 313 n. 1; Brown, *John 13–21*, p. 577; Lindars, *John*, p. 458; Barrett, *St John*, p. 446; Carson, *John*, p. 473; Brodie, *John*, pp. 452–3; Stibbe, *John*, pp. 149–50; Morris, *John*, p. 555 n. 53; O'Day, *John*, p. 729; Witherington, *John's Wisdom*, p. 238; Moloney, *John*, p. 387; Malina and Rohrbaugh, *John*, p. 226; Beasley-Murray, *John*, p. 238; Conway, *Men and Women*, pp. 180–1; Keener, *John*, p. 918; Köstenberger, *John*, p. 414; Edwards, *John*, p. 134; Waetjen, *Beloved Disciple*, p. 334; Lincoln, *John*, p. 378; Michaels, *John*, p. 749; von Wahlde, *Gospel of John*, p. 606; Bruner, *John*, p. 782.

33 This becomes particularly clear when John is compared with Matthew, Mark and Luke, who never specifically mention either the love of the Father for the Son or the love of the Son for the Father.

34 As seems to be indicated by John 17.5, which suggests Jesus will be glorified in the Father's presence as he was before creation, and John 17.24, which suggests that this glory results from the Father's love for the Son in heaven (literally, 'before the creation of the world', so it would have to be in heaven).

35 Such speculation can be found in fifth century BC papyri from Elephantine in Egypt which speak of a goddess Anath Ya'u, who has been identified as a female goddess and presumably a consort of YHWH the god of Israel (CAP 44.3). See A. E. Cowley, *Aramaic Papyri of the Fifth Century B.C.*, Ancient Texts and Translations (Eugene, OR: Wipf & Stock, 2005), p. 148.

36 Or, with Jeremias and many commentators, the image of the best man waiting outside the bridal chamber to receive the proof of virginity and/or evidence that the marriage has been consummated.

37 On this and what follows on love in the Gospel of John, see Moloney, *Love*.

38 John uses the Greek words *tēreō* (keep) and the plural *entolai* (commandments). The LXX most often uses the verbs *phulassō* (guard), *eisakouō* (obey) and *akouō* (hear) with *entolai*. Sirach uses cognates of *tēreō* – *suntēreō* (Sir. 15.15; 37.12) and *diatēreō* (Sir. 1.26) and the noun *tērēsis* (Sir. 32.23) – with *entolai*. Proverbs uses *tēreō* with the singular *entolē* (commandment). There is a clear difference between John's vocabulary and that of the greater part of the LXX. This dissimilarity suggests that caution is needed with respect to the views of some commentators (e.g. Köstenberger, *John*, p. 434) who suggest that Jesus' language here recalls the Old Testament commands. John may echo this language but certainly does not imitate or use it.

39 So Brown, *John 13–21*, p. 638. Paul uses the phrase *tērēsis entolōn* (keeping the commandments).

40 So Lindars, *John*, p. 490; Barratt, *St John*, pp. 461, 477; Morris, *John*, p. 575; Michaels, *John*, pp. 782–3; cf. e.g. Schnackenburg, *John 13–21*, p. 74. Even if Brown (*John 13–21*, p. 638) and Beasley-Murray (*John*, p. 256) are right that the commands are not simply moral but involve a way of life in loving union with Christ, they are still moral. Although I am not sure I can read this way of life into the term 'command' in John, Brown's point about obeying commands being part of loving intimacy with the Father and the Son is certainly true within the wider message of the Gospel.

41 So Brown, *John 13–21*, p. 638; Michaels, *John*, pp. 782–3.

42 The nearest he comes to an allusion would be the woman taken in adultery (John 8.1–11), a story not found in the earliest surviving manuscripts and which therefore may well not have been part of the original Gospel.

43 This seems to be the implication of the plain meaning of the plural noun 'commandments' (so Hendriksen, *John*, p. 303; Sanders and Mastin, *John*, pp. 325, 339; Lindars, *John*, p. 490; Barrett, *St John*, pp. 461, 477; Morris, *John*, p. 597; Keener, *John*, p. 1003; Michaels, *John*, p. 810). Some commentators interpret 'commandments' as Jesus' 'word' or self-revelation (so Schnackenburg, *John 13–21*, p. 74; Moloney, *John*, pp. 405, 421–2). If this were so, surely John would have used the word *logos*, which would convey this sense. Carson (*John*, p. 498) observes that 'commandments' (*entolai*) likely focuses on ethical commands, whereas 'teaching' (*logos*) refers to all that Christ reveals. Nor should we succumb to the temptation to reduce Jesus' plural commandments (John 15.10) to an undefined and only mildly challenging 'love' (e.g. Brodie, *John*, p. 481; Bruner, *John*, pp. 888–9) or single love command by way of reference to v. 12 (so Schnackenburg, *John 13–21*, p. 103). If John does not use the singular 'command' in v. 10, there is

no reason for us to do so in interpreting him. It is interesting how some commentators write of obedience to Jesus' word or words rather than commands (e.g. Witherington, *John's Wisdom*, p. 259; Lincoln, *John*, p. 405). Keener (*John*, p. 1003) comments that 'protestant scholars may feel uncomfortable with the condition of obedience for God's love in this passage, but throughout John the initiative comes from God, who then provides more love in response to human obedience'; this is true enough, but it is not only Protestants who seem to experience this discomfort.

44 It is worth noting that the Pharisees approach Jesus with a question about divorce law (relating to Deut. 24.1–4) which Jesus answers from the law (Gen. 1.27; 2.24). Jesus assumes that obedience to divine commands (as he interprets them) is central to faith – whatever one makes of Jesus' pronouncement that no one should separate what God has joined, the exception clause ('except for adultery/sexual immorality'), or whether Jesus did or did not permit divorce or remarriage. On Jesus' discussion of divorce with the Pharisees, see further Loader, *Septuagint*, pp. 79–86; W. D. Davies and Dale C. Allison, *A Critical and Exegetical Commentary on the Gospel According to Saint Matthew, volume III: XIX–XXVIII*, 2nd edn, ICC (London: T&T Clark, 2004), pp. 4–30; Joseph A. Fitzmyer, *The Gospel According to Luke X–XXIV*, AB 28A (New York: Doubleday, 1985), pp. 1119–24.

45 William Sanday in *The Criticism of the Fourth Gospel* (Oxford: Clarendon, 1905), pp. 97–9 estimated 'a stripling . . . of sixteen to eighteen, or even fifteen to seventeen'.

46 Michael L. Satlow, 'Jewish Constructions of Nakedness in Late Antiquity', *JBL* 116 (1997), pp. 436–7, cites rabbinic evidence of men working naked, esp. *t. Ber.* 2.14. Although the basic meaning of *gymnos* (the Greek word John uses in 21.7) is 'naked', it can mean 'lightly clad' (LSJ 362; BDAG 208). Satlow's evidence renders redundant the suggestion that Peter must have been clothed at least in underwear as Jewish men would not work naked (so e.g. Brown, *John 13–21*, p. 1072; Michaels, *John*, p. 1034). Peter may well be naked (so e.g. Barrett, *St John*, p. 580; Lincoln, *John*, p. 512). Given that they are all fishing, there is every reason to suppose that all the disciples are in a similar state of undress or complete nakedness.

47 Many scholars are perplexed at why Peter should put on his outer garment to swim when one normally takes clothes off to go swimming. Bernard (*St John*, pp. 697–8) suggests that Peter (already wearing underwear) tucks in his outer garment in order to wade ashore in shallow water. However, wading ashore does not fit John's language of Peter throwing himself into the sea. Brown (*John 13–21*, p. 1072) suggests that Peter is only naked underneath his outer garment and so tucks it in to swim rather than taking it off (so also e.g. Witherington, *John's Wisdom*,

p. 354; Moloney, *John*, p. 553; Beasley-Murray, *John*, p. 394; Keener, *John*, pp. 1229–30; Köstenberger, *John*, p. 591; Michaels, *John*, p. 1034). However, wearing an outer garment is hardly being naked or even nearly so, yet John uses the word *gymnos*. Citing the rabbis (t. Ber. 2.20), Barrett (*St John*, pp. 580–1) suggests that Peter was naked, and put on his loose outer garment so as not to greet Jesus naked, for this would have gone against religious custom (similarly e.g. Morris, *John*, pp. 672–3, esp. n. 19; Lincoln, *John*, p. 512).

48 For which see the works of Plato, especially his *Republic* and *Euthyphro*. For accessible translations, see Plato, *The Republic*, trans. Desmond Lee, rev. edn (London: Penguin Books, 1987); Plato, *The Last Days of Socrates*, trans. Hugh Tredennick and Harald Tarrant, rev. edn (London: Penguin Books, 1993).

49 E.g. Juvenal, *Satires* 9; Martial, *Epigrams* 1.96; 2.51; 3.71, 89. There is plenty more.

50 Most obviously in the character of Eumolpus in Petronius' *Satyricon* (see particularly *Satyricon* 140).

51 Contemporary Jewish attitudes towards homoerotic actions were almost universally negative and some preferred to believe such things did not happen in their communities. As the Sages put it in later times, 'Israel is not suspected of this', *t. Qidd.* 5.2; see Michael L. Satlow, *Tasting the Dish: Rabbinic Rhetorics of Sexuality*, BJS 303 (Atlanta: Scholars Press, 1995), p. 209. For a very thorough survey of Jewish attitudes to homosexuality in this period, see the relevant sections in the works of William Loader, *Enoch, Levi and Jubilees on Sexuality: Attitudes towards Sexuality in the Early Enoch Literature, the Aramaic Levi Documents, and the Book of Jubilees*, Attitudes towards Sexuality in Judaism and Christianity in the Hellenistic Greco-Roman Era (Grand Rapids: Eerdmans, 2007); *The Dead Sea Scrolls on Sexuality: Attitudes towards Sexuality in Sectarian and Related Literature at Qumran*, Attitudes towards Sexuality in Judaism and Christianity in the Hellenistic Greco-Roman Era (Grand Rapids: Eerdmans, 2009); *The Pseudepigrapha on Sexuality: Attitudes towards Sexuality in Apocalypses, Testaments, Legends, Wisdom, and Related Literatures*, Attitudes towards Sexuality in Judaism and Christianity in the Hellenistic Greco-Roman Era (Grand Rapids: Eerdmans, 2011); *Philo, Josephus, and the Testaments on Sexuality: Attitudes towards Sexuality in the Writings of Philo and Josephus and in the Testaments of the Twelve Patriarchs*, Attitudes towards Sexuality in Judaism and Christianity in the Hellenistic Greco-Roman Era (Grand Rapids: Eerdmans, 2011).

52 The debate around Paul and homosexuality is enormous and far too complex to summarize here. Given that little in terms of the overall presentation of this book hangs on which way the debate swings, I shall content myself with only two references, both to Joseph Fitzmyer, who

to my mind sums up the primary texts and their implications at least as well as anyone else. On Rom. 1.26–27, see Joseph A. Fitzmyer, *Romans* (New York: Doubleday, 1993), pp. 285–8; on 1 Cor. 6.9, see Joseph A. Fitzmyer, *First Corinthians* (New Haven: Yale University Press, 2008), pp. 255–8.

53 C. S. Lewis, *The Four Loves* (London: HarperCollins, 1977), p. 58.

54 Lewis, *Four Loves*, pp. 59–60. He gives the examples of Beowulf and Hrothgar, Johnson and Boswell, and Roman centurions as described by Tacitus. David Halperin (*One Hundred Years*, pp. 75–87) would add David and Jonathan, Gilgamesh and Enkidu, and Achilles and Patroclus.

5 Peter, Mary and the woman caught in adultery

1 Most famously by Dan Brown, *The Da Vinci Code* (New York: Doubleday, 2003), pp. 245–6.

2 For this translation, see Wesley W. Isenberg, 'The Gospel of Philip (II, 3)', in *The Nag Hammadi Library in English*, ed. James M. Robinson, 4th edn (Leiden: Brill, 1996). For brief introductions to this text (including its dating to the second or third century AD), see both the translation and notes by Isenberg and Hans-Martin Schenke, 'The Gospel of Philip', in *New Testament Apocrypha, Volume One: Gospels and Related Writings*, ed. Wilhelm Schneemelcher, trans. R. McL. Wilson, rev. edn (Louisville: Westminster John Knox, 1991).

3 Robert McL. Wilson, in *The Gospel of Philip: Translated from the Coptic Text, with an Introduction and Commentary* (London: Mowbrays, 1962), p. 115, describes this reconstruction as 'fairly certain'. Bart Ehrman, *Lost Christianities: The Battles for Scripture and the Faiths We Never Knew* (Oxford: Oxford University Press, 2003), p. 122, questions whether we can be certain of such a reconstruction.

4 Schenke, 'Philip', p. 207 n. 34.

5 This reading is understandable, if unlikely. The Greek words *hon ephilei ho Iēsous* (John 20.2), which we normally translate 'whom Jesus loved', could be translated 'whom Jesus used to kiss regularly'. The parallel phrase, *hon ēgapa ho Iēsous* (John 13.23; 19.26; 21.7, 20, 'whom Jesus loved'), and the lack of any sexual action between Jesus and this disciple make it most unlikely that we should read John 20.2 as referring to Jesus kissing the disciple. This does not, clearly, preclude the possibility that Jesus did kiss his disciples – after all, the famous kiss from Judas (Mark 14.45) might suggest this was his regular way of greeting them.

6 William E. Phipps, *Perspectives*, pp. 67–9, where he refers to 'physical relations'. Phipps softens his language in his later work *Sexuality of Jesus*, pp. 132, 231 n. 92.

7 The present imperative can imply that some already existing condition must stop – hence it is quite legitimate to suppose that whatever touching Mary Magdalene is doing must stop. So, given Phipps' assumption

that *haptomai* signifies sex here, he is within his grammatical rights to assume a prior sexual relationship.

8 So Matt. 8.3, 15; 9.20, 21, 29; 14.36 (twice); 17.7; 20.34; Mark 1.41; 3.10; 5.27, 28, 30, 31; 6.56 (twice); 7.33; 8.22; 10.13; Luke 5.13; 6.19; 7.14; 8.16, 44, 45, 46, 47; 11.33; 15.8; 18.15; 22.51; Acts 28.2; 2 Corinthians 6.17; Colossians 2.21; 1 John 5.18. Luke 7.39 may well be ambiguous. 1 Corinthians 7.1 is clearly sexual.

9 Even if Mary does not yet fully understand the significance of the empty tomb (so Conway, *Men and Women*, pp. 187–8), it does not mean that she does not follow Jesus with the commitment appropriate to her understanding.

10 As we saw in Chapter 3, it is most unlikely that the wedding of Cana was Jesus' own wedding – as suggested by Charlesworth, *Historical Jesus*, p. 83 – because Jesus was a guest at the wedding.

11 On this apostolic role of Mary Magdalene, see e.g. Schneiders, 'Women', pp. 43–4; Conway, *Men and Women*, pp. 197–8.

12 The present imperative *mē haptou* could mean 'do not hug me' or 'stop hugging me'. Jesus' command implies that Mary is either embracing Jesus already or is about to do so. So Barrett, *St John*, p. 595. For her seeking to embrace Jesus as a natural reaction (as Matt. 28.9 suggests), see e.g. Barrett, *St John*, p. 565; Carson, *John*, p. 644; Morris, *John*, p. 742; Köstenberger, *John*, p. 569. For brief discussions of the interpretation of Jesus' command, see Brown, *John 13–21*, pp. 992–3, 1011–17; Carson, *John*, pp. 641–5.

13 Tilborg, *Imaginative Love*, pp. 199–207. For his reading of John 20.11–18 as a 'recognition scene' familiar from ancient Greek novels, see especially *Imaginative Love*, pp. 203–6.

14 Tilborg (*Imaginative Love*, pp. 207–8) reads his relationships with his mother, Mary, Martha and the Samaritan woman at the well similarly.

15 Tilborg, *Imaginative Love*, pp. 237–52.

16 For examples of this form, see Chariton, *Callirhoe*; Achilles Tatius, *Leucippe and Clitophon*; Xenophon of Ephesus, *Anthia and Habrocomes*.

17 Not least given John 13.13, where Jesus says that his disciples quite rightly call him 'teacher' and 'lord'.

18 Conway, *Men and Women*, p. 137.

19 For details see Michaels, *John*, pp. 669–70, especially n. 43.

20 So Moloney, *John*, pp. 357–8.

21 So e.g. Brown, *John 1–12*, p. 449; Köstenberger, *John*, pp. 363–4.

22 So e.g. Brown, *John 1–12*, p. 454; Haenchen, *John 1*, p. 85.

23 For details, see Haenchen, *John 1*, p. 85.

24 Barrett, *St John*, pp. 414–15.

25 Generally, the NT uses *mnēmoneuō, mimnēskomai, anamimnēskō, hupomimnēskō, mneian echō* and *mneian poieō*. John uses *mimnēskomai* (John 2.17, 22; 12.17) and *mnēmoneuō* (John 15.20; 16.4, 21).

26 So Michaels, *John*, p. 670.

27 Lindars (*John*, p. 416) claims it was 'not unheard of in ancient literature'. Moloney (*John*, p. 357) claims that the anointing of feet is unique to this text and Luke 7.38. Even Matt. 26.7 and Mark 14.3 have perfume poured on Jesus' head. The relationship between these texts is complex and it is not necessary to discuss it here. For one discussion, see e.g. Brown, *John 1–12*, pp. 449–54.

28 Lindars, *John*, pp. 416–17.

29 Brant, 'Husband Hunting', p. 217.

30 On Ruth 3.4, 7, see Edward F. Campbell, *Ruth*, AB 7 (New Haven: Yale University Press, 1975), p. 121; Robert L. Hubbard, *The Book of Ruth*, NICOT (Grand Rapids: Eerdmans, 1988), p. 203. On 2 Samuel 11.8, see P. Kyle McCarter, *2 Samuel*, AB 9 (New Haven: Yale University Press, 1984), p. 286; David G. Firth, *1 & 2 Samuel*, ApOTC 8 (Nottingham: Apollos, 2009), p. 418.

31 For anointing feet as sexual action in ancient Greek literature, see Tilborg, *Imaginative Love*, pp. 197–8.

32 Brant, 'Husband Hunting', pp. 217–18.

33 Nard may also be found in a description of paradise (*1 En.* 32.1), a magic spell (*T. Sol.* 6.10) and the story of what Adam was allowed to take out of the garden (*Apoc. Mos.* 29.6) in the OT Pseudepigrapha. Of these only the *Testament of Solomon* makes clear possible uses for nard – one of which was magic.

34 Brant ('Husband Hunting', pp. 218–19), who also mentions Song of Sol. 4.1. However, there the lover describes the eyes behind his beloved's veil before describing her hair – which implies he is imagining what lies behind the veil. For wearing hair loose as a prelude to sexual intercourse in Roman literature, see Tilborg, *Imaginative Love*, p. 198, citing Apuleius, *Metamorphoses* 2.9, 17.

35 Similarly, Brant, who suggests ('Husband Hunting', p. 219) that Mary offers herself as a wife.

36 Commentators tend to read Mary's response in terms of her faith – for a nice summary, see Köstenberger, *John*, pp. 337–8. Given the actions of the sisters to date and Jesus' apparent failure to act in a timely manner, it seems to me that Mary is not best pleased. I think she finds herself in that confusing situation of believing in Jesus, loving him and wanting to be absolutely furious with him.

37 Ironically, the people who had come to comfort Mary and Martha read this as his grief for Lazarus (John 11.36).

38 The Greek verb *embrimaomai* (translated 'greatly disturbed' in NRSV) refers to horses snorting, and so to human beings being deeply emotionally moved (LSJ 540).

39 The Greek verb *tarassō* (NRSV has 'deeply moved') means 'stir' or 'trouble'.

40   Brant, 'Husband Hunting', pp. 219–22. For this reason, I cannot agree
     with the conclusion of Tilborg (*Imaginative Love*, pp. 193–9) that Jesus'
     interaction with Mary of Bethany fits the alleged pattern according to
     which Jesus has good relationships with women which he closes down
     when they come near. His evidence for this in the case of Mary of Bethany
     is that he interprets her letting her hair down – which had a sexual
     meaning for her (*Imaginative Love*, p. 198) – as a sign of mourning
     (*Imaginative Love*, p. 198) thus rejecting her advances. The likelihood of
     any respectable ancient Jewish man making public such an action even
     if he wants to marry her seems most unlikely; cf. the way Boaz follows
     up Ruth's actions with subtlety and discretion (Ruth 3—4), and the
     way Joseph seeks to cover Mary's alleged indiscretion graciously (Matt.
     1.18–19). Jesus' interpretation of the event reads most naturally as a
     defence of Mary in the face of someone attacking her actions. This kind
     of defence is what one would expect from someone who cares. If Jesus
     had 'gone cold' on Mary, he would more likely respond as Simon does
     in Luke 7.39.

41   Martin, *Single Saviour*, pp. 99–100. His point throughout the chapter
     concerned ('Sex and the Single Saviour') is that the early Church fa-
     thers and modern historical critics have to exercise some imagination
     to come to their conclusions, so what is to stop others with differ-
     ent perspectives from doing the same? Given the failure of the
     historical-critical project to produce assured and universally accepted
     results, he recommends that we simply accept that there are different
     readings. I can only accept this so far: the historical-critical project has
     not been a complete failure and must have bettered our understanding
     of the text, as it is still the common language of scholars of differing
     and competing ideologies and methodologies (not unlike utilitarian-
     ism in ethical discourse when it hits real politics). Hence I stick to my
     judgement that we must see whether the text will accept a reading or
     stand as a witness against it when interpreting the biblical text.

42   Martin, *Single Saviour*, pp. 99–100.

43   For Jesus and the beloved disciple, see *agapaō* in John 13.23; 19.26; 21.7,
     20; and *phileō* in John 20.2. For the Father and the Son, see *agapaō* in
     e.g. John 3.35; and *phileō* in John 5.20.

44   Martin, *Single Saviour*, p. 100.

45   *HALOT* 2.387. See e.g. the Hebrew text of Isa. 57.8, which the LXX
     translators render idiomatically as 'those you sleep with'.

46   Martin, *Single Saviour*, p. 100.

47   Searching LXX, Josephus, Philo and the Greek OT Pseudepigrapha on
     the Bibleworks 10 search engine. Having located a reference to *huios
     anthrōpou* in *Joseph and Aseneth* in the early 2000s which was not then
     on *TLG*, I am aware that search engines are only as accurate as the data
     (including variants) that are put into them. So I am not claiming that

this search is exhaustive, but it is certainly thorough and indicative until further data appears.

48 Martin, *Single Saviour*, p. 100.

49 There is a long history of interpretation with regard to the alleged comparisons of Peter and the beloved disciple. I do not intend to go into it here as there is no need.

50 He uses *agapaō* in vv. 15 and 16, and *phileō* in vv. 15, 16 and 17.

51 So, e.g. Brown (*John 13–21*, pp. 1107–8) and Barrett (*St John*, p. 585) on John 21.18–19.

52 For details, see e.g. Brown, *John 1–12*, pp. 335–6; Lindars, *John*, pp. 305–8; Barrett, *St John*, pp. 589–91; Carson, *John*, pp. 333–4; Morris, *John*, pp. 778–9; Moloney, *John*, p. 259; Keener, *John*, pp. 735–6; Köstenberger, *John*, pp. 245–9; Michaels, *John*, p. 746.

53 So e.g. Morris, *John*, p. 781.

54 The law (Lev. 20.10; Deut. 22.22) does not specify in which order adulterers are to be stoned or whether they are to be executed together. If the scribes and Pharisees had already stoned the man, this would explain why they suggest that Moses prescribed stoning for 'such as these' (in the feminine form).

55 So e.g. Keener, *John*, pp. 737, 1104–9.

56 So e.g. Michaels, *John*, p. 496.

57 Lindars, *John*, p. 311.

58 Morris, *John*, p. 786.

Bibliography

Allison, Dale C. *Jesus of Nazareth: Millenarian Prophet*. Minneapolis: Fortress, 1998.

Allison, Dale C. *Constructing Jesus: Memory, Imagination and History*. London: SPCK, 2010.

Alter, Robert. *The Art of Biblical Narrative*. Rev. edn. New York: Basic Books, 2011.

Angel, Andrew R. 'From Wild Men to Wise and Wicked Women: An Investigation into Male Heterosexuality in Second Temple Interpretations of the Ladies Wisdom and Folly.' In Deborah W. Rooke (ed.), *A Question of Sex? Gender and Difference in the Hebrew Bible and Beyond*. Hebrew Bible Monographs 14, pp. 145–61. Sheffield: Sheffield Phoenix, 2007.

Angel, Andrew R. '*Crucifixus Vincens*: The "Son of God" as Divine Warrior in Matthew.' *CBQ* 73 (2011), pp. 299–317.

Angel, Andrew R. *Angels: Ancient Whispers of Another World*. Eugene, OR: Cascade, 2012.

Arterbury, Andrew E. 'Breaking the Betrothal Bonds: Hospitality in John 4'. *CBQ* 72 (2010), pp. 63–83.

Ashton, John. *Understanding the Fourth Gospel*. Oxford: Clarendon, 1991.

Balla, Ibolya. 'Ben Sira/Sirach.' In William Loader, *The Pseudepigrapha on Sexuality: Attitudes towards Sexuality in Apocalypses, Testaments, Legends, Wisdom and Related Literature*, pp. 363–98. Attitudes towards Sexuality in Judaism and Christianity in the Hellenistic Greco-Roman Era. Grand Rapids: Eerdmans, 2011.

Barrett, Charles Kingsley. *The Gospel according to St John: An Introduction with Commentary and Notes on the Greek Text*. 2nd edn. London: SPCK, 1978.

Beasley-Murray, G. R. *John*. 2nd edn. WBC 36. Nashville: Nelson, 1999.

Bennema, Cornelis. *Encountering Jesus: Character Studies in the Gospel of John*. Milton Keynes: Paternoster, 2009.

Bernard, J. H. *A Critical and Exegetical Commentary on the Gospel according to St. John*. 2 vols. ICC. London: T&T Clark, 1928.

Black, C. Clifton. 'Rhetorical Criticism.' In Joel B. Green (ed.), *Hearing the New Testament: Strategies for Interpretation*, pp. 166–88. 2nd edn. Grand Rapids: Eerdmans, 2010.

Bligh, John. 'Jesus in Samaria.' *HeyJ* 3 (1962), pp. 329–46.

Botha, J. Eugene. *Jesus and the Samaritan Woman: A Speech Acts Reading of John 4:1-42*. NovTSup 65. Leiden: Brill, 1991.

Botha, J. Eugene. 'John 4.16: A Difficult Text Speech Act Theoretically Revisited.' In Mark W. G. Stibbe (ed.), *The Gospel of John as Literature: An Anthology of Twentieth-Century Perspectives*, pp. 183–92. Leiden: Brill, 1993.

Brant, Jo-Ann A. 'Husband Hunting: Characterization and Narrative Art in the Gospel of John.' *BibInt* 4 (1996), pp. 205–23.

Brant, Jo-Ann A. 'Hammering Out a Response from One Mennonite's Perspective.' *Semeia* 77 (1997), pp. 285–90.

Brant, Jo-Ann A. *Dialogue and Drama: Elements of Greek Tragedy in the Fourth Gospel.* Peabody, MA: Hendrickson, 2004.

Brant, Jo-Ann. *John.* Paideia. Grand Rapids: Baker Academic, 2011.

Brodie, Thomas L. *The Gospel According to John: A Literary and Theological Commentary.* Oxford: Oxford University Press, 1993.

Brown, Dan. *The Da Vinci Code.* New York: Doubleday, 2003.

Brown, R. E. *The Gospel according to John: 1–12.* AB 29. New Haven: Yale University Press, 1966.

Brown, R. E. *The Gospel according to John: 13–21.* AB 29A. New Haven: Yale University Press, 1970.

Bruce, F. F. *The Gospel of John: Introduction, Exposition and Notes.* Grand Rapids: Eerdmans, 1983.

Bruner, Frederick Dale. *The Gospel of John: A Commentary.* Grand Rapids: Eerdmans, 2012.

Bultmann, Rudolph. *The Gospel of John: A Commentary.* Translated by G. R. Beasley-Murray. Oxford: Blackwell, 1971.

Burge, Gary M. *John.* NIV Application Commentary. Grand Rapids: Zondervan, 2000.

Byrne, Brendan. 'Beloved Disciple.' *ABD* 1, pp. 658–61.

Byrskog, Samuel. *Jesus the Only Teacher: Didactic Authority and Transmission in Ancient Israel, Ancient Judaism and the Matthean Community.* ConBNT 24. Stockholm: Almqvist & Wiksell, 1994.

Calvin, John. *Commentary on the Gospel according to John. Volume 1.* Translated by William Pringle. Calvin's Commentaries volume 18. Grand Rapids: Baker Books, 2009.

Campbell, Edward F. *Ruth.* AB 7. New Haven: Yale University Press, 1975.

Cantarella, Eva. *Bisexuality in the Ancient World.* Translated by Cormac Ó Cuilleanáin. New Haven: Yale University Press, 2002.

Cantwell, Laurence. 'Immortal Longings in Sermone Humili: A Study of John 4.5-26.' *SJT* 36 (1983), pp. 73–86.

Carlson, Stephen C. *The Gospel Hoax: Morton Smith's Invention of Secret Mark.* Waco, TX: Baylor University Press, 2005.

Carmichael, Calum M. 'Marriage and the Samaritan Woman.' *NTS* 26 (1980), pp. 332–46.

Carson, D. A. *The Gospel according to John.* Pillar New Testament Commentaries. Grand Rapids: Eerdmans, 1991.

Carter, Warren. *John and Empire: Initial Explorations.* New York: T&T Clark, 2008.

Casey, Maurice. *Is John's Gospel True?* London: Routledge, 1996.

Casey, Maurice. *Jesus of Nazareth: An Independent Historian's Account of His Life and Teaching.* London: T&T Clark, 2010.

Charlesworth, James H. *The Historical Jesus.* Nashville: Abingdon, 2008.

Colwell, E. C. 'A Definite Rule for the Use of the Article in the Greek New Testament.' *JBL* 52 (1933), pp. 12–21.

Conway, Colleen M. *Men and Women in the Fourth Gospel: Gender and Johannine Characterization.* SBLDS 167. Atlanta: Society of Biblical Literature, 1999.

Cowley, A. E. *Aramaic Papyri of the Fifth Century B.C.* Ancient Texts and Translations. Eugene, OR: Wipf & Stock, 2005.

Crossan, John Dominic. *The Historical Jesus: The Life of a Mediterranean Jewish Peasant.* Edinburgh: T&T Clark, 1991.

Culpepper, R. Alan. *Anatomy of the Fourth Gospel: A Study in Literary Design.* Foundations and Facets. Philadelphia: Fortress, 1983.

Culpepper, R. Alan. *The Gospel and Letters of John.* Interpreting Biblical Texts. Nashville: Abingdon, 1998.

Danker, Frederick W., Walter Bauer, William F. Arndt and F. Wilbur Gingrich. *Greek-English Lexicon of the New Testament and Other Early Christian Literature.* 3rd edn. Chicago: University of Chicago Press, 2000.

Daube, David. 'Jesus and the Samaritan Woman: The Meaning of *sugchraomai.*' *JBL* 69 (1950), pp. 137–47.

Davies, W. D. and Dale C. Allison. *A Critical and Exegetical Commentary on the Gospel According to Saint Matthew. Volume III: XIX–XXVIII.* 2nd edn. ICC. London: T&T Clark, 2004.

Day, Janeth Norfleete. *The Woman at the Well: Interpretation of John 4:1-42 in Retrospect and Prospect.* BibInt 61. Leiden: Brill, 2002.

Depuydt, Leo. 'The Alleged *Gospel of Jesus' Wife:* Assessment and Evaluation of Authenticity.' *HTR* 107 (2014), pp. 172–89.

Derrett, J. Duncan M. *Law in the New Testament.* London: Darton, Longman & Todd, 1970.

Deutsch, Celia. 'The Sirach 51 Acrostic: Confession and Exhortation.' *ZAW* 94 (1982), pp. 400–9.

Dover, Kenneth J. *Greek Homosexuality.* Rev. edn. Cambridge, MA: Harvard University Press, 1989.

Duke, Paul D. *Irony in the Fourth Gospel.* Atlanta: John Knox, 1985.

Dunn, James D. G. *Christianity in the Making. Volume 1: Jesus Remembered.* Grand Rapids: Eerdmans, 2003.

Edwards, Mark. *John.* Blackwell Bible Commentaries. Oxford: Blackwell, 2004.

Ehrman, Bart. *Lost Christianities: The Battles for Scripture and the Faiths We Never Knew.* Oxford: Oxford University Press, 2003.

Eslinger, Lyle. 'The Wooing of the Woman at the Well: Jesus, the Reader and Reader-Response Criticism.' In Mark W. G. Stibbe (ed.), *The Gospel of John as Literature: An Anthology of Twentieth-Century Perspectives*, pp. 165–82. Leiden: Brill, 1993.

Fewell, Danna Nolan and Gary A. Phillips. 'Drawn to Excess, or Reading Beyond Betrothal.' *Semeia* 77 (1997), pp. 23–58.

Fiorenza, Elisabeth Schüssler. *In Memory of Her: A Feminist Theological Reconstruction of Christian Origins.* London: SCM Press, 1983.

Firth, David G. *1 & 2 Samuel.* ApOTC 8. Nottingham: Apollos, 2009.

Fitzmyer, Joseph A. *The Gospel according to Luke X–XXIV.* AB 28A. New York: Doubleday, 1985.

Fitzmyer, Joseph A. *Romans.* AB 33. New York: Doubleday, 1993.

Fitzmyer, Joseph A. *Tobit.* CEJL. Berlin: de Gruyter, 2003.

Fitzmyer, Joseph A. *First Corinthians.* AB 32. New Haven: Yale University Press, 2008.

Fox, Michael V. *Proverbs 1–9.* AB 18A. New York: Doubleday, 2000.

Fox, Michael V. *Proverbs 10–31.* AB 18B. New Haven: Yale University Press, 2009.

Goodman, David. 'Do Angels Eat?' *JJS* 37 (1986), pp. 160–75.

Green, Joel B. *Hearing the New Testament: Strategies for Interpretation.* 2nd edn. Grand Rapids: Eerdmans, 2010.

Greenberg, Moshe. *Ezekiel 1–20.* AB 22. New Haven: Yale University Press, 1983.

Greenberg, Moshe. *Ezekiel 21–37.* AB 22A. New Haven: Yale University Press, 1997.

Haenchen, Ernst. *John 1: A Commentary on the Gospel of John Chapters 1–6.* Translated by Robert W. Funk. Hermeneia. Philadelphia: Fortress, 1984.

Haenchen, Ernst. *John 2: A Commentary on the Gospel of John Chapters 7–21.* Translated by Robert W. Funk. Hermeneia. Philadelphia: Fortress, 1984.

Halperin, David M. *One Hundred Years of Homosexuality and Other Essays on Greek Love.* New Ancient World. London: Routledge, 1990.

Hayman, A. P. 'Monotheism – A Misused Word in Jewish Studies?' *JJS* 42 (1991), pp. 1–15.

Heil, John Paul. *Jesus Walking on the Sea: Meaning and Gospel Functions of Matt 14:22-33, Mark 6:45-52 and John 6:15b-21.* AnBib 87. Rome: Biblical Institute Press, 1981.

Hendriksen, William. *The Gospel of John.* London: Banner of Truth Trust, 1954.

Hess, Richard S. *Song of Songs.* BCOTWP. Grand Rapids: Baker Academic, 2005.

Holladay, William L. *Jeremiah 1.* Hermeneia. Philadelphia: Fortress, 1986.

Hollander, H. W. and Marinus de Jonge. *The Testaments of the Twelve Patriarchs: A Commentary.* SVTP 8. Leiden: Brill, 1985.

Hornblower, Simon, Antony Spawforth and Esther Eidinow (eds). *The Oxford Classical Dictionary.* 4th edn. Oxford: Oxford University Press, 2012.

Hoskyns, E. C. *The Fourth Gospel.* Edited by Francis Noel Davey. 2nd edn. London: Faber and Faber, 1947.

Howard, Wilbur F. and Arthur J. Gossip. *The Gospel according to St. John.* IB 12. Nashville: Abingdon, 1952.

Hubbard, Robert L. *The Book of Ruth*. NICOT. Grand Rapids: Eerdmans, 1988.

Isenberg, Wesley W. 'The Gospel of Philip (II, 3).' In James M. Robinson (ed.), *The Nag Hammadi Library in English*, pp. 139–60. 4th edn. Leiden: Brill, 1996.

Jeffery, Peter. *The Secret Gospel of Mark Unveiled: Imagined Rituals of Sex, Death and Madness in a Biblical Forgery*. New Haven: Yale University Press, 2007.

Käsemann, Ernst. *The Testament of Jesus: A Study in the Gospel of John in the Light of Chapter 17*. Translated by Gerhard Krodel. NTL. London: SCM Press, 1968.

Kazantzakis, Nikos. *The Last Temptation of Christ*. Translated by P. A. Bien. New York: Simon & Schuster, 1960.

Keener, Craig S. *The Gospel of John: A Commentary*. 2 vols. Peabody, MA: Hendrickson, 2003.

Kim, Jean K. 'A Korean Feminist Reading of John 4:1-42.' *Semeia* 78 (1997), pp. 109–19.

King, Karen L. 'Jesus said to them, "My wife . . .": A New Coptic Papyrus Fragment'. *HTR* 107 (2014), pp. 131–59.

Kittel, Gerhard and Gerhard Friedrich, eds. *Theological Dictionary of the New Testament*. Translated by Geoffrey W. Bromiley. 10 vols. Grand Rapids: Eerdmans, 1964–1976.

Kobel, Esther. *Dining with John: Communal Meals and Identity Formation in the Fourth Gospel and its Historical and Cultural Context*. BibInt 109. Leiden: Brill, 2011.

Koehler, L., W. Baumgartner and J. J. Stamm. *The Hebrew and Aramaic Lexicon of the Old Testament*. Translated and edited under the supervision of M. E. J. Richardson. 4 vols. Leiden: Brill, 1994–1999.

Koester, Craig R. 'Hearing, Seeing and Believing in the Gospel of John.' *Bib* 70 (1989), pp. 327–48.

Koester, Craig R. '"The Savior of the World" (John 4:42).' *JBL* 109 (1990), pp. 665–80.

Köstenberger, Andreas J. *John*. BECNT. Grand Rapids: Baker Academic, 2004.

Kruse, Colin G. *The Letters of John*. Pillar New Testament Commentary. Grand Rapids: Eerdmans, 2000.

Kysar, Robert. *John: The Maverick Gospel*. 3rd edn. Louisville: Westminster John Knox, 2007.

Lawrence, D. H. *The Escaped Cock*. Isle of Skye: Aquila, 1982.

Lewis, C. S. *The Four Loves*. London: HarperCollins, 1977.

Liddell, Henry George, Robert Scott and Henry Stuart Jones. *A Greek-English Lexicon*. 9th edn with revised supplement. Oxford: Clarendon, 1996.

Lightfoot, R. H. *St. John's Gospel: A Commentary*. Oxford: Clarendon, 1956.

Lincoln, Andrew T. *The Gospel according to St John*. BNTC. London: Continuum, 2005.

Lindars, Barnabas. *The Gospel of John*. NCB. London: Oliphants, 1972.

Loader, William. *The Septuagint, Sexuality and the New Testament: Case Studies on the Impact of the LXX in Philo and the New Testament*. Grand Rapids: Eerdmans, 2004.

Loader, William. *Sexuality and the Jesus Tradition*. Grand Rapids: Eerdmans, 2005.

Loader, William. *Enoch, Levi, and Jubilees on Sexuality: Attitudes towards Sexuality in the Early Enoch Literature, the Aramaic Levi Document, and the Book of Jubilees*. Attitudes towards Sexuality in Judaism and Christianity in the Hellenistic Greco-Roman Era. Grand Rapids: Eerdmans, 2007.

Loader, William. *The Dead Sea Scrolls on Sexuality: Attitudes towards Sexuality in Sectarian and Related Literature at Qumran*. Attitudes towards Sexuality in Judaism and Christianity in the Hellenistic Greco-Roman Era. Grand Rapids: Eerdmans, 2009.

Loader, William. *Sexuality in the New Testament: Understanding the key texts*. London: SPCK, 2010.

Loader, William. *Philo, Josephus, and the Testaments on Sexuality: Attitudes towards Sexuality in the Writings of Philo and Josephus and in the Testaments of the Twelve Patriarchs*. Attitudes towards Sexuality in Judaism and Christianity in the Hellenistic Greco-Roman Era. Grand Rapids: Eerdmans, 2011.

Loader, William. *The Pseudepigrapha on Sexuality: Attitudes towards Sexuality in Apocalypses, Testaments, Legends, Wisdom and Related Literature*. Attitudes towards Sexuality in Judaism and Christianity in the Hellenistic Greco-Roman Era. Grand Rapids: Eerdmans, 2011.

Loader, William. *Making Sense of Sex: Attitudes towards Sexuality in Early Jewish and Christian Literature*. Grand Rapids: Eerdmans, 2013.

Longman III, Tremper. *Proverbs*. BCOTWP. Grand Rapids: Baker Academic, 2006.

McCarter, P. Kyle. *2 Samuel*. AB 9. New Haven: Yale University Press, 1984.

Maccini, Robert Gordon. 'A Reassessment of the Woman at the Well in John 4 in the Light of the Samaritan Context.' *JSNT* 53 (1994), pp. 35–46.

McHugh, John F. *A Critical and Exegetical Commentary on John 1–4*. ICC. London: T&T Clark, 2009.

McNally, Terrence. *Corpus Christi*. New York: Grove Press, 1998.

McWhirter, Jocelyn. *The Bridegroom Messiah and the People of God: Marriage in the Fourth Gospel*. SNTSMS 138. Cambridge: Cambridge University Press, 2006.

Makowski, John F. 'Greek Love in the Greek Novel.' In Edmund P. Cueva and Shannon N. Byrne (eds), *A Companion to the Ancient Novel*, pp. 490–501. Blackwell Companions to the Ancient World. Oxford: Wiley Blackwell, 2014.

Malina, Bruce J. and Richard L. Rohrbaugh. *Social-Science Commentary on the Gospel of John*. Minneapolis: Fortress, 1998.

Marsh, John. *Saint John*. PNTC. London: Penguin, 1968.

Martin, Dale B. *Sex and the Single Saviour*. Louisville: Westminster John Knox, 2006.

Martin, Michael W. 'Betrothal Journey Narratives.' *CBQ* 70 (2008), pp. 505–23.

Meier, John Paul. *A Marginal Jew: Rethinking the Historical Jesus. Volume 1: The Roots of the Problem and the Person*. ABRL. New York: Doubleday, 1991.

Meier, John Paul. *A Marginal Jew: Rethinking the Historical Jesus. Volume 2: Mentor, Message, and Miracles*. ABRL. New York: Doubleday, 1994.

Meier, John Paul. *A Marginal Jew: Rethinking the Historical Jesus. Volume 3: Companions and Competitors*. ABRL. New York: Doubleday, 2001.

Meier, John Paul. *A Marginal Jew: Rethinking the Historical Jesus. Volume 4: Law and Love*. ABRL. New York: Doubleday, 2009.

Meyers, Carol L. and Eric M. Meyers. *Zechariah 9–14*. AB 25C. New York: Doubleday, 1993.

Michaels, J. Ramsey. *The Gospel of John*. NICNT. Grand Rapids: Eerdmans, 2010.

Milne, Bruce. *The Message of John*. BST. Leicester: Inter-Varsity Press, 1993.

Moloney, Francis J. *Glory not Dishonour: Reading John 13–21*. Minneapolis: Fortress, 1998.

Moloney, Francis J. *The Gospel of John*. SP 4. Collegeville, MN: Liturgical Press, 1998.

Moloney, Francis J. *Love in the Gospel of John: An Exegetical, Theological, and Literary Study*. Grand Rapids: Baker Academic, 2013.

Montefiore, Hugh. 'Jesus, the Revelation of God.' In Norman Pittenger (ed.), *Christ for Us Today: Papers from the Fiftieth Annual Conference of Modern Churchmen, held at Somerville College Oxford, 24-28 July, 1967*, pp. 101–16. London: SCM Press, 1968.

Moore, George Foot. *Judaism in the First Centuries of the Christian Era: The Age of the Tannaim Volume 2*. Cambridge, MA: Harvard University Press, 1927.

Moore, Stephen D. 'Are There Impurities in the Living Water that the Johannine Jesus Dispenses? Deconstruction, Feminism, and the Samaritan Woman.' *BibInt* 1 (2003), pp. 207–27.

Morales, Helen. *Vision and Narrative in Achilles Tatius' Leucippe and Clitophon*. Cambridge Classical Studies. Cambridge: Cambridge University Press, 2004.

Morris, Leon. *The Gospel according to John*. Rev. edn. Grand Rapids: Eerdmans, 1995.

Munro, Winsome. 'The Pharisee and the Samaritan in John: Polar or Parallel?' *CBQ* 57 (1995), pp. 710–28.

Muraoka, Takamitsu. 'Sir. 51:13-20: An Erotic Hymn to Wisdom?' *JSJ* 10 (1979), pp. 166–78.

Murphy, Roland E. 'Wisdom and Eros in Proverbs 1–9.' *CBQ* 50 (1988), pp. 600–3.

Murphy, Roland E. *The Song of Songs*. Hermeneia. Minneapolis: Fortress, 1990.

Newbigin, Lesslie. *The Light Has Come: An Exposition of the Fourth Gospel*. Grand Rapids: Eerdmans, 1982.

Neyrey, Jerome H. 'Jacob Traditions and the Interpretation of John 4:10-26.' *CBQ* 41 (1979), pp. 419–37.

Neyrey, Jerome H. *The Gospel of John*. NCBC. Cambridge: Cambridge University Press, 2007.

O'Day, Gail R. *Revelation in the Fourth Gospel: Narrative Mode and Theological Claim*. Fortress: Philadelphia, 1986.

O'Day, Gail R. *The Gospel of John*. *NIB* 9. Nashville: Abingdon, 1995.

Okure, Teresa. *The Johannine Approach to Mission: A Contextual Study of John 4:1-42*. WUNT 31. Tübingen: J. C. B. Mohr, 1888.

Olsson, Birger. *Structure and Meaning in the Fourth Gospel: A Text-Linguistic Analysis of John 2:1-11 and 4:1-42*. ConBNT 6. Lund: Gleerup, 1974.

Painter, John. *1, 2, and 3 John*. SP 18. Collegeville, MN: Liturgical Press, 2002.

Parsenios, George L. *Departure and Consolation: The Johannine Farewell Discourses in Light of Greco-Roman Literature*. NovTSup 117. Leiden: Brill, 2005.

Pazdan, Mary Margaret. 'Nicodemus and the Samaritan Woman: Contrasting Models of Discipleship.' *BTB* 17 (1987), pp. 145–8.

Perkins, Pheme. *The Gospel according to St. John: A Theological Commentary*. Herald Scriptural Library. Chicago: Franciscan Herald Press, 1978.

Phipps, William E. *Was Jesus Married? The Distortion of Sexuality in the Christian Tradition*. New York: Harper & Row, 1970.

Phipps, William E. *The Sexuality of Jesus: Theological and Literary Perspectives*. New York: Harper & Row, 1973.

Phipps, William E. *The Sexuality of Jesus*. Cleveland, OH: Pilgrim Press, 1996.

Rabinowitz, Isaac. 'The Qumran Hebrew Original of Ben Sira's Concluding Acrostic on Wisdom.' *HUCA* 42 (1971), pp. 173–84.

Reinhartz, Adele. 'The Gospel of John.' In Elisabeth Schüssler Fiorenza (ed.), *Searching the Scripture. Volume Two: A Feminist Commentary*, pp. 561–600. London: SCM Press, 1995.

Sakenfeld, Katherine Doob. 'Whose Text Is It?' *JBL* 127 (2008), pp. 5–18.

Sanday, William. *The Criticism of the Fourth Gospel*. Oxford: Clarendon, 1905.

Sanders, E. P. *Jesus and Judaism*. London: SCM Press, 1985.

Sanders, J. A. *The Psalms Scroll of Qumran Cave 11 (11QPsa)*. DJD 4. Oxford: Clarendon, 1971.

Sanders, J. N. and B. A. Mastin. *The Gospel according to John*. BNTC. London: Black, 1968.

Satlow, Michael L. *Tasting the Dish: Rabbinic Rhetorics of Sexuality.* BJS 303. Atlanta: Scholars Press, 1995.

Satlow, Michael L. 'Jewish Constructions of Nakedness in Late Antiquity.' *JBL* 116 (1997), pp. 429–54.

Satlow, Michael L. *Jewish Marriage in Antiquity.* Princeton: Princeton University Press, 2001.

Schenke, Hans-Martin. 'The Gospel of Philip.' In Wilhelm Schneemelcher (ed.), *New Testament Apocrypha. Volume One: Gospels and Related Writings,* pp. 179–208. Translated by R. McL. Wilson. Rev. edn. Louisville: Westminster John Knox, 1991.

Schnackenburg, Rudolph. *The Gospel according to John, volume 1: Introduction and Commentary on Chapters 1–4.* Translated by Kevin Smyth. HThKNT. New York: Herder, 1968.

Schnackenburg, Rudolph. *The Gospel according to John, volume 2: Commentary on Chapters 5–12.* Translated by Cecily Hastings, Francis McDonagh, David Smith and Richard Foley. HThKNT. New York: Crossroad, 1982.

Schnackenburg, Rudolph. *The Gospel according to John, volume 3: Commentary on Chapters 13–21.* Translated by David Smith and G. A. Kon. HThKNT. New York: Crossroad, 1982.

Schneiders, Sandra M. 'Women in the Fourth Gospel and the Role of Women in the Contemporary Church.' *BTB* 12 (1982), pp. 35–45.

Schneiders, Sandra M. *The Revelatory Text: Interpreting the New Testament as Sacred Scripture.* San Francisco: HarperSanFrancisco, 1991.

Schnelle, Udo. *Antidocetic Christology in the Gospel of John: An Investigation of the Place of the Fourth Gospel in the Johannine School.* Translated by Linda M. Maloney. Minneapolis: Fortress, 1992.

Schottroff, Luise. 'The Samaritan Woman and the Notion of Sexuality in the Fourth Gospel.' In Fernando F. Segovia (ed.), *'What is John?' Volume II: Literary and Social Readings of the Fourth Gospel,* pp. 157–81. SBL Symposium Series 7. Atlanta: Scholars Press, 1998.

Segovia, Fernando F. *'What is John?' Volume II: Literary and Social Readings of the Fourth Gospel.* SBL Symposium Series 7. Atlanta: Scholars Press, 1998.

Shanks, Hershel. 'The Saga of "The Gospel of Jesus' Wife."' *BAR* 41.3 (2015), pp. 54–9.

Skehan, Patrick W. and Alexander A. di Lella. *The Wisdom of Ben Sira.* AB 39. New York: Doubleday, 1987.

Sloyan, Gerard. *John.* Interpretation. Louisville: Westminster John Knox, 1988.

Smith, Morton. *Clement of Alexandria and the Secret Gospel of Mark.* Cambridge, MA: Harvard University Press, 1973.

Spencer, F. Scott. 'Feminist Criticism.' In Joel B. Green (ed.), *Hearing the New Testament: Strategies for Interpretation,* pp. 289–325. 2nd edn. Grand Rapids: Eerdmans, 2010.

Staley, Jeffrey Lloyd. *The Print's First Kiss: A Rhetorical Investigation of the Implied Reader in the Fourth Gospel.* SBLDS 82. Atlanta: Scholars Press, 1988.

Steinberg, Leo. *The Sexuality of Christ in Renaissance Art and in Modern Oblivion,* 2nd edn. Chicago: University of Chicago Press, 1996.

Stibbe, Mark W. G. *John.* Readings. Sheffield: JSOT Press, 1993.

Strack, Hermann Leberecht and Paul Billerbeck. *Kommentar zum Neuen Testament aus Talmud und Midrasch.* 6 vols. Munich: Beck, 1922–1961.

Strecker, Georg. *The Johannine Letters: A Commentary on 1, 2, and 3 John.* Translated by Linda M. Maloney. Hermeneia. Minneapolis: Fortress, 1996.

Talbert, Charles H. *Reading John: A Literary and Theological Commentary on the Fourth Gospel and the Johannine Epistles.* Reading the New Testament Series. London: SPCK, 1992.

Tenney, Merrill C. *The Gospel of John.* Expositor's Bible Commentary. London: Pickering & Inglis, 1981.

Trible, Phyllis. *God and the Rhetoric of Sexuality.* London: SCM Press, 1978.

Vanhoozer, Kevin J. 'The Reader in New Testament Interpretation.' In Joel B. Green (ed.), *Hearing the New Testament: Strategies for Interpretation,* pp. 259–88. 2nd edn. Grand Rapids: Eerdmans, 2010.

van Tilborg, Sjef. *Imaginative Love in John.* BibInt 2. Leiden: Brill, 1993.

von Wahlde, Urban C. *The Gospel and Letters of John. Volume 2: Commentary on the Gospel of John.* ECC. Grand Rapids: Eerdmans, 2010.

Waetjen, Herman C. *The Gospel of the Beloved Disciple: A Work in Two Editions.* London: T&T Clark, 2005.

Waltke, Bruce K. *The Book of Proverbs Chapters 1–15.* NICOT. Grand Rapids: Eerdmans, 2004.

Watson, Alan. *Jesus and the Jews: The Pharisaic Tradition in John.* Athens, GA: University of Georgia Press, 2012.

Westcott, B. F. *The Gospel According to John.* London: John Murray, 1908.

Wilson, R. McL. *The Gospel of Philip: Translated from the Coptic Text, with an Introduction and Commentary.* London: Mowbrays, 1962.

Winston, David. *The Wisdom of Solomon.* AB 43. New York: Doubleday, 1979.

Witherington III, Ben. *John's Wisdom: A Commentary on the Fourth Gospel.* Louisville: Westminster John Knox, 1995.

Wright, N. T. *Jesus and the Victory of God.* Christian Origins and the Question of God, vol. 1. London: SPCK, 1996.

Wright Knust, Jennifer. *Unprotected Texts: The Bible's Surprising Contradictions About Sex and Desire.* New York: HarperOne, 2011.

Yarborough, Robert W. *1–3 John.* BECNT. Grand Rapids: Baker Academic, 2008.

Index of ancient sources

OLD TESTAMENT

Genesis 12, 24,
  127 n.65
1 121 n.30
1.1 LXX 12
1.1—2.4a 12
1.27 144 n.44
2.21 LXX 29
2.23 LXX 24, 29
2.24 144 n.44
16.5 LXX 112 n.10
16.7 LXX 127 n.66
17.21 29
21.19 LXX 40
24 108 n.3, 121
  n.30
24.1–27 36
24.10–27 122
  n.34
24.11–13 123 n.44
24.13 LXX 126
  n.63, 127 n.66
24.15–20 36
24.16 123 n.42
24.18–20 40
24.20 LXX 126 n.63
24.28–51 36
24.43 LXX 127
  n.66
26.19 LXX 125
  n.56
29–30 127 n.65
29.1–12 36, 122
  n.34
29.1–20 120 n.30
29.3–4 123 n.44
29.9–14 40
29.10 37
29.20 37
41.45 108 n.3

Exodus 49
2.15–21 36
2.16 123 n.44
2.19 40
2.20 40
3.14 17, 19
3.14 LXX 17, 18,
  47, 54
20.1–17 121 n.30
33.20 111 n.2
40.34–35 26

Leviticus
11.36 LXX 127
  n.66
14.5–6 LXX 40
14.50–52 LXX 125
  n.57
15 26
15.16 26
20.10 95, 150
  n.54

Numbers
5.17 LXX 125 n.57
11.12 LXX 112
  n.10
19.17 LXX 125
  n.57

Deuteronomy
  121 n.30
8.15 LXX 127 n.66
13.7 LXX 112 n.10
18.18 133 n.97
22.22 95, 150 n.54
24.1–4 144
  n.44
32.15 LXX 136
  n.130
32.39 17

Joshua
15.9 LXX 127 n.66
18.15 LXX 127
  n.66
24 121 n.30

Judges
3.9 LXX 137 n.130
3.15 LXX 137
  n.130
11.12 32
11.12 LXX 114
  n.27
12.3 LXX 137
  n.130

Ruth
3—4 149 n.40
3.4 89, 148 n.30
3.7 89, 148 n.30
4.16 LXX 112
  n.10

1 Samuel
10.19 LXX 136
  n.130

2 Samuel
11.8 89, 148 n.30

1 Kings
17.18 LXX 114
  n.27

2 Kings
  130 n.77
3.13 LXX 114
  n.27
3.19 LXX 127
  n.66
3.25 LXX 127 n.66

13.4 114 n.27
17.24 130 n.77

**3 Kingdoms
(LXX)**
17.10 33

**4 Kingdoms
(LXX)**
3.13 32

2 Chronicles
10.10 LXX 92
35.21 33, 114 n.10

Nehemiah
6.27 LXX 137
  n.130

Esther
5.1 LXX 136
  n.130
8.12 LXX 137
  n.130

Job
9.8 18

Psalms
23.5 LXX 136
  n.130
24.5 LXX 136
  n.130
26.1 LXX 136
  n.130
26.9 LXX 136
  n.130
61.3 LXX 136
  n.130
61.7 LXX 136
  n.130

64.6 LXX 136
n.131
78.9 LXX 136
n.130
80.14–15 140 n.19
94.1 LXX 136
n.130
104 121 n.30

Proverbs 4,
13–14, 27–9
1—9 27, 28
4.5–9 27
5.15 36, 123 n.45
5.15–18 LXX 38
5.15–20 50
5.18 LXX 127 n.66
7 27, 109 n.13
7.1–27 3–4
7.4 27
8 14
8.22–31 12
23.27 LXX 38

**Song of
Solomon** 38,
41, 89
1.3 89
1.12 89
4.1 148
4.12 38
4.12–15 50
4.13 89
4.14 89
4.15 38, 123 n.45
4.15 LXX 41, 125
n.59

Isaiah 49
12.2 LXX 137
n.130
12.3 LXX 126 n.63
17.10 LXX 137
n.130
35.7 LXX 127 n.66

41.4 17
41.13 LXX 40
43.10 17
43.25 17
45.15 LXX 137
n.130
45.18–19 17
45.19 LXX 47, 54,
113 n.14
45.21 LXX 137
n.130
46.4 17
51.12 17
52.6 17
52.6 LXX 17, 47,
54, 124 n.53,
133 n.101
54.4–8 32
57.8 149 n.45
62.4–5 32
62.11 LXX 137
n.130
66.10 119 n.19

Jeremiah
2.2–3 32
2.13 125 n.58
2.13 LXX 40, 41,
127 n.66
3.1–11 32
3.20 32
7.32–34 LXX 120
n.22
16.9 120 n.22
25.10 120 n.22
33.10–11 120 n.22

Ezekiel
16 32
23.20 LXX 29

Hosea 52
2.1–15 32
2.14–23 133
n.102

14.4–7 133 n.102
14.8 114 n.27

Micah
7.7 LXX 137 n.130

Habakkuk
3.18 LXX 137
n.130

Zechariah
14.8 125 n.58
14.8 LXX 40

**APOCRYPHAL
(DEUTERO-
CANONICAL)
BOOKS**

Tobit
12.11–15 20

Judith
7.12 127 n.66
9.11 136 n.130
12.7 127 n.66

**Wisdom of
Solomon** 13,
14, 28
7.24—8.1 13
7.24 13
7.26 13
7.27 13
8.1 13
9.4 13
9.7 13
9.10 13
16.7 136 n.130

**Wisdom of Ben
Sira (Sirach)**
14, 27–8, 42,
143 n.38
1.26 143 n.38

9.1–9 106 n.3
9.3–9 3
15.15 143 n.38
24.2 14
24.3 14
24.4 14
24.5–6 14
24.7 14
24.8 14
24.9 14
24.19–21 42
32.23 143 n.38
37.12 143 n.38
51.1 136 n.130
51.13–21 27
51.16 28
51.18 28
51.19 28
51.20 28, 116
n.41
51.21 28

1 Esdras
1.24 33, 114 n.27

Baruch
2.23 120 n.22

1 Maccabees
4.30 136 n.130

3 Maccabees
6.29 136 n.130
6.32 136 n.130
7.16 136 n.130

NEW TESTAMENT

Matthew 18, 68,
76, 141 n.21,
141 n.23
1.18–19 149 n.40
1.19 134 n.113
5.43–46 141 n.21
8.3 147 n.8

8.15 147 n.8
9.20 147 n.8
9.21 147 n.8
9.29 147 n.8
10.2 141 n.23
10.37 141 n.21
14.22–33 18
14.36 141 n.8
16.18 68
17.1–9 141 n.23
17.7 147 n.8
17.24 141 n.23
19.3–9 77, 95
19.4–7 xi
19.17 76
19.19 141 n.21
20.34 147 n.8
22.37–39 141 n.21
24.12 141 n.21
26.6 88
26.7 148 n.27
26.37 141 n.23
28.9 147 n.8

Mark xii, 18, 68, 76, 141 n.21, 141 n.23
1.41 147 n.8
3.10 147 n.8
3.16–17 141 n.23
5.7 33, 114 n.27
5.27 147 n.8
5.28 147 n.8
5.30 147 n.8
5.31 147 n.8
5.37 141 n.23
6.45–52 18, 113
6.56 147 n.8
7.33 147 n.8
8.22 147 n.8
9.2–9 141 n.23
10.2–9 77
10.6–9 xi
10.13 147 n.8

10.35–45 138 n.7
12.18–23 131 n.84
12.30–31 141 n.21
12.33 141 n.21
13.3–37 141 n.23
14.3 89, 148 n.27
14.33 141 n.23
14.45 146 n.5

Luke 68, 76, 141 n.21, 141 n.23
5.13 147 n.8
6.14 141 n.23
6.19 147 n.8
6.27 141 n.21
6.32 18, 141 n.21
6.35 141 n.21
7.14 147 n.8
7.38 148 n.27
7.39 147 n.8, 149 n.40
7.47 141 n.21
8.16 147 n.8
8.28 33, 114 n.27
8.42 117 n.53
8.44 147 n.8
8.45 147 n.8
8.46 147 n.8
8.47 147 n.8
8.51 141 n.23
9.28–36 141 n.23
10.27 141 n.21
10.38–42 87
11.33 147 n.8
11.42 141 n.21
15.8 147 n.8
16.22 112 n.10
18.15 147 n.8
18.28 141 n.23
22.51 147 n.8

John
1.1 11–12

1.1–14 117 n.53
1.1–18 xiv, 9, 11–12
1.2 12
1.2–3 11
1.3 12
1.10 75
1.10–13 52, 129 n.71
1.11–13 23, 38
1.12 36
1.13 23, 24, 25, 29, 31, 115 n.35
1.14 5, 11, 12, 13, 15, 20, 23, 24, 25, 26, 115 n.35, 115 n.37
1.15 29, 33
1.16b–17 11, 29, 42
1.17 3, 11
1.18 12, 15, 29, 71, 72, 75, 77, 111 n.2
1.20 33, 46
1.29–30 33
1.34 19
1.35–36 33
1.45 20
1.46 19
2.1–2 32, 118 n.9
2.1–11 31, 32, 35
2.4 22
2.6 118 n.14
2.10 33, 118 n.14
2.12 22
2.14 24
2.17 147 n.25
2.21 21, 25, 40
2.22 147 n.25
3.1–21 31
3.6 24
3.16 15, 141 n.21
3.16–17 52

3.16–18 15
3.19 141 n.21
3.22–36 31, 33
3.25 118 n.14
3.27–30 33
3.28 46
3.28–29 31, 33, 46
3.29 34, 35, 53, 74, 119 n.19, 119 n.22
3.30 118 n.14
3.35 16, 72, 74, 141 n.21, 149 n.43
3.35–36 89, 74, 141, 149
4 94, 106 n.20, 108 n.3, 121 n.30, 122 n.36, 128 n.69, 128 n.70
4.5 121 n.30
4.6 21, 24, 38, 121 n.30
4.7 39, 49, 129 n.71, 133 n.116
4.7–8 39, 49
4.8 21, 36
4.9 37, 39
4.11 38, 41, 136 n.127
4.11–12 38, 41, 127 n.69
4.12 121 n.30, 126 n.65
4.14 38, 41
4.14–15 124 n.51
4.15 38, 40, 109 n.9, 127 n.69, 128 n.69, 129 n.71, 129 n.72, 136 n.127
4.15–16 126 n.64, 128 n.71

4.15–20 40
4.16 43, 44, 127 n.69, 129 n.71
4.16–18 25
4.17 43, 44, 51, 124 n.51, 127 n.69
4.17–18 43, 86
4.18 43, 44, 124 n.51, 131 n.90
4.19 20, 45
4.20 45
4.21–24 46
4.23–24 54
4.24 15, 73
4.25 17, 46, 47, 133 n.97
4.25–26 46, 48
4.26 17, 54, 124 n.51, 133 n.103
4.27 xiii, 1, 25, 130 n.77, 132 n.92
4.27–28 43
4.28 1, 49
4.28–29 49
4.29 20, 25, 51, 52, 53, 54, 133 n.97, 133 n.103
4.31 20
4.31–33 52
4.31–38 133 n.104
4.34 52
4.35–36 53
4.35–38 53
4.36b 53
4.39 52, 53, 115 n.37
4.39–42 37, 115, 138 n.123
4.40 136 n.123
4.42 31, 54, 137 n.138
5.12 25

5.19 16
5.19–20 74
5.20 72, 74, 141 n.21, 149 n.43
5.21–29 74
5.30 16
5.42 141 n.21
6.1–14 21
6.16–20 18
6.35 18
6.38–40 18
6.40 15
6.41 18
6.42 20
6.46 18
6.48 18
6.51 18, 24
6.53–56 24
6.63 24
6.68 76
7.1–9 22
7.37–38 41
7.38–39 46
7.39 41
7.46 25
8.1–11 94, 143 n.42
8.6 95
8.7 95
8.8 95
8.11 95
8.12 18, 24
8.22 135 n.118
8.28 16, 19
8.36 76
8.38 16
8.42 141 n.21
8.48 37
8.58 18
9.11 25
9.16 25
9.38 115 n.37
10.7 18
10.9 18
10.10 50
10.11 18

10.14 18
10.14–18 19
10.16 37
10.17 16, 72, 74, 141 n.21
10.17–18 15, 73, 76
10.18 114
10.22–39 16
10.27–29 19
10.30 16, 19
10.33 20, 25
10.36 16
10.38 16
11.1–44 22, 87
11.2 87, 90
11.3 90
11.4 90
11.5 87, 91, 92
11.6 90
11.19 91
11.20 90
11.25 18
11.27 19
11.28 90
11.32 90
11.33–35 90
11.35 22, 87, 90
11.36 91, 92, 148 n.37
11.40–44 90
11.47 25
11.47–53 89
11.50 25
12.1–2 88
12.1–8 22, 87, 88
12.3 88
12.4–8 88, 91
12.7 88
12.17 147 n.25
12.25 141 n.21
13 62, 64, 89, 108 n.3, 140 n.19
13—17 62, 64, 65, 68, 71, 89, 138 n.9, 139 n.9,

139 n.13, 140 n.19, 141 n.25
13.1 68, 75, 77
13.1–11 93
13.2 64
13.3–12 63
13.4 64, 139 n.13
13.4–5 62
13.13 85, 147 n.17
13.13–14 63, 68
13.13–17 62, 63, 64, 68, 71, 147
13.22 77
13.23 15, 61, 62, 68, 69, 71, 72, 77, 146 n.5, 149 n.43
13.24 78
13.24–25 68
13.25 62, 69, 78, 138 n.4
13.26 93
13.26–27 139 n.13
13.27 140 n.19
13.28 62
13.30 64, 93
13.31—17.26 64
13.34 76, 77, 141 n.21
13.34–35 75
13.35 77, 141 n.21
14.6 18, 63, 80
14.8–24 16
14.15 xv, 42, 75, 76, 77, 141 n.21
14.19–21 75
14.21 77, 141 n.21
14.23 75, 141 n.21
14.23–24 77
14.24 141 n.21
14.28 77, 141 n.21

14.31 72, 74, 75, 141 n.21
15.1 18
15.1–11 18, 65
15.5 18
15.6–7 24
15.9 77, 141 n.21
15.9–10 72, 74, 75
15.9–11 76
15.10 xv, 19, 74, 76, 141 n.21, 143 n.43
15.12 75, 77, 141 n.21, 143 n.43
15.13 16, 77, 141 n.21
15.14 141 n.21
15.14–15 77
15.15 141 n.21
15.17 77, 141 n.21
15.18 75
15.19 141 n.21
15.20 147 n.25
16.4 147 n.25
16.20 87
16.21 147 n.25
16.27 77, 141 n.21
17.1–26 16
17.2 24
17.5 142 n.34
17.21–23 74
17.21–26 16, 74
17.22–26 75
17.23 75, 141 n.21
17.23–24 72, 74, 77
17.24 74, 141 n.21, 142 n.34
17.26 68, 72, 74, 75, 77, 141 n.21
18.14 25
18.17 25
18.21 14, 106 n.1
18.29 25
18.35 135 n.118

19.1–3 21
19.5 25
19.6 95
19.25 85
19.25–27 78
19.26 61, 77, 146 n.5, 149 n.43
19.26–27 23
19.27 78
19.28 114 n.24
19.31 21, 25
19.34 22, 92
19.34–35 22, 92
19.38 21, 25
19.40 21, 25
20 87
20.1–2 85
20.1–9 68
20.2 61, 77, 78, 85, 87, 146 n.5, 149 n.43
20.8 78
20.9 61, 78
20.11 86
20.12 21, 25, 93
20.13 86, 87
20.15 87
20.16 85, 88
20.17 73, 85, 86
20.24ff 92
20.24–29 22
20.25 19
20.27 19, 92
20.27–28 22
20.27–29 92
20.28 19
20.30 35
20.30–31 xiv, 110 n.19
20.31 xi, xiv, 9, 18, 24
21 106 n.19, 110 n.19
21.5 135 n.118
21.7 54, 61, 68,

77, 78, 138 n.4, 144 n.46, 146 n.5, 149 n.43
21.9 21
21.15 141 n.21, 150 n.50
21.15–19 93
21.16 141 n.21, 150 n.50
21.17 141 n.21, 150 n.50
21.18–19 150 n.50
21.20 54, 61, 62, 77, 94, 138 n.4, 146 n.5, 149 n.43
21.21 93

Acts
28.2 147 n.8

Romans
1.26–27 146 n.52
7.5 24
7.14 24
7.18 24
7.25 24
13.13 65

1 Corinthians
1.18–31 134 n.105
5.11 65
6.9 146 n.52
6.10 65
6.17 147
7.1 85, 147 n.8
7.19 76

2 Corinthians
6.17 147 n.8
11.2 34

Galatians
5.21 65

Ephesians
5.18 65
5.25–33 34
5.29 24

Colossians
2.21 147 n.8

1 Timothy
3.3 65

Hebrews
4.15 xi

1 Peter
4.3 65

1 John 110 n.20
4.14 54
4.18 9
5.18 147 n.8

SECOND TEMPLE JEWISH LITERATURE

Elephantine papyri
44.3 142 n.35

Apocalypse of Moses
29.6 148 n.33

1 Enoch
32.1 148 n.33

4 Ezra
13.39–50 133 n.102

Psalms of Solomon
3.6 136 n.130
8.33 136 n.131
16.4 137 n.131
17.3 137 n.131

Testament of Solomon
6.10 148 n.33

Testaments of the Twelve Patriarchs
T. Benj.
3.8 136 n.129

T. Levi
10.2 136 n.129
14.2 136 n.129

Dead Sea Scrolls
11Q5 116 n.51
XXI 14 28
XXI 15 28
XXI 15–16 28

11QTemple
XLV 7–12 26

Josephus 26
Jewish Antiquities
2.6.1§94 57
3.11.3§261 26
3.11.5§269 26
6.11.10§240 57
9.14.3§287 130 n.77
9.14.3§288–291 135 n.116
12.1.1§1–11 137 n.134
12.5.5§257–262 137 n.134
14.15.8§439–444 56
15.7.5§231 56
16.8.1§230 56

Jewish War
1.26.4§530 137 n.139

1.32.2§625 137 n.134
2.8.5§133 140 n.19
3.9.8§459 56
4.3.5§146 137 n.139
4.9.11§575 137 n.139
7.4.1§63–74 56

Philo 14, 27–8, 55
Allegorical Interpretation
1.65 14

On the Cherubim
127 14

On the Confusion of Tongues
146 14

On Dreams
1.215 14
1.238–239 14
2.242–245 14

On Flight and Finding
101 14

On the Sacrifices of Cain and Abel
21–28 27
21–25 27
26–28 27

On the Special Laws
1.81 14
2.198 55, 136 n.128
3.9 27

RABBINIC LITERATURE

Tosefta
t. Ber.
2.14 144 n.46
2.20 145 n.47

t. Qidd.
5.2 145 n.51

Mishnah
m. 'Abot
1.5 2–3, 106 n.3, 108 n.3

m. Ketub.
2.10 89
7.6 89
7.9–10 44

m. Pesaḥ.
2.8 143 n.13
10.1 65
10.4–5 143 n.13

m. Soṭah
3.4 106 n.3

Talmud
b. 'Erub.
53b 2, 106 n.3

b. Ketub.
7b–8a 120 n.25
12a 34

b. Qidd.
70a 106 n.3

Other rabbinic works
'Abot R. Nat.
2.1d 106 n.3

APOSTOLIC FATHERS

Didache 76

NAG HAMMADI TEXTS

Gospel of Philip 84
3 59.6–11 84
3 63.30–35 84

CLASSICAL AND ANCIENT CHRISTIAN WRITINGS

Achilles Tatius 7, 64
Leucippe and Clitophon 7, 64
1.7 125 n.55
2.35–38 64, 65
2.38.4 7

Apollodorus
Bibliotheca
2.4.10 57

Apuleius 72
Metamorphoses
2.9 148 n.34
2.17 148 n.34
8.25–29 72

Augustine 4, 24, 119 n.16
Tractates of the Gospel of John
2.14 24
13.12–16 119 n.16
15.6–7 24
15.29 4

Chariton 72, 147 n.16
Callirhoe
1.5.2 72

Euripides
Heracles
922–1015 57

Eusebius
Ecclesiastical History
7.25.6 110 n.20

Herodotus
Histories
4.8–9 57

Homer
Iliad
20.231–235 73

Odyssey
5.129 57
5.207–227 57
6.110–332 121 n.30
15.403–54 121 n.30

Irenaeus 5, 9
Against Heresies
3.3.4 6
3.16.5 110 n.20
3.16.8 110 n.20

John Chrysostom 5, 101, 119 n.16
Homilies on John
29.3 119 n.16
32.2 129 n.75
33.3 5

Juvenal 81
Satires
9 125 n.55, 145 n.49

Lucian
Lexiphanes 140 n.16

Martial 7, 81, 113 n.19
Epigrams
1.23 8
1.96 145 n.49
1.96.12–13 8
2.51 145 n.49
3.51 8
3.71 145 n.49
3.72 8
3.89 145 n.49
5.8.1 19
7.34.8 19
8.2.6 19
10.72.3 19
14.201 8

Meleager 69
Anthology
5.8 69
130 69
173 69

Origen
Commentary on the Gospel of John
2.2.13–15 111 n.2

Ovid
Metamorphoses
1.588–621 55
9.14–15 57
9.98–272 57
9.241–272 57
10.155–161 55

Petronius 8, 69, 81
Satyricon 69, 72, 81, 140 n.16, 145 n.50
9 70
9–10 70

79–92 70
85–87 142 n.26
92 8
105 70
113 70
125–132 70
133–138 70
140 70, 145 n.50

Plato 64–9, 71
Symposium 64–9, 141 n.25
175C–E 64
178A–180B 66
180C–185C 66, 72
181B 79
181C–E 79
184D 79
188C–193D 66, 72
192C 66
194E–197E 66
210A–212A 66, 72
211C–212A 79
222B 69
222E–223B 69, 71
223A 69

Plutarch
Erotikos
761d 57

Suetonius
Divus Julius
2 56
6.1–2 56
49.1–4 56
50–52 56
52.3 56
88 56

Domitian
13.2 19

Vespasianus
3 56
13.1 56
21–22 56

Tertullian
Against Praxeas
15 110 n.20

Antidote for the Scorpion's Sting
12 110 n.20

Theocritus
Idylls
13 57

Tibullus
2.4 125 n.55

Virgil
Aeneid
4.165–72 57
4.630–705 57

Xenophon 64–8, 88, 139 n.13, 139 n.16, 140 n.16, 141 n.25
Symposium 67–8, 139 n.13, 140 n.16, 141 n.25
1.2–4 67
1.8–10 67
2.4 67
4.7–9 139 n.13
4.10–22 67
4.23–28 67
4.53–54 67
4.63 67
5 67
8 67
8.3–6 71

Xenophon of Ephesus 7, 147 n.16
Anthia and Habrocomes 7, 147 n.16
3.2.2 7

Index of modern authors

Allison, Dale C. 104 n.6, 144 n.44

Alter, Robert 117 n.2, 120 n.30, 122 n.33, 122 n.34, 123 n.40

Angel, Andrew R. 113 n.15, 114 n.23, 116 n.44, 116 n.47, 116 n.49

Arterbury, Andrew E. 121 n.30

Ashton, John 113 n.16

Balla, Ibolya 116 n.49, 116 n.50

Barrett, Charles Kingsley 106 n.19, 107 n.3, 108 n.4, 110 n.19, 111 n.2, 112 n.3, 112 n.4, 115 n.35, 118 n.11, 119 n.18, 119 n.20, 124 n.48, 125 n.59, 126 n.61, 126 n.62, 127 n.67, 130 n.77, 131 n.80, 132 n.97, 133 n.98, 133 n.101, 134 n.106, 135 n.118, 136 n.129, 137 n.1, 138 n.7, 139 n.13, 140 n.17, 141 n.24, 142 n.32, 143 n.43, 144 n.46, 145 n.47, 147 n.12, 147 n.24, 150 n.51, 150 n.52

Beasley-Murray, G. R. 107 n.3, 108 n.4, 115 n.29, 115 n.32, 115 n.35, 119 n.20, 130 n.77, 131 n.80, 132 n.97, 138 n.4, 142 n.32, 143 n.40, 145 n.47

Bernard, J. H. 106 n.3, 108 n.4, 115 n.32, 115 n.35, 119 n.18, 128 n.71, 130 n.77, 131 n.80, 132 n.97, 133 n.101, 135 n.118, 136 n.129, 138 n.7, 144 n.47

Black, C. Clifton 120 n.30, 122 n.34, 125 n.58

Bligh, John 109 n.9, 120 n.30, 124 n.48, 126 n.61, 130 n.77

Botha, J. Eugene 108 n.4, 109 n.16, 122 n.38, 123 n.43, 126 n.64, 127 n.69, 128 n.71, 129 n.71, 131 n.91, 132 n.97, 133 n.101, 134 n.106, 136 n.122, 136 n.123

Brant, Jo-Ann A. 24, 97, 106 n.20, 108 n.5, 110 n.19, 112 n.10, 114 n.27, 115 n.31, 115 n.35, 118 n.8, 118 n.10, 118 n.12, 120 n.30, 121 n.30, 122 n.32, 122 n.39, 123 n.39, 123 n.43, 124 n.51,125 n.60, 126 n.65, 127 n.69, 129 n.73, 129 n.75, 131 n.87, 132 n.96, 133 n.101, 135 n.118, 138 n.8, 140 n.18, 140 n.19, 148 n.29, 148 n.32, 148 n.34, 148 n.35, 149 n.40

Brodie, Thomas L. 107 n.3, 109 n.12, 110 n.19, 120 n.30, 130 n.77, 142 n.32, 143 n.43

Brown, Dan 96, 146 n.1

Brown, R. E. 107 n.3, 108 n.4, 110 n.19, 111 n.1, 112 n.9, 112 n.11, 113 n.13, 113 n.18, 113 n.19, 113 n.20, 114 n.24, 114 n.25, 114 n.27, 115 n.29, 115 n.32, 115 n.35, 115 n.38, 118 n.10, 119 n.14, 119 n.17, 119 n.18, 124 n.48, 125 n.59, 126 n.62, 127 n.67, 127 n.68, 130 n.77, 131 n.80, 133 n.101, 134 n.106, 135 n.118, 136 n.129, 137 n.1, 138 n.4, 138 n.5, 142 n.32, 143 n.39, 143 n.40, 143 n.41, 144 n.46, 144 n.47, 147 n.12, 147 n.21, 147 n.22, 148 n.27, 150 n.51, 150 n.52

Bruce, F. F. 107 n.3, 109 n.6, 109 n.8, 110 n.19, 112 n.10, 115 n.25, 115 n.32, 116 n.45, 130 n.77, 131 n.83, 133 n.99, 138 n.4

Bruner, Frederick Dale 108 n.3, 108 n.4, 110 n.19, 113 n.19, 115 n.35, 131 n.91, 132 n.97, 136 n.129, 142 n.32, 143 n.43

Bultmann, Rudolph 107 n.3, 108 n.4, 110 n.19, 115 n.35, 130 n.78, 132 n.97, 135 n.120

Burge, Gary M. 107 n.3, 108 n.4, 115 n.35, 120 n.30, 131 n.80

Byrne, Brendan 114 n.26

Byrskog, Samuel 141 n.25

Calvin, John 24, 115 n.30, 115 n.34
Campbell, Edward F. 148 n.30
Cantarella, Eva 110 n.17, 142 n.29
Cantwell, Laurence 130 n.77
Carlson, Stephen C. 104 n.9
Carmichael, Calum M. 106 n.2, 119 n.19, 120 n.30, 123 n.45, 124 n.48, 128 n.71
Carson, D. A. 105 n.17, 107 n.3, 109 n.9, 110 n.19, 111 n.2, 112 n.11, 114 n.25, 114 n.27, 115 n.29, 115 n.32, 115 n.35, 115 n.38, 118 n.8, 122 n.32, 124 n.48, 126 n.61, 126 n.62, 128 n.71, 129 n.75, 130 n.77, 131 n.80, 132 n.97, 133 n.101, 134 n.110, 134 n.111, 135 n.118, 136 n.129, 137 n.1, 138 n.4, 138 n.7, 138 n.8, 139 n.13, 140 n.17, 142 n.32, 143 n.43, 147 n.12, 150 n.52
Carter, Warren 113 n.19, 137 n.131
Casey, Maurice 104 n.6, 127 n.68
Charlesworth, James H. 117 n.4, 118 n.7, 147 n.10
Colwell, E. C. 111 n.2
Conway, Colleen M. 107 n.3, 108 n.4, 120 n.30, 121 n.30, 122 n.36, 124 n.46, 125 n.60, 126 n.60, 131 n.89, 138 n.8, 142 n.32, 147 n.9, 147 n.11, 147 n.18
Cowley, A. E. 142 n.35
Crossan, John Dominic 104 n.6
Culpepper, R. Alan xiii, 105 n.15, 108 n.4, 117 n.3, 120 n.30, 122 n.32, 131 n.79

Daube, David 124 n.48
Davies, W. D. 144 n.44
Day, Janeth Norfleete 105 n.13, 130 n.77, 131 n.89
Depuydt, Leo 104 n.9
Derrett, J. Duncan M. 118 n.11, 119 n.20
Deutsch, Celia 116 n.49, 116 n.51
Dover, Kenneth J. 108 n.17, 142 n.29
Duke, Paul D. 117 n.6, 120 n.30, 128 n.71, 130 n.78, 132 n.95, 134 n.112
Dunn, James D. G. 104 n.6

Edwards, Mark 108 n.4, 113 n.19, 115 n.35, 131 n.80, 142 n.32
Ehrman, Bart 146 n.3
Eslinger, Lyle 105 n.14, 120 n.30, 122 n.32, 122 n.33, 122 n.39, 123 n.39, 124 n.46, 124 n.50, 124 n.52, 125 n.60, 126 n.65, 127 n.69, 128 n.71, 129 n.72, 129 n.74, 132 n.97, 133 n.99, 136 n.122

Fewell, Danna Nolan 106 n.20, 121 n.30, 131 n.78, 131 n.88, 131 n.90, 132 n.95
Fiorenza, Elisabeth Schüssler 108 n.3
Firth, David G. 148 n.30.
Fitzmyer, Joseph A. 114 n.21, 144 n.44, 145 n.52
Fox, Michael V. 122 n.39, 123 n.41

Goodman, David 114 n.23
Gossip, Arthur J. 106 n.3, 108 n.4, 115 n.35
Greenberg, Moshe 117 n.54

Haenchen, Ernst 106 n.19, 107 n.3, 108 n.4, 111 n.2, 114 n.24, 115 n.35, 130 n.77, 131 n.80, 131 n.92, 136 n.129, 147 n.22, 147 n.23
Halperin, David M. 108 n.17, 146 n.54
Hayman, A. P. 112 n.5
Heil, John Paul 113 n.15
Hendriksen, William 107 n.3, 108 n.4, 115 n.35, 130 n.78, 132 n.97, 143 n.43
Hess, Richard S. 123 n.39, 125 n.59
Holladay, William L. 125 n.58
Hollander, H. W. 136 n.128
Hoskyns, E. C. 106 n.3, 108 n.4, 115 n.32, 115 n.35
Howard, Wilbur F. 106 n.3, 108 n.4, 115 n.35
Hubbard, Robert L. 148 n.30

Isenberg, Wesley W. 146 n.2

Jeffery, Peter 104 n.9
Jonge, Marinus de 136 n.128

Käsemann, Ernst 114 n.28
Kazantzakis, Nikos 96, 104 n.4
Keener, Craig S. 59, 105 n.17, 107 n.3,
    109 n.11, 113 n.15, 113 n.19, 115
    n.32, 115 n.35, 120 n.30, 126 n.61,
    126 n.62, 129 n.74, 130 n.77, 131
    n.80, 131 n.86, 133 n.97, 133 n.101,
    134 n.110, 136 n.129, 137 n.1, 137
    n.143, 138 n.6, 138 n.7, 140 n.17,
    140 n.19, 142 n.27, 142 n.32, 143
    n.43, 144 n.43, 145 n.47, 150 n.52,
    150 n.55
Kim, Jean K. 120 n.30, 129 n.71, 131
    n.89, 132 n.93, 134 n.109, 134
    n.116, 135 n.121
King, Karen L. 104 n.8
Knust, Jennifer Wright 130 n.77
Kobel, Esther 140 n.19
Koester, Craig R. 117 n.3, 135 n.116,
    136 n.128, 137 n.135
Köstenberger, Andreas J. 107 n.3, 109
    n.8, 112 n.9, 113 n.14, 113 n.19,
    114 n.27, 115 n.29, 115 n.32, 115
    n.35, 115 n.36, 118 n.10, 120 n.30,
    129 n.75, 131 n.80, 131 n.82, 131
    n.90, 132 n.97, 138 n.4, 138 n.7,
    138 n.8, 142 n.32, 143 n.38, 145
    n.47, 147 n.12, 147 n.21, 148 n.36,
    150 n.52
Kruse, Colin G. 110 n.20
Kysar, Robert 131 n.89

Lawrence, D. H. 96, 104 n.4
Lella, Alexander A. di 109 n.13, 112
    n.7, 112 n.8
Lewis, C. S. 82, 146 n.53, 146 n.54
Lightfoot, R. H. 115 n.35, 131 n.80,
    135 n.119
Lincoln, Andrew T. 107 n.3, 108 n.4,
    112 n.11, 113 n.14, 113 n.15, 113
    n.17, 113 n.18, 113 n.19, 114 n.27,
    115 n.29, 115 n.32, 115 n.33, 118
    n.10, 119 n.21, 120 n.30, 122 n.32,
    125 n.60, 126 n.61, 127 n.67, 128
    n.71, 130 n.77, 131 n.80, 131 n.84,
    133 n.101, 136 n.122, 136 n.129,

138 n.4, 140 n.19, 142 n.32, 144
    n.43, 144 n.46, 145 n.47
Lindars, Barnabas 107 n.3, 108 n.4,
    112 n.10, 113 n.19, 115 n.29, 115
    n.32, 115 n.35, 119 n.21, 122 n.35,
    130 n.77, 131 n.80, 132 n.97, 133
    n.101, 135 n.118, 138 n.4, 138 n.7,
    138 n.8, 142 n.32, 143 n.40, 143
    n.43, 148 n.27, 148 n.28, 150 n.52,
    150 n.57
Loader, William 103 n.1, 103 n.3, 109
    n.12, 115 n.40, 115 n.41, 116 n.42,
    116 n.43, 116 n.46, 116 n.47, 116
    n.49, 118 n.6, 120 n.27, 120 n.30,
    137 n.137, 144 n.44, 145 n.51
Longman III, Tremper 116 n.45, 123
    n.38, 123 n.41

McCarter, P. Kyle 148 n.30
Maccini, Robert Gordon 124 n.46
McHugh, John F. 107 n.3, 108 n.4,
    111 n.1, 114 n.27, 115 n.29, 115
    n.32, 115 n.33, 115 n.35, 115 n.38,
    117 n.3, 117 n.5, 118 n.10, 118
    n.13, 119 n.15, 119 n.20, 120 n.28,
    120 n.30, 122 n.37, 125 n.54, 125
    n.59, 127 n.67, 130 n.77, 132 n.97,
    133 n.100, 133 n.101, 133 n.102,
    135 n.118, 136 n.124, 136 n.125,
    136 n.129
McNally, Terrence 96, 104 n.4
McWhirter, Jocelyn 117 n.5, 118 n.13,
    119 n.22, 120 n.30
Makowski, John F. 139 n.11
Malina, Bruce J. 107 n.3, 108 n.4, 118
    n.12, 140 n.19, 142 n.32
Marsh, John 107 n.3, 108 n.4, 115
    n.29, 115 n.32, 115 n.35, 130 n.77,
    130 n.78, 132 n.97
Martin, Dale B. xii, 91, 92, 93, 96,
    104 n.10, 105 n.11, 149 n.41, 149
    n.42, 149 n.44, 149 n.46, 150
    n.48
Martin, Michael W. 120 n.30
Mastin, B. A. 107 n.3, 108 n.4, 113
    n.19, 115 n.29, 115 n.32, 120 n.30,

130 n.77, 131 n.83, 131 n.87, 132 n.97, 138 n.7, 142 n.32, 143 n.43

Meier, John Paul 103 n.2, 104 n.5, 104 n.6

Meyers, Carol L. 125 n.58

Meyers, Eric M. 125 n.58

Michaels, J. Ramsey 105 n.17, 106 n.19, 108 n.3, 109 n.10, 110 n.19, 113 n.17, 114 n.27, 115 n.29, 115 n.32, 115 n.33, 115 n.35, 115 n.38, 118 n.10, 118 n.12, 118 n.13, 119 n.21, 120 n.30, 124 n.47, 124 n.48, 129 n.75, 130 n.77, 131 n.83, 132 n.97, 138 n.4, 141 n.24, 142 n.32, 143 n.40, 143 n.41, 143 n.43, 144 n.46, 145 n.47, 147 n.19, 148 n.26, 150 n.52, 150 n.56

Milne, Bruce 109 n.6

Moloney, Francis J. 107 n.3, 109 n.12, 112 n.9, 113 n.19, 114 n.27, 115 n.29, 115 n.35, 115 n.39, 118 n.10, 118 n.11, 120 n.30, 128 n.71, 130 n.77, 131 n.78, 132 n.97, 137 n.2, 138 n.4, 138 n.7, 138 n.8, 138 n.9, 140 n.19, 142 n.27, 142 n.32, 143 n.37, 143 n.43, 145 n.47, 147 n.20, 148 n.27, 150 n.52

Montefiore, Hugh 103 n.3

Moore, George Foot 4, 109 n.14

Moore, Stephen D. 127 n.69, 128 n.69, 137 n.145

Morales, Helen 139 n.11

Morris, Leon 107 n.3, 108 n.4, 114 n.27, 115 n.29, 115 n.32, 115 n.33, 115 n.35, 115 n.36, 115 n.38, 118 n.10, 130 n.77, 131 n.78, 132 n.97, 135 n.119, 136 n.129, 138 n.5, 138 n.7, 142 n.32, 143 n.40, 143 n.43, 145 n.47, 147 n.12, 150 n.52, 150 n.53, 150 n.58

Munro, Winsome 117 n.3, 120 n.30, 129 n.75, 131 n.85

Muraoka, Takamitsu 116 n.49

Murphy, Roland E. 116 n.45, 123 n.39, 125 n.59

Newbigin, Lesslie 107 n.3, 108 n.4, 115 n.35, 130 n.77, 130 n.78

Neyrey, Jerome H. 108 n.4, 115 n.35, 117 n.3, 117 n.6, 118 n.9, 120 n.30, 125 n.54, 131 n.78, 134 n.112, 136 n.129

O'Day, Gail R. 120 n.30, 121 n.30, 129 n.75, 132 n.93, 132 n.97

Okure, Teresa 107 n.3, 109 n.10, 109 n.12, 121 n.30, 129 n.71, 130 n.77, 133 n.97, 133 n.103, 134 n.107, 135 n.121, 136 n.124

Olsson, Birger 107 n.3, 108 n.4, 109 n.10, 118 n.10, 118 n.13, 120 n.30, 122 n.38, 125 n.59

Painter, John 111 n.20

Parsenios, George L. 138 n.9, 139 n.10, 139 n.12, 139 n.14, 139 n.15, 139 n.16, 140 n.16, 140 n.19, 141 n.20

Pazdan, Mary Margaret 117 n.3

Perkins, Pheme 115 n.35, 131 n.81

Phillips, Gary A. 106 n.20, 121 n.30, 131 n.78, 131 n.88, 131 n.90, 132 n.95

Phipps, William E. xii, 85, 104 n.5, 146 n.6, 146 n.7

Rabinowitz, Isaac 116 n.49

Reinhartz, Adele 109 n.15, 115 n.35, 116 n.52, 120 n.30

Rohrbaugh, Richard L. 107 n.3, 108 n.4, 118 n.12, 140 n.19, 142 n.32

Sakenfeld, Katharine Doob 135 n.116

Sanday, William 144 n.45

Sanders, E. P. 104 n.6

Sanders, J. A. 116 n.49

Sanders, J. N. 107 n.3, 108 n.4, 113 n.19, 115 n.29, 115 n.32, 120 n.30, 130 n.77, 131 n.83, 131 n.87, 132 n.97, 138 n.7, 142 n.32, 143 n.43

Satlow, Michael L. 103 n.3, 119 n.17, 119 n.22, 120 n.23, 120 n.24, 120 n.26, 144 n.46, 145 n.51

Schenke, Hans-Martin 146 n.2, 146 n.4

Schnackenburg, Rudolph 105 n.17, 106 n.1, 106 n.19, 107 n.3, 108 n.4, 111 n.1, 111 n.2, 113 n.13, 113 n.17, 113 n.18, 113 n.19, 114 n.25, 114 n.27, 115 n.35, 115 n.38, 118 n.10, 119 n.20, 120 n.27, 126 n.62, 127 n.67, 130 n.77, 131 n.80, 132 n.97, 133 n.101, 135 n.117, 136 n.129, 138 n.7, 138 n.8, 139 n.13, 140 n.17, 141 n.22, 141 n.24, 143 n.40, 143 n.43

Schneiders, Sandra M. 118 n.6, 120 n.30, 130 n.77, 133 n.104, 134 n.104, 135 n.119, 135 n.121, 147 n.11

Schnelle, Udo 113 n.20

Schottroff, Luise 108 n.3, 109 n.7, 122 n.31, 131 n.83, 131 n.90, 132 n.95, 134 n.114, 134 n.115, 136 n.127, 142 n.28

Shanks, Hershel 104 n.9

Skehan, Patrick W. 109 n.13, 112 n.7, 112 n.8

Sloyan, Gerard 108 n.4, 113 n.19, 115 n.35, 131 n.78

Smith, Morton 104 n.7

Spencer, F. Scott 109 n.12

Staley, Jeffrey Lloyd 105 n.15, 117 n.6, 118 n.13, 120 n.30, 122 n.32, 122 n.33

Steinberg, Leo 104 n.4

Stibbe, Mark W. G. 105 n.14, 108 n.4, 115 n.35, 117 n.3, 120 n.30, 128 n.71, 142 n.32

Strecker, Georg 110 n.20

Talbert, Charles H. 107 n.3, 108 n.4, 136 n.126

Tenney, Merrill C. 108 n.4, 109 n.11, 115 n.35

Tilborg, Sjef van 87, 105 n.14, 119 n.22, 140 n.19, 142 n.27, 142 n.28, 142 n.30, 142 n.31, 147 n.13, 147 n.14, 147 n.15, 148 n.31, 148 n.34, 149 n.40

Trible, Phyllis 105 n.13

Vanhoozer, Kevin J. 120 n.30, 125 n.60

Waetjen, Herman C. 107 n.3, 108 n.4, 115 n.35, 120 n.30, 122 n.36, 127 n.66, 128 n.71, 130 n.77, 131 n.83, 133 n.101, 138 n.7, 140 n.17, 142 n.32

Wahlde, Urban C. von 107 n.3, 108 n.4, 110 n.19, 112 n.9, 112 n.10, 115 n.35, 120 n.30, 130 n.77, 138 n.4, 138 n.5, 138 n.7, 142 n.32

Waltke, Bruce K. 116 n.45

Watson, Alan 123 n.45, 124 n.45, 125 n.60, 126 n.63, 128 n.69, 128 n.71

Westcott, B. F. 114 n.25, 115 n.35, 119 n.18, 130 n.77, 131 n.83, 132 n.97

Wilson, R. McL. 146 n.3

Winston, David 112 n.6

Witherington III, Ben 138 n.7, 140 n.19, 142 n.32, 144 n.43, 144 n.47

Wright, N. T. 104 n.6

Yarborough, Robert W. 110 n.20

Index of subjects

adultery 4, 38, 44, 50, 56, 60, 84, 94–6, 125 n.57, 129 n.72, 130 n.77, 143 n.42, 144 n.44
attraction *see* sexual attraction

baths 5–9, 79, 110 n.18
beauty xiv, 3, 8, 44, 66–7, 72, 77, 79–80, 83; physical 8, 66–7
beloved disciple xiii–xiv, 5, 15, 22, 61–3, 68–9, 70–2, 76–9, 81, 86, 91–4, 105 n.14, 137 n.1, 137 n.3, 138 n.3, 138 n.4, 141 n.24, 142 n.27, 149 n.43, 150 n.49
betrothal narrative xiv, 36–40, 47–8, 51–4, 58, 60, 106 n.20, 120 n.30, 122 n.31, 122 n.33, 123 n.45, 124 n.50, 136 n.122
bisexuality xi
bosom 12, 62–3, 68, 112 n.10
breast 15, 62–3, 69, 71–2, 74–5, 77–8, 112 n.10
bridegroom 31–7, 40, 46–9, 51, 53, 118 n.12, 119 n.16, 119 n.22, 120 n.22, 142 n.36; Messiah 35–7, 40, 47–9, 51

chastity 56, 58, 60
chest 62–3, 69, 71, 80, 94, 100
Christ 11, 15, 48, 52, 78, 86, 96, 101–2, 110 n.19, 135 n.120, 136 n.121, 143 n.43; love of Christ 5, 9, 82, 100–1; (the) sexual healer 52
Christology 48, 113 n.20, 121 n.30
commandments xiii, xv, 16, 19, 26, 60, 73–7, 80–1, 86, 94–5, 98, 100–1, 105 n.18, 106 n.18, 143 n.38, 143 n.39, 143 n.40, 143 n.43, 144 n.43, 144 n.44, 147 n.12
courtship 32–3, 39
covenant: bride 74; commands 76; God 48; language 76; marriage 47,

51, 123 n.45; people 32–5, 37, 47–8, 122 n.36; relationship 48, 52–3, 133 n.102; texts 121 n.30

desire: physical 50; sexual xiv, 24–5, 27–8, 30–1, 48, 58–9, 71–2, 98–9, 101
divorce xi, 32, 39, 44, 56, 60, 89, 144; law 44, 89, 144 n.44
Docetism 20, 113 n.20

Encolpius 69–70, 72, 74
encounters, sexual 9, 56–7, 77, 79–81, 97
ethics *see* sexual ethics
exercise (physical) 6–8
expression *see* sexual expression

father 20, 24, 40, 51, 55, 92, 123 n.42, 149 n.41
Father (God) xiv, 9, 11–13, 15–20, 24, 47, 52–4, 61, 71–7, 79–82, 92–4, 99, 105 n.18, 129 n.71, 142 n.33, 142 n.34, 143 n.40, 149 n.43
feet 32, 62–4, 87–90, 93, 97, 108 n.3, 138 n.6, 138 n.7, 148 n.27, 148 n.31
fertility 36, 44, 126 n.65
flesh xiii–xiv, 5, 9, 11, 20, 23–30, 36, 59, 98–9, 102, 115 n.35, 117 n.54, 140 n.19
fountain 38, 40, 74, 76, 125 n.60
freedom *see* sexual freedom
friend 22, 33–4, 53, 58, 61, 66, 77–8, 81–2, 87, 90, 96, 98, 141 n.21
friendship 22, 30, 34, 67, 79–80, 82, 92, 94, 99–100
fulfilment *see* sexual fulfilment

Ganymede 55, 65, 67, 73–4
gay 72, 91, 96, 103 n.3; imagination 91, 93, 96

genitalia 66, 89, 126 n.63

glory of God xiv, 13, 25–8, 30–1, 49, 58, 98, 102, 114 n.28, 115 n.28, 115 n.39, 142 n.34

God xi–xiv, 5, 9–20, 23–8, 30–8, 40–2, 46–55, 58, 60–1, 73–7, 81, 83, 92, 96–7, 98–102, 111 n.2, 112 n.2, 112 n.5, 114 n.28, 115 n.39, 116 n.52, 121 n.30, 122 n.37, 123 n.45, 124 n.53, 129 n.71, 133 n.101, 133 n.102, 144 n.43, 144 n.44; creator of the world 12, 14; of Israel 12, 17–20, 55, 73, 111 n.2, 112 n.2, 114 n.28, 142 n.35; king of the universe 34; Lord God Almighty 18–19, 47, 49; only begotten god xiv, 12, 74–5, 77; *see also* Father (God); incarnate (God); Spirit of God

gods and goddesses 9, 13, 29, 54–8, 66–7, 72–3, 80, 108 n.3, 111 n.2, 113 n.19, 115 n.28, 130 n.77, 137 n.142, 142 n.35

gratification *see* sexual gratification

groom 31–7, 118 n.12, 119 n.19, 119 n.22

gymnasia 6–8, 65, 79, 110 n.18

healing *see* sexual healing

heterosexual relationships 100

homoerotic relationships xiv, 61, 63, 71, 79–81

homoeroticism xii, xiv, 7–8, 61, 63–4, 69–72, 74, 79, 82, 91–4, 97, 99–101, 103 n.3, 145 n.51

homosexuality xi, 82, 100, 103 n.3, 145 n.51. 145 n.52

husband 27, 43–4, 46–7, 50–1, 55, 89, 103 n.3, 119 n.19, 121 n.30, 123 n.42, 130 n.77, 131 n.79, 131 n.89, 131 n.90, 136 n.121, 148–3; of Israel 32, 47

I AM 17–19, 46–7, 54, 113 n.14; 'before Abraham was . . .' 18; bread of life 18; (the) gate 18; (the) good shepherd 18; (the) light of the world 18; (the) resurrection and the life 18; (the) vine 18; (the) way, truth, life 18

imitation of Christ xii

impropriety *see* sexual impropriety

incarnate (God) xii, 5, 28, 35, 49, 54, 58–9, 97, 102, 129 n.71; incarnation 15, 29, 30, 73, 98–9, 102, 110 n.18

intimacy xiv, 15, 61, 63, 66, 68, 71–5, 78–83, 86, 92, 94, 97, 100, 138 n.4, 143 n.40; emotional 80–1; physical 15, 62–3, 79–83, 94, 100; spiritual 75, 81–2, 100

kiss 65, 82, 84, 146 n.5

lap xiv, 62–3, 69, 94

lesbian 72

levirate marriage 44, 60

limitations *see* physical limitations

living water 38, 40–8, 96, 122 n.37, 125 n.58, 125 n.59, 125 n.60, 126 n.60, 126 n.61, 127 n.69, 128 n.69, 128 n.71, 129 n.71, 132 n.93, 132 n.94, 132 n.95, 133 n.96, 134 n.106

love: affection (Greek noun *philia*, verb *phileō*) 66–8, 77, 92, 141 n.21, 149 n.43, 150 n.50; intimacy (Greek *oikeitotēs*) 66; love (Greek noun *agape*, verb *agapaō*) 68, 77, 92, 141 n.21, 149 n.43, 150 n.50; love (Greek noun *erōs*) 28, 66–7, 82; loved one/beloved (Greek *eromenos*) 69, 123 n.39, 148 n.34; lover vii, 27, 40, 55–7, 60, 65, 67, 69–71, 73, 79–80, 86–7, 89, 125 n.55, 128 n.70, 142 n.26, 148 n.34; lover (Greek *erastēs*) 69, 71

marriage xi, 27, 32, 34–40, 44–5, 47, 50–1, 53, 57–8, 60, 74, 77, 103 n.3, 109 n.9, 117 n.4, 119 n.19, 120 n.27, 121 n.30, 122 n.30,

123 n.45, 130 n.77, 133 n.101, 142 n.36; courtship 32–3, 39; marital status xii, 45; of the Messiah 32; *see also* covenant, marriage; levirate marriage
Martha 19, 22, 87–8, 90, 92, 96, 147 n.14, 148 n.37
Mary of Bethany 84, 87, 91–3, 96–7, 99, 149 n.40
Mary Magdalene 68, 78, 84–8, 96–7, 146 n.7, 147 n.11
metrosexual 83

nakedness 6–8, 28, 65, 78–9, 144 n.46, 144 n.47, 145 n.47
nard 88–9, 148 n.33
needs *see* physical needs
nudity 8, 79

obedience 60, 75–8, 80–1, 95, 101, 144 n.43, 144 n.44
oil 6–7, 89

passion *see* sexual passion
patriarchal oppression 60
patristic imagination 91
pederasty 80
penis 8, 29, 92, 126 n.63
perfume 27, 87–90, 148 n.27
physical, the/physicality 5–6, 8–9, 15, 21–5, 27, 29, 50, 60, 62–3, 65–7, 79–83, 93–4, 100; *see also* beauty; desire; intimacy
physical body 15, 21, 22, 24–5, 60, 62–3
physical limitations 21
physical needs 58
physical pleasure 6, 27, 65

relationships, sexual *see* sexual relationships
ritual 7, 26, 28, 39–40, 116 n.51, 119 n.19, 125 n.57, 140 n.19
ritual uncleanness 39–40
romance 40, 60, 90, 97, 100

salvation 32, 40–2, 46–8, 50, 52, 60, 100–1, 124 n.53, 125 n.58, 126 n.63, 127 n.66, 129 n.71, 135 n.119, 136 n.121
saviour 31, 54–9, 136 n.121, 137 n.139; saviour of the world 31, 54–6, 58–9
sex *see* sexual intercourse
sex (gender) 8, 66
sex life 50–2, 54–5, 60, 96, 100, 136 n.121
sexual attraction 8, 38, 59, 89, 92, 99
sexual drive 50–1, 54
sexual ethics 77, 98
sexual expression xi, 59, 148 n.31, 149 n.40
sexual freedom xi, 83, 101
sexual fulfilment 96
sexual gratification 79, 100
sexual healing 51, 60
sexual impropriety xiii, 4, 86, 95, 99, 144 n.44
sexual innuendo 3, 46, 125 n.59, 125 n.60, 126 n.63, 126 n.64
sexual intercourse 8, 9, 25–8, 34–6, 38, 45–6, 50, 53, 58–60, 69–70, 72–3, 80, 85–6, 96, 98, 103 n.1, 112 n.10, 121 n.30, 124 n.52, 126 n.64, 128 n.69, 129 n.71, 131 n.90, 146 n.5, 147 n.7, 148 n.34
sexual judgementalism 48, 60, 96
sexual motivations 2, 10, 49, 82, 134 n.104
sexual overtures 41, 59, 99, 127 n.69
sexual passion 27
sexual prowess 7, 58, 126 n.65
sexual relationships 24, 42–3, 45, 56, 60–1, 66, 72–3, 84–6, 96, 100, 127 n.66, 131 n.90, 147 n.7
sexuality xi–xii, xiv, 5, 9, 10, 23–30, 36, 48, 50, 53, 59–60, 72–3, 83, 94, 98–102, 110 n.17, 115 n.35, 128 n.69, 34 n.78; difficulties of 25, 59; female 29; of God 35, 49, 73–5, 101–2; of Jesus xi–xii, xiv–xv,

5, 9–11, 23, 26, 30–1, 36, 48–50, 54, 58–9, 84, 95, 98–9, 104 n.4, 110 n.16, 110 n.18, 110 n.19, 132 n.92; male xii, 29; of Wisdom 23, 28–9
shame 50–1, 60, 100, 134 n.115, 135 n.116
singleness xi
son of God 9, 12, 15–19, 24, 36, 52, 54, 61, 71–7, 80–2, 92–3, 99, 105 n.18, 129 n.71, 142 n.33, 142 n.34, 143 n.40
son of Joseph 20
son of Mary 22
Spirit of God 13, 15–17, 24, 41, 46
spiritual intimacy 75, 81–2, 100
spiritualizing of sex 47–60, 101
spring 38, 40–1, 127 n.66
symposium 63–9, 71–2, 79, 99, 138 n.9, 139 n.9, 139 n.13, 139 n.15, 140 n.16, 140 n.17, 140 n.19, 141 n.25

temptation xi, 25, 30
transsexuality xi

Venus 57
virgin 3, 34, 36, 38, 51, 123 n.42

water *see* living water
wedding 22, 32–5, 37, 40, 47, 53, 65, 89, 118 n.9, 119 n.22, 120 n.24, 147 n.10
well xiii, 1, 4, 9, 20, 21, 24, 25, 31, 35–8, 40–2, 45, 47–51, 54, 58–9, 122 n.31, 122 n.37, 123 n.44, 123 n.45, 124 n.45, 125 n.54, 127 n.65, 127 n.66, 129 n.71, 147 n.14
Wisdom 12–15, 23, 27–9, 42, 84, 112 n.6, 116 n.52
woman at the well xiii, 4, 25, 31, 35, 47, 51, 58, 60, 95, 99
Word xiii–xiv, 5, 9, 11–20, 23–30, 31, 33, 35–6, 42, 47, 54, 73, 98, 111 n.1, 111 n.2, 112 n.2, 116 n.52, 117 n.53, 129 n.71
wrestling 6–8, 65, 67